John "Buck" O'Neil,
The Rookie, His Words, His Voice

Phil S. Dixon

Front cover: Cobe LaBron Bowie in uniform photographed by Cory Davis of KrisDavi Photography, Ebbets Field Flannels for KC patch, Muehlebach Field/Ruppert Stadium, Kansas City, Missouri, Buck O'Neil photograph Wilborn & Associates Collection, colorized by Lorenxo Dow. Back cover photograph by Jerry Lockett.

Dedicated to Robby Jermaine "Robb" Madden,

My nephew, a family historian,

who died in the 2020 Covid-19 pandemic at the young age of 41.

John "Buck" O'Neil.

Contents

Acknowledgments

I had the good fortune of beginning this publication in the 1980s when I first met and later interviewed John "Buck" O'Neil for an oral history project about the Kansas City Monarchs. For the next twenty-plus years, our continuous dialogue never stopped. There were plenty of things to talk about, and so, at big-league baseball games, social events, at libraries, churches, community centers, speaking engagements, book openings, and during the period when the Negro League Baseball Museum was incorporated, seldom did we miss an opportunity to converse about baseball history. These tidbits of information from our everyday conversations impacted my knowledge of the Monarchs team and enlightened me on baseball history. Some of our conversations were much longer; these were actual interviews. One interview specifically, the one recorded on January 24, 1985, stood out among all others. O'Neil and I connected because of our similar experiences and talked past the time allotted. On a uniquely different level, he appreciated my sincere effort to depict his career, the Monarchs team, and life as a Black American as no one had ever done before while addressing a baseball topic. He saw right off that I had a proclivity for small details and that I genuinely cared about this history.

I had been a traveling musician during the 1970s, and some of the cities that O'Neil had played in as a ballplayer I had visited as a musician. We had both traveled on the "Chitlin' Circuit." Having toured on that circuit, which for me was a series of bars and nightclubs in African American communities, allowed us to talk about the world of segregation, for he had experienced many of the same challenges. In that taped interview, he provided candid conversation about his Kansas City Monarchs' teammates.

We sat down in the living room of O'Neil's South Benton Avenue residence and discussed the 1938 Kansas City Monarchs in vivid detail. When "Buck," told stories, he was more lucid than most; his memory was sharp and on target. His gigantic personality resonated throughout as he answered question after question. That initial taped conversation led to an hour-long television documentary recorded in 1986, which featured O'Neil and myself in a video session recorded at Kansas City Kansas Community College. It predated his feature in the now famous Ken Burns documentary, "Baseball," by several years.

During this same period, I was fortunate to interview other former Monarchs with whom I was connected. It was an exciting period. I took my work seriously, and with fervor, passion, and a knack for mobility, I traveled to the homes of Junius "Rainey" Bibbs in Indianapolis, Indiana, to speak with his widow Dorothy; I was a regular visitor to Tom Baird's daughter's home in Kansas City, Kansas. His daughter, Harriett Wickstrom, lived in the family home where Tom, a former Monarch owner, once lived. I sat in the same living room where Tom suffered his fatal heart attack and conducted many interviews with his daughter. I visited Hilton Smith and his wife Louise on numerous occasions at their home in Kansas City, Missouri. I interviewed Newton Henry Allen, who was also living in Kansas City, Missouri, at the time and continued our dialog when he moved to Cincinnati, Ohio. I traveled to Georgia to interview Joe Greene and to North Carolina to interview "Buck" Leonard. Talking to Byron "Mex" Johnson at his Denver, Colorado home by telephone was a common occurrence. I was also in touch with Dick Bradley and the widow of I.V. Barnes. It was a fascinating time to do research, and I was blessed to hear first-hand accounts from many former players. Five of O'Neil's 1938 teammates were consulted for this project. Many non-Monarchs were also interviewed.

I had the pleasure of interviewing two managers of Negro American League teams from the 1938 season--James "Gabby" Kemp and Ted "Double Duty" Radcliffe. Many Negro American and Negro National League players from other teams have portions of their interviews added to this publication. The list includes the following list of athletes:

Cowan "Bubba" Hyde

Felix "Chin" Evans

George Giles

Herbert "Doc" Bracken

James "Joe" Greene

James "Red" Moore

Jesse Askew

Jessie Williams

John Huntley

Marcus Haynes

Marlin Carter

Marshall Riddle

Maurice "Doolittle" Young

Quincy Trouppe

Richard "Subby" Byas

Roy Partlow

Walter "Buck" Leonard

Willard "Sonny" Brown

William "Jack" Marshall

William "Sug" Cornelius

These ballplayers, their wives, and other family member interviews were a welcome addition to my research. Ora O'Neil, O'Neil's wife, graciously assisted this work on numerous occasions. A retired Kansas City, Kansas, elementary school teacher, she willingly relayed messages to her husband for appointments and provided me with lots of general information that only a wife can experience. In some years, I talked with Ora far more than Buck as he was busy scouting for the Chicago Cubs and the Kansas City Royals. Georgia Dwight, Francis Armour, Dorothy I. Brown, Dorothy Bibbs, Sarah Barnes, and Louise Smith were also interviewed. Dwight was always vocal about her husband Eddie Dwight, who had been a neighbor of ours while I was growing up in Kansas City, Kansas. She was transparent and straightforward in our many conversations about baseball and her husband's lifetime achievements. Armour was interviewed over the telephone about her husband Alfred "Buddy" Armour. Brown, who was living in Kansas City, provided a wealth of anecdotes about her Hall of Fame husband, Willard Brown. During a visit to Indianapolis, Dorothy Bibbs, the wife of infielder Julius Bibbs, provided me with an entertaining array of details on her late husband. Barnes a graduate of Piney Woods College, was equally encouraging as she provided information on her husband, I. V. Barnes, over the telephone. Louise Smith, the wife of Hilton Smith--a native of Monroe, Louisiana--gave detailed descriptions of her past recollections when I visited her home in Kansas City, Missouri. Together, they teamed with Bernice Duncan, Frank Duncan's widow, to tell a more personal side of their Monarch husbands. Each in this wonderful and inspirational group of ladies embraced me with love and support years before the subject was popular. For the record, there were others--many others--who helped this history to survive.

Willa Simms gave detailed documentation on her brother Floyd Kranson from her home in California. Lorraine McGee was helpful with information on her father, Robert Dean, and her grandfather Nelson Dean. Reverend Newton H. Allen Jr. and Myrtle Vanoy shared information about Newt Allen's celebrated career with the Monarchs. And of course, Turk Taylor, who came to Kansas City, Kansas, from a vacation trip he was taking in Hot Springs, Arkansas, to personally deliver information and pictures on his brother, Olan "Jelly" Taylor.

Harriet Wickstrom provided descriptive accounts about her father, Thomas Younger "T. Y." Baird, as did Baird's brother Floyd. Floyd was equally resourceful as he discussed the Monarchs second team, known as the Satchel Paige All-Stars of 1939 and 1940. Samuel R. Brown, the Memphis Red Sox traveling secretary, also contributed mightily to this publication.

Most of the research for this manuscript was completed over a 30-year period. I spent lots of time looking for games. Many hours were spent researching inside the Kansas State Historical Society in Topeka, Kansas, and the Missouri State Historical Society in Columbia, Missouri. My time at the Kenneth Spencer Research Library in Lawrence, Kansas, added important facts to this effort. Others helped me hunt for data. These important individuals assisted with the development of this book. I am forever grateful for their resourcefulness.

Thank you to Jason Stewart, Library Assistant at the Shawnee, Oklahoma Public Library and to Mary Woods, Historian at the Black River Falls, Wisconsin Public Library, for sending information on an important game played in those cities. Michael Sellman, the Reference Specialist at the Dorothy Bramlage Public Library in Junction City, Kansas, dug deeply into their newspaper archives. His was a superman effort that produced great results. James F. Shearouse, Reference Librarian at the Rock Island Public Library in Illinois, was equally essential in helping me understand what occurred during the House of David tour. My special thank you is extended to Emily Hobson of the Marshall, Texas Public Library; Barbara Galbreath, Access Associate of the Tyler, Texas Public Library; and Rachel Garret Howell, Assistant Manager at the Texas/Dallas History and Archives Division of the Dallas Public Library for information originating from Texas. Lending their assistance from Louisiana, the Louisiana Division/City Archives and Special Collections of the New Orleans Public Library were very resourceful. In Oklahoma, the Enid Public Library, and the Oklahoma City Public Library provided data for games played in that state. Michelle Andrews of the Birmingham Public Library directed me to games against the Black Barons in Birmingham. Doris Jarvis and Jan Culbreth of the Leeds Library of Leeds, Alabama, assisted with games played in other parts of Alabama. I also received help from Shane Molander, a staff member for the State Historical Society of North Dakota; Margaret W. Morford of the Jacksonville, Florida Public Library; Tim Novak at the Saskatchewan Archives Board; Judy Mathison, an employee at the Vernon County Historical Society in Viroqua, Wisconsin and Chris Marshall of the Marion County Public Library in Indianapolis. Judith Johnson of Memphis was more than generous as she extracted articles from the Memphis Commercial Appeal and Memphis Press-Scimitar. Thank you also to Jon Hamilton for your assistance in locating information from Lincoln, Nebraska. Also, thanks to Sharon Canter for her diligent effort to search through the St. Joseph News-Press and St. Joseph Gazette. My special thanks to Robert Langenderfer, who assisted with the editing of this manuscript. He is much appreciated. One final review by editor Erin Rivers polished the manuscript for publication. I am still singing my praises to all of you for the outstanding job everyone did in helping me to reconstruct the Monarchs' 1938 season.

Other participating libraries and contributors included the Madison, Wisconsin Public Library; the Fargo Public Library in North Dakota; the Charles City, Iowa Public Library; the Arkansas History Commission of Little Rock; the Louisville Free Public Library and St. Paul, Minnesota Public Library. I wish to extend a special thank you to Suzana Bursich, Reference Assistant at the East Chicago Public Library, for her assistance with history and photographs on Henry Milton. James F. Shearouse, Reference Librarian at the Rock Island, Illinois Public Library, was helpful on several levels. Robert Mapes of Des Moines, Iowa, assisted with locating Monarchs' games played in that city, as did Jeremy Krock for games in Peoria, Illinois. Herbert Brown of Moberly, Missouri's Gatewood Browns, gave insight as to how that team scheduled a Monarchs' appearance. These are the unsung individuals and institutions that helped me produce a publication that will entertain and inform researchers and fans for generations to come. Although I had lots of support putting this book together, it was no easy task.

There are several gaps in the games' dates that I have been unable to locate. Missing are games played by the Monarchs between June 8 to June 11, four days, June 22 to June 25, four days, September 9 and 10, two days, September 15 to the 17, three days, and part of the House of David tour played on September 22 to September 25, four days. We tried our best without success to fill in the missing dates.

Conducting research and interviews took away my evenings at home, but I always had the support of a loving family. My mother, Margaret Elizabeth, now deceased, deserves my special gratitude for her unwavering support of everything I did in baseball during her lifetime. My father, Arthur Howard Dixon, a longtime Kansas City Monarchs fan, was also proud of this endeavor and provided much inspiration and financial support before his death in 1988. My mother-in-law Sidney Mae Carroll chipped in with a few furious comments, suggestions, and some editing, for which I am forever grateful.

Finally, I must thank my wife, Dr. Kerry Dixon, and our three children. They listened as I rehashed stories and accompanied me to libraries and visits to ballplayers' homes. Thank you for loving me when the going was tough. Kerry pitched in with suggestions and edited parts of the work. She was equally supportive in seeing that this story is shared with the many people who loved, admired, and cherished the rookie, the man, and the legacy of John "Buck" O'Neil. He thought well of her also. I am indebted to Kerry and my classmate Bernice Keith for creating the catchy title and subtitle of this publication that you are about to read.

Preface

Because of the many unique features in *John "Buck" O'Neil, The Rookie, His Words, His Voice,* we wanted to make readers aware of certain omissions and additions. The author made an extreme and dedicated effort to reconstruct the Monarchs' 1938 season. In so doing, we faced many obstacles. Luckily, no one covers a Negro League season with such creativity as Phil S. Dixon, and we finished our task with amazing results. The challenges we faced were many.

Games in Memphis against the Red Sox, of which there were almost a dozen, had no printed box scores. The *Memphis Commercial Appeal* did not print box scores, and copies of that year's minority-owned *Memphis World* were destroyed in a fire. In addition, box scores for games in Oklahoma City were never printed, and this pattern was repeated often. Southern newspapers in Birmingham, Little Rock, and Louisville were equally as lax in publishing box scores of games played by the Monarchs and other Negro American League teams in these cities. There were also lots of missing box scores for games played in Missouri and Chicago. Ten days of box scores were not printed during the Monarchs' visit to Chicago from June 17, 1938, to June 27, 1938, which included a rainout. Fielding statistics was also a problem.

Some games, especially those in Illinois and Wisconsin, did not include putouts or assist. They had a category titled chances and thus some of the fielding is lost forever. In some of these box scores, only errors were listed. Finding newspaper reports of games played was also problematic. There were times when a particular newspaper was no longer available, partially destroyed, or skipped dates. For example, the Friday, July 1 edition of the *Charles City Press* is missing. The Saturday, July 2, edition of the same newspaper has the bottom left corner of the sports page is torn off. These are some of the many misfortunes of covering Negro League baseball during the era of segregation. To help readers understand the nature of the information located, I used the following keys to simplify our findings.

Where box scores were located, the city is underscored in this manner **July 24-Bismarck (DH)** as a marker, and an added **(DH)** is attached if it was played as part of a doubleheader. If the date and city are not underlined, no box score was located, and only written accounts of that day's results were available. The author added other information to heighten our understanding of what historical information was found.

In our statistical totals, we show if O'Neil's performance was against a Negro National League team **(NNL)**, a Negro American League opponent **(NAL)**, or Western Association minor league competition **(WA)**, or simply an exhibition **(E)** against a local town team. Each set of statistics has a unique identifier. I did not separate official league games between rival **(NAL)** teams from those that were termed exhibition games. The "exhibition games" were not listed in the league's official standings, but we combined them into our games played. The Kansas City Monarchs' season-ending series against the House of David and the Oklahoma All-Stars are both listed as exhibitions **(E)**.

"His face covered with sweat, his body itching in the heat and muck, teen-ager Buck O'Neil grimaced as he logged boxes across a Sarasota celery field in the 1920s. 'Damn,' he said. 'There's got to be something better than this.' O'Neil's father, the foreman of the celery crew, told him there was, 'But you can't get it here. You're gonna have to go somewhere else.'"

Charlie Huisking, Sarasota Herald-Tribune, March 5, 1995

Buck O'Neil says...

"One of the women I loved like my mother was Miss Emma E. Booker. She was the elementary teacher at our school. Miss Booker...what she told us, was 'anything you're big enough to do, you can do it. Now, these people aren't going to give you but eight grades here in this school. See, but I tell you what you can do. You can come back here to school at nights, and when you get out, you're going to have just as much as they got at Sarasota High School'--which I couldn't go to."

Somewhere Else, Someplace Better

It was the opening day of the 1938 baseball season, on Sunday, May 15, to be exact, in Kansas City, Missouri, when 26-year-old John "Buck" O'Neil, a Monarchs' rookie, first stepped into spacious Ruppert Stadium. Feeling as if he had entered the Roman Coliseum as a Christian ready for slaughter, O'Neil's auspicious beginning, as it happened numerous other times, was smothered in fate and circumstantial favor. And yet, it was more than coincidental that Kansas City was where he found himself on this day.

Ruppert Stadium, the old ballpark at 22nd and Brooklyn Avenue, also home to Kansas City's American Association Blues, was the site of the Monarchs' home opener against the Chicago American Giants. Before reaching Kansas City, William "Bill" Simms, the Monarchs' right fielder, was abruptly traded to the American Giants. Monarchs' manager, Andy Cooper, needing to adjust his line-up, looked to his bench for an adequate outfield replacement. The rookie John "Buck"

O'Neil, a first baseman held in reserve, was summoned. O'Neil, mighty surprised to see his name penciled in as the Monarchs' opening day right fielder, appeared anxious as he reached into his grip, rumbling past his first baseman's mitt, and fumbling around until his fielder's glove was located. Encouraged by his manager's selection, O'Neil side-stepped an assortment of wooden Louisville Slugger bats laid cluttered in front of the Monarchs' dugout and never hesitated while jogging to the outfield. Along the way, he reached into his back pocket where his cap was wedged and sort of screwed it into game time compliance. Naturally enough, those around him acknowledged and supported the rookie's unanticipated outfield berth.

(L to R) Elwood Knox, Andrew "Rube" Foster, J. D. Howard and C. I. Taylor. Foster participated in Florida's Winter League as early as 1909. Taylor had taken his entire ABCs team to Florida in 1916. (Authors collection)

Studying his surroundings, O'Neil stood and gazed at his teammates, several of whom were considered to be the league's top stars. To his right, shagging fly balls in centerfield stood Willard Brown, perhaps the hardest-hitting outfielder in baseball. Turning for a better view of the infield, O'Neil's eyes sought out Newton Henry Allen, peer of all second basemen. On the mound, warming up with a world of confidence, was Hilton Smith, one of the Negro American League's best right-handed pitchers. Down the foul line, standing on the steps of his team's dugout, were Manager Andy Cooper and Coach Wilber "Bullet" Rogan. Perched on first base, where O'Neil originally intended to play, stood Eldridge Mayweather. Also appearing with O'Neil in that memorable home opener were men like Henry Milton in left field, Roosevelt Cox at third base, Frank Duncan in full catcher's gear, and shortstop Byron "Mex" Johnson. In Chicago's dugout along the third baseline stood another group of illustrious Negro Leaguers. American Giants' pitchers Ted Trent, Jess Houston, William "Sug" Cornelius along with third baseman Alex Radcliffe and outfielder Norman "Turkey" Stearnes were there playing under the tutorship of Manager Jim "Candy Jim" Taylor. Each eagerly awaited the umpire's directive to "play ball." It is ironic, perhaps, that such memorable occasions are often carved out of easily forgettable moments. For the rookie O'Neil, this was a moment to savor, for the journey to Kansas City was cloaked in years of disillusionment, lofty exuberance, and sometimes downright humiliation.

John Jordan O'Neil Jr., nicknamed "Buck," was born in Carrabelle, Florida, roughly fifty-five miles south of Tallahassee, on November 13, 1911. He was the middle son of three O'Neil children. There was also Fanny, an older sister born in 1910 and Warren, a younger brother born in 1918.[1] His parents, John O'Neil Sr. and Luella O'Neil, were both Floridians by one account, but another record named his father's birthplace as Georgia in 1871.[2] His mother was twelve years younger than the father, so most of his siblings' rearing fell on her, as John O'Neil Sr. labored endlessly for a sawmill that traversed Florida, working in forests for weeks on end, and was frequently away from the family. In O'Neil's mind, his father was a combination of the lumberjack Paul Bunyan and the steel-driving John Henry. The 1920 census is synonymous with Buck's early childhood.

In that census, the family name is incorrectly spelled as O'Neal. They were living in the town of Carrabelle in Franklin County, Florida, where the father worked at a town Sawmill. When the elder O'Neil grew tired of the constant separation from his family, sometime after 1924, the entire O'Neil family relocated to Sarasota, more than three hundred miles into Southern Florida, where field employment was plentiful. They left the unpaved streets of Carrabelle for greener pastures. Sarasota was thriving!

Booming, growing, and expanding, Sarasota was buzzing with opportunities. Buck recalled, "The Ringling Brothers Circus had just moved from Indiana to Florida, and O'Neil's mother was hired as a cook by Ida Ringling North, who was John Ringling's sister."[3] In 1923, John McGraw's New York Giants, a team that historically trained in Texas, moved their spring training headquarters to Sarasota.[4] Equally exciting was the agricultural progress of the region. "Florida's celery growing had become a highly developed and specialized industry,"

> Four states were in the celery business on a large scale, but Florida led in production. Figuring mere returns on the acre, Florida growers received $1,112, California growers $435, New York growers $447, and Michigan growers $318.[5]

O'Neil's father went to work in the celery fields, and his sons followed, although new laws prohibited the children from working in this capacity.[1] Celery harvesting was a specialized

---

[1] The Fair Labor Standards Act (FLSA) was passed in 1938. This act prohibited the employment of any child under the age of fourteen and children under sixteen while school is in session.

occupation. To keep the celery from deteriorating, it had to be harvested within a few days after reaching marketable sizes. Growers scheduled plantings to ensure that O'Neil and his fellow workers had weekly work. On weekends the adult workers would leave the fields to fellowship at church and watch the men play baseball.

Having watched his father perform with the sawmill team since early childhood and by attending games between workers from the celery fields, young John grew to love baseball. Ironically, Buck never saw his father as a very young man. Depending on the source, his father was either 38 or 40 when John Jr. was born. Young John had no equipment, not even a ball, so his mother helped. She made baseballs out of pieces of brick and old socks, keeping a ready supply of these homemade balls for her son and his friends.[6] When his work permitted, young John snuck over to see McGraw's Giants. As a teenager, he watched from a tree beyond the outfield fence while major league teams trained at Payne Park.[7] "I guess [I wanted to play baseball] practically all of my life because I was raised in Sarasota, Florida, and the major league ball clubs trained in Florida. So, I had seen good baseball all my life," offered O'Neil. He countered,

> I think most of the kids wanted to be professional baseball players. Now I had
>
> no idea about playing Black baseball. I was just thinking about professional
>
> baseball. Because I didn't realize that the major leagues were not for me at that
>
> time, I thought anybody could play before I realized the social situation.[8]

The so-called "social situation" was also affecting O'Neil in other ways. Like many African American boys and girls in their adolescent years, John was denied the opportunity to attend high school in Sarasota because of Florida's mandated segregation. Emma E. Booker, his teacher at Booker Elementary and Principal of the school, had done her best to educate the young people in the community. Since early in his childhood, Booker found young O'Neil to be one of the most ravenous learners in the one-room county schoolhouse. O'Neil shifted uneasily as he recalled, "The eighth grade was as high as our school [the Negro School] went. I walked past the Sarasota High School every day, but I couldn't go there."[9] O'Neil added, "I don't know how in the hell he [White Americans] figured I could learn as much [by] the eighth grade as his boy would learn in twelve." [10] Consequently, young John continued to work as child labor in the same celery fields with his father, but his studies and baseball remained a priority. His school had two baseball teams, a first and second team. He started playing baseball with Booker Grammar School in 1924.[11] About 1927, when he was in the eighth game, Andrew Brown showed up at the school and asked the principal if O'Neil could play first base for his team. She consented, so I became a member of the Sarasota Nine Devils. They really needed a first baseman and invited O'Neil to play."[12] Still, homework always came first,"

> I used to get in trouble when I played ball until dark, but when I came home,
> whether it was dark or not, I still had to cut the wood. But I got smart; I started
> cutting the wood first. I'd play ball after that, come in for dinner time and after
> dinner, then I would do my homework.[13]

O'Neil also considered himself to be a clever box boy in the celery fields. They were paying $1.00 for a day's work. He did so well that they boosted his pay to $1.25 a day for placing boxes along the road to be loaded on trucks. The work was as punishing as it was dull for a young boy working alongside the men. He told the story often of how he used foul language for the first time,

> When I was 12 years old, I worked in the celery fields, and I was a box boy. I
> would put the boxes out so they could pack the celery in the boxes to ship it. I
> was sitting behind the boxes one day in the fall of the year, and it was hot in
> Florida, and I was sweating and itching in that muck. My father was the foreman
> on this job, and he was on [one] side of the boxes, and I was on the other side.

21

And I said, 'Damn. There's got to be something better than this.' So, when we got off the truck that night, my daddy said, 'I heard what you said behind the boxes.' I thought he was going to reprimand me for saying 'damn,' because he had never heard me say 'damn.' I doubt if I had ever said 'damn,' to tell you the truth. But he said, 'I heard what you said about there being something better than this. There is something better, but you can't get it here; you're gonna have to go someplace else.[14]

That 'someplace' else was Jacksonville, Florida, two hundred miles north. The 'something better' was an education. Therefore, after working that last summer as child labor in Sarasota, O'Neil's parents sent him to Jacksonville to live in a better environment with an aunt and uncle. At the time, according to O'Neil, there were only four high schools for African American children in the entire state of Florida. One was in Miami, another in Tampa, another in Jacksonville, and the other in Pensacola. In Jacksonville, he attended high school at Edward Waters College, a coeducational institution serving both high school and college-aged students. Founded by the African Methodist Episcopal Church in 1866, Edward Waters School was created to educate newly freed slaves and their children through a curriculum designed to emphasize practical and professional skills. Since O'Neil's family, being the devout A.M.E. parishioners that they were, wanted John to have an education, going to Edward Waters was a natural forward progression. It was about that same time that O'Neil saw his first African American professional baseball team. O'Neil remembered,

I had an uncle who was a railroader, and he came to Sarasota to visit us and took my father and me down to West Palm Beach to see the great Rube Foster at the Royal Poinciana Hotel.[15] Every year the Chicago American Giants and the

Indianapolis A.B.C.s would come to Florida to play, and they played at the Breakers Hotel [in] Palm Beach. They had two outstanding hotels; the Royal Poinciana was one of the hotels, and these guys would play ball all winter down there. And, they were actually waiters, bellhops in the hotel, but they played ball for the enjoyment of the guests at the hotel. So, my father took me down there, and I got a chance to see 'Rube' [Foster] and all the great Black ballplayers at that time. I was sold then after I saw them. I wanted to play with one of those ball clubs.[16] When I got back, now I'm telling everybody about these ballplayers. So, my father then started getting the Amsterdam News which was the black weekly, sent to me. And we got the *Pittsburgh Courier* from Pittsburgh and the *Chicago Defender*. So now I'm also reading about these great black baseball players.[17]

Young O'Neil never forgot these experiences. When he returned home, he began to share stories with other boys his age: "I learned more about baseball in college. I had a great coach in Ox Clemons. He taught me quite a bit about baseball. The guys on the ball club they would go east every year to play baseball--[People] like [Dean] Everett and [Schute] Merritt, he [eventually] played with the Black Yankees."[18] Joe Dugan, an infielder who had gone north to join the Syracuse New York Red Caps, was also a native of Sarasota.[19] The census of 1930 provided further insight into O'Neil's youth.

In the 1930 census, 18-years-old O'Neil was listed with the family in Sarasota. His occupation was given as shoe repair at a local shop. He worked in shoe repair and as a shoe-shining boy for Adolph Roth, who he thought was a German Jew but was Hungarian. Mr. Roth was teaching him the shoe repair business.[20] O'Neil Sr. was said to be working as a laborer on a Truck Farm for Palmer Farms on Fruitville Road, and Luella as a servant at a private facility, more than likely for Ida Ringling

North.[21] The O'Neil's home was valued at $1,000 in that census. By comparison, Ida, a 56-year-old widow, had her house valued at $10,000 in the same census. O'Neil's neighbors had similar jobs as laborers in celery and orange groves. They worked and lived in improvised and near destitute situations. Around that same time, Luella opened her restaurant, and young O'Neil headed for Jacksonville to attend college in hopes of improving their lives. When Mr. Roth heard that O'Neil was going away to school, he slapped $50 in the youngster's hand. "That was a whole lot of money," added O'Neil. Ida Ringling North gave O'Neil two of her deceased husband's suits to wear in college. He had to resize and cut them down because her husband had been a big man.

O'Neil eventually finished school at Edward Waters, graduating from its high school branch in 1929. He added two more years of college, graduating in 1931. Attending school in Jacksonville only intensified his desire to play professional baseball. Shortly thereafter, O'Neil, with more bravado than common sense, started working towards his goal to play for one of those league teams in professional Negro baseball.

"Sarasota's lineup will probably see O'Neil at first base, Brown catching; Thomas cavorting around short, Milton at second, McClain at the hot corner, Toronto in leftfield, Yarber in center garden, Martin in right, and Ben or Hollamon catcher for Morris, Houston or Pittman on the mound."

Sarasota Herald-Tribune, October 20, 1929

Buck O'Neil says...

"I started playing baseball when I was 12-years-old. My Daddy was a baseball player, and I followed him around watching them play, and I always had good hands see, and the old men would throw me the ball, and I would catch it, and I was a ham. I enjoyed it."

A Whole New Ballgame

Young O'Neil was ready to play baseball anywhere his talent took him. In his travels,

he would become more acclimated to segregation and second-class citizenship as it was practiced all

over America. He played in towns that had no place for them to stay, and in cities where they had

to get their food at a side window or a back door, and almost always to go. He traveled thousands of

miles in cars, from Florida to New York playing one-nighters, often participating in a small town or a major metropolitan city tournament that prohibited his use of restrooms and post-game showers. In every town and community where segregation permitted nine or ten good Black men to use a local park, baseball was being played. Sarasota had its Nine Devils, which is where O'Neil got his start on the diamond, the place where he began playing a game that became his lifetime passion.

In 1930, civic-minded "white fans" led by O'Neil's employer, Adolph Roth, started a movement to equip the Nine Devils team of "Colored Boys" to take on teams of their same race in some regional competition as activities for the young men, and entertainment for the adults in Sarasota. They dropped the Devils name and changed it to Tigers. An article in the *Sarasota Herald Tribune* dated April 22, 1930, announced,

"The Negroes need shoes and uniforms, not to mention gloves, mitts, and other implements used in the diversion. The idea formulated by a number of fans is to have a large number of enthusiasts take season tickets at so much per taking, thereby assuring the past-timers' outfits and audiences."[22]

Numerous fund-raising campaigns continued throughout April of 1930 when another published statement said, "It will cost $175 to provide 10 complete uniforms, 10 pairs of shoes, and a supply of one dozen baseballs."[23] A later article asked for thirty-five men to step forward with $5 contributions and that a list of those who had paid would be posted at Roth's El Toro Pocket Billiard Parlor on Main Street."[24] With these requests behind them, games were scheduled on Thursday and Sunday afternoons at Payne Park. These were said to be good days for the ballplayers to get permission to be absent from their jobs. H.C. Wynn, a white farmer in the district, was put in charge of the team's local affairs. Andrew Brown acted as manager on the field and pitched. The old Nine Devils team was renamed the Sarasota Tigers. O'Neil affirmed,

When I was about 14, I was asked to play with the Sarasota Nine Devils. Brown was the manager, and we played Sundays and Thursdays at Payne Park. Needless to say, I did nothing for them, mostly because I was scared to death. But I stayed with them until I left here.[25]

(L to R) John "Buck" O'Neil and Homer "Goose" Curry. Shown here kissing the Delta Queen in Greenville, Mississippi. Curry was O'Neil's manager at Memphis in 1937 before O'Neil joined the Monarchs in 1938. (Authors collection)

O'Neil's local team was well-known and widely publicized as a "Crack local Negro" squad. Their games were covered in part by the *Sarasota Herald-Tribune*, absent of important details that allowed fans to track the team's progress. The Giants of Mulberry, the Atlanta Gray Sox, Tampa Tappers, the Florida Cuban Giants of Jacksonville, and Tampa Cuban Stars provided the opposition. Teams from Orlando, Fort Pierce, Ocala, Bowling Green, Port Tampa, and Winter Haven came to Sarasota but were simply noted as "Colored teams" or "Colored Champions." A few of Buck's teammates managed to get their names printed in the newspapers, unfortunately, and in most cases, it was only their last names. "Dizzy" Martin, Ferguson, Lloyd Haisley, Calvin, Harvard, Smith, Belford, and Shann were among the named. Not once was Buck's name mentioned in any of these articles, and there were many in the *Sarasota Herald-Tribune* and *Tampa Tribune*. Box scores were absent in these same newspapers. This was O'Neil's start in baseball and also the start of a new nickname, "Foots," which he got after his return from college. He left Sarasota as a boy but returned as a man seeking to do the things that men do,

> That first year when I came back to Sarasota, I was a big shot; I had been to
>
> college, and all of this, and that's when I ran into Big Knox. We called him Big
>
> Knox. He was a gambler and a hustler around the street, and he liked me, and I
>
> liked Big Knox. Big Knox wore a size twelve shoe, and I wore a ten. He gave me
>
> a pair of Florsheim shoes, black and pretty. I put cotton and newspaper in the
>
> toe, and then they started calling me "Foots."[26]

The 1930 season concluded with a gala Labor Day celebration that included a barbecue, races, a quartet singing contest, a pole climbing contest, and a boxing battle royal.[27] It was an interesting year in other ways.

While some thought that "Hallelujah," the all-talking motion picture that came to Sarasota's Edwards Theater, was the greatest "Colored" movie of the 1920's it had serious racial undertones. It was advertised as a "Story of Negro Life." In reality, it was yet another stereotypic version of tap dancers, dancing waiters mixed in with some Negro spirituals and religious stereotypes. Released in 1929, it starred Daniel Haynes as the male lead and Nina Mae McKinney as the female lead. Fannie Belle De Knight played a southern mammy. It wasn't produced by Blacks, but they were proud of it because it was all they had. There were two new songs by Irving Berlin, who was not African American, "The End of the Road" and Swanee Shuffle," that were used in the cabaret, and cotton-marketing sequences on this Metro Goldwyn Mayer production.[28] This was the kind of propaganda making its way across America and into Sarasota during the summer of 1930, the same year local residents fell in love with its new Negro nine. The Tiger's success during the summer of 1930 set the stage for 1931.

The Sarasota Tigers became the Sarasota Black Tigers in 1931 and continued with a schedule of games at Payne Park. New to the team was a player called "Red Sox" from Pittsburg, Florida, brothers "Fats" Major and Doby Major, along with a ballplayer named "Flukie." A player nicknamed "Blue," last name "Yarbrough," was said to be the team's "Homerun King."[29] The Orlando Gray Sox were added to the schedule, as were the Red Caps of Jacksonville. On June 4, 1931, 8-4 defeat of the Smokers, their arch-rivals from Tampa, a report in the *Sarasota Herald-Tribune* reported that Haisley, O'Neil, and Brown led with the willow work for the Tigers, each rapping out a triple. Although his name was often misspelled, Buck was making his presence felt.[30] He returned for a third season with the Tigers in 1932 when he, as a 21-years-old infielder, was one of the most popular players on the local diamond.

Much more was written about the 1932 team as their popularity increased and their importance resonated within the community. For the first time rosters, and lineups were printed in the local newspapers. The Black Tigers also moved to a new park in the Nicetown area of Sarasota. To start the 1932 season, the city of Sarasota set aside a plot of land in Newtown to be used as a baseball field. The ball diamond ran from an area on Osprey Avenue to Orange Avenue to Thirty-Third Street. Bradenton, Azuka, Lake Walls, Sebring, Bartow, and Punta Gorda were added to the schedule in a region where Black teams dominated the turf.

On June 5, 1932, O'Neil's name was mentioned along with others in a 9-1 win over Sebring. The lineup read, "Carlo [Carlos Suarez], 3b; Lloyd Haisley, p; John O'Neal, 2b; Ferguson, c; Major, 1b; Doby "Fats" Major, rf; Williams, ss; Wilson, LF; C. Major, cf," along with a statement that said, "O'Neal, Tiger second-sacker, led the local nine with the stick work with three hits in four times up."[31] Although his last name was misspelled, he received a similar mention after an 8-4 win over Sebring the following afternoon while playing first base,

> [Fats] Major, who hurled for the Tigers, held the Sebring team to four scattered
>
> hits. He also got two hits out of four trips to the plate and scored one run. C.
>
> Major, Carlo, and O'Neal also connected for two hits in four times at-bat.

O'Neil picked up the story from there. "About 1933, I hooked up with my first professional team, the Tampa Black Smokers," he recalled as he reflected on a past fused by time. "I left home, traveling all the way to southern Georgia. After a month with the Smokers, I got an offer to join the Miami Giants."[32] The Giants were managed by Wayne Carr. A much-renowned pitcher, Carr entered professional play with the St. Louis Giants of the Negro National League in 1920. Also listed among O'Neil's 1933 teammates were veteran players Oliver "Ghost" Marcelle and Orville "Bill" Riggins, who were good friends of Manager Carr. It was a step in a different direction.

Marcelle, born June 24, 1895, in Thibodaux, Louisiana, was a seasoned veteran, having already played for such illustrious teams as the New York Lincoln Giants and Bacharach Giants of Atlantic City, New Jersey. He was easily admired since his career had taken him everywhere that Buck dreamed of going. On the road, Marcelle was a tremendous drawing card, especially for crowds that wanted to see one of the better third basemen in baseball. Like other celebrities, Marcelle chose another well-known city to call home. O'Neil recalled, "He [Marcelle] always said he was from New Orleans."[2] Riggins, a second baseman, also had extensive experience, previously having performed for the New York Lincoln Giants, the Harlem Stars, the Detroit Stars, and Cleveland Hornets.

O'Neil, proud that he was finally getting paid for something he would have done for free, added, "For the first time in my life, I actually got a salary for playing baseball: ten dollars a week, plus room and board."[33] One of the nice aspects about Florida was that you could play baseball year-round and draw a crowd from the tourist. As always, there was segregation in the bleachers, sections where special seats were reserved for white fans adhering to southern customs. That same summer, he took his iconic nickname, "Buck" from Miami Giants co-owner Buck O'Neal.[34] For the moment, many would continue to call him "Foots," as they were slow to adapt to the new nickname.

The summer, and winter of 1933, was nondescript. O'Neil did have the good fortune to familiarize himself with Winfield Welch, a team manager and scout who eventually introduced him to Monarchs' owner J. L. Wilkinson. Welch was the manager of Shreveport's Acme Giants. The summer of 1934 was also a smooth one as O'Neil, and his Miami Giants teammates left Florida headed north toward New York, and Pennsylvania where they started to get some well-deserved media attention. The team was in Miami on April 1 to start a two-game series with the Jacksonville

---

[2] Oliver Marcelle was inducted into the Louisiana Sports Hall of Fame in 1996. His name is sometimes spelled, Marcell.

Red Caps, losing the opener 6-3 with Marsh and McGee as the battery.[35] On May 27, Buck's Giants were back in Miami for another pair of games which they lost to the local Red Caps in a 4-2 final in the opener with Bubber pitching for Miami against Mitchell of the Red Caps.[36] After splitting a doubleheader at Navy Field with the Key West All-Stars, the team headed north.[37] Navy Field and the other fields in the South, where the "Colored" teams played, were subpar for baseball. One traveling fan was compelled to complain to the *Key West Citizen* newspaper after watching Buck's Miami Giants,

> I was out at the baseball game Thursday afternoon at the Navy Field. Two colored
>
> teams played a very good game, and it was interesting from start to finish. I have
>
> been in the city for two days, and I expect to come back again soon. I hope that
>
> on my return in the near future, the city will have a field fit to play on because it
>
> seems impossible to play on these grounds. I hope the fans here will do
>
> something about this.[38]

The Miami Giants remained in Key West for an additional day to play the local Pirates team before motoring north. There were some good teams around Florida, such as the Fort Lauderdale Giants, the Key West Coconuts, the Florida Pelicans, Florida Tigers, and others, but the money was not enough to survive on, so off to the north, they dashed for more games.

Unfortunately, their team received little notoriety up north as most of that year's coverage was reserved for the better-known teams and numerous historical events in the news. In 1934 Eastern baseball circles were dominated by the Philadelphia Stars, the Pittsburgh Crawfords, the Homestead Grays, the Nashville Elite Giants, Chicago American Giants, the Baltimore Black Sox, and Kansas City Monarchs. They were teams considered atop of everyone else in the Negro League hierarchy. On the second rung were teams like the Cleveland Red Sox, the Newark Dodgers, and Bacharach

Giants. O'Neil's Miami Giants, more-than-likely were a third rung team, were joined by such touring squads as the New Orleans Crescents, the Detroit Black Tigers, and Columbus Stars. That year's newspaper coverage highlighted such major events as the Kansas City Monarchs versus Satchel Paige, who pitched for the House of David in the Denver Post Tournament; Chicago's second annual East-West game; New York's four-team doubleheaders at Yankee Stadium, and the Dizzy and Daffy Dean's tour in October. Seldom, if ever, did national minority newspaper coverage trickle down to the circuit of baseball in which O'Neil's team was engaged.

Buck estimated that it took "two weeks in two old jalopies to get from Florida up to there [New York], playing our way up by day, and driving at night. And, when we got to Harlem, we stayed at the Woodside Hotel."[39] In an October edition of the *Colored Baseball and Sports Monthly*, one writer took note of the team and put his observations into words,

The [Miami] club as a whole would not impress you. The fans called the players a bunch of farmers. But the Florida bunch was really a great outfit. They left a lasting impression on Baltimore and Newark. They shut out Baltimore 2-0 [on] August 20 and were defeated by the Black Sox 7-3. Penns Grove [New Jersey] (white) were defeated 9-1. The Newark Dodgers beat them 4-2 in the opening game of a doubleheader, but the Florida Tossers came back with that do-or-die spirit, and 'Bubber' Hubert beat the Dodgers 6-3.[40]

While summarizing, the writer ensured, "The Florida team has won nine games and lost two at this writing. Had they arrived in the East earlier in the season, their booking would have been much easier.[41] There were other games where media attention was given to Buck's Miami Giants. On August 14, 1934, they were in Richmond, Virginia, to play the Capital City All-Stars at the local Mayo Island Park, where "Special seats were reserved for white patrons."[42] The Giants won 7-4 behind Carr's pitching as he held the All-Stars scoreless through eight innings.[43] They also lost a 2-1 game in Richmond, but they were so well-liked that another game was scheduled at the same park on August 17 against the Petersburgh Giants.[44]

As late as August 25, 1934, the Miami Giants were in Chester, Pennsylvania, losing 2-0 to manager Herbert "Rap" Dixon's renowned Baltimore Black Sox.[45] It was one of the few games his team could get against higher-up competition.[46] There were also a series of games in Syracuse, New York, against the Detroit Clowns in September. An edition of the *Baltimore Afro-American* wrote,

> Little need be said of the Miami aggregation. Their record of 49 wins in 60 starts
>
> is enough to make them an attraction wherever their appearance is announced.
>
> The Giants have a large number of clashes with major league teams to their
>
> credit.[47]

In early September, the Miami team was booked in Schenectady, New York, for games against the American Laundry-Edisons.[48] They were back in Richmond, on September 27 and 28, for more games against the Richmond Virginia Stars.[49] In early October, while returning to Florida, O'Neil's team stopped in Burlington, North Carolina, for a doubleheader against that city's African American team, the Yellow Jackets.[50] O'Neil returned home feeling not so prosperous but certainly a bit wiser for having taken the excursion.

Riding the success of 1934, O'Neil ventured out with the Miami Giants in 1935 and headed south towards Louisiana to begin the season. He quickly discovered that "Depression" was more than a vocabulary word. O'Neil recollected, "We left Sarasota that spring in these two old seven-passenger cars, Cadillacs with jump seats on them, one which my father had bought for a hundred dollars. Doby Major, a friend of mine from Sarasota, joined us, and off we went seeking fame and fortune."[51] Riggins did not return to the Miami Giants in 1935, but Jacksonville's Sylvester Sneed, Marcelle, and Carr were all there at the tour's start.

Before traveling east, one of the team's first stops was Monroe, Louisiana. O'Neil, testifying on the difficulties of this experience, recalled, "In Monroe, we fell so far behind with the rent, we couldn't pay the landlady. So, she said, 'Here's what I'll do. I'll take one of your cars until you can pay me and come back and get the car.' Well, we didn't ever get back."[52] Instead, crammed into one car, the team headed off to nearby Shreveport, Louisiana, with eleven ballplayers--prime candidates for whatever road hazards a set of dangerously worn-out U.S. Royals tires might supply. O'Neil jokingly remembered with some hesitation,

> We would ride packed up in there--we'd have three people on the backseat,
> three people in the jump seat (where there ought to be only two), and three
> people in the front seat. That's nine people. So, after we would ride so long, well
> then, two guys that were sitting inside would get out on the bumper. I was on the
> right bumper, and my friend was on the left bumper. I'd put my left hand over,
> and he'd put his right hand, and we would hold each other this way. We would
> ride fifty, a hundred miles like this. And then two other guys would get out and
> get on the bumpers, and we'd get in the car and ride. This is the way we traveled.[53]

Finances remained unstable, and when O'Neil's struggling teammates defaulted on their rent at their rooming house in Shreveport, he recollected, "We snuck out the back window in the middle of the night."[54] As the team anxiously motored toward Wichita Falls, Texas, the remaining car gave out from pure exhaustion. O'Neil and his teammates sought refuge in a nearby rail yard and decided to hobo the remainder of the way to Texas. Hobos weren't all that unusual during the 1930s. Often the only way poor people traveled was by hopping on freight trains illegally, a process that was called

35

hoboing. One reference estimated, "More than two million men and perhaps eight thousand women became hoboes during the 1930s. At least sixty-five hundred traveling hoboes were killed, either in accidents or by railroad 'bulls,' brutal guards hired by the railroads to make sure trains carried only paying customers."[55] Listed among the people who rode the rails illegally are novelists Louis L'Amour, television host Art Linkletter, oil billionaire H. L. Hunt journalist Eric Sevareid, and former Supreme Court Justice William O. Douglas.[56] As young African American men, the well-publicized Scottsboro case kept everyone on alert while hoboing on trains.

Back on March 25, 1931, nine African American teenagers were arrested for alleged gang rape of two white girls, Victoria Price and Ruby Bates, while hoboing on a Southern Railroad freight run from Chattanooga to Memphis. Arrested in Paint Rock, Alabama, and taken to Scottsboro, Alabama, a crowd of several hundred white men, hoping for a good old-fashioned lynching, surrounded the Scottsboro jail. Their plans were foiled, however, when Alabama's governor, B. M. Miller, ordered the National Guard to Scottsboro to protect the suspects. When the trial ended (all eight of the Scottsboro boys went to trial together), eight of the nine were convicted and sentenced to death. Bates later recanted her testimony and said there was no rape, that none of the defendants touched her or even spoke to her, and that the accusations of rape were made after Price told her "To frame up a story" to avoid morals charges for prostitution. Still, seven of the nine Scottsboro Boys remained jailed in 1937.[57]

In Wichita Falls, O'Neil's Miami Giants were scheduled to play Texas' Black Spudders. After jumping off in a nearby rail yard, stepping into puddles of rainwater, and beating a muddy path to the park, it became evident that there would be no ball games in Wichita Falls. The town was nearly flooded by a continuous rainstorm. Marooned and stuck without transportation, he resorted to "hustling pool rooms" to keep afloat. O'Neil called it "sheer survival" as he refused to return home broke and dejected. In a stroke of optimism, Carr heard that a Denver merchant named Joe Alpert was looking for an African American team to represent his clothing store in the *Denver Post* newspaper tournament. When Texas' Black Spudders, who was headed to Denver to perform in the Post tournament, offered transportation for some of O'Neil's Miami Giants, "Carr," explained O'Neil, "got him [Mr. Alpert] on the telephone and [he] agreed to sponsor us--if we [all of us] could get to Denver."[58] O'Neil continued, "The Spudders were kind enough to pack six of our older players and all our equipment in one of their cars. The rest of us hopped another freight train out of Wichita Falls for the twenty-four-hour ride to Colorado."[59]

O'Neil, having reached Colorado, appeared in the Denver Post Tournament as a first baseman with the Joe Alpert Clothiers. Ultimately, they were beaten out in the late rounds by Denver's United Fuel, a team that won Colorado's state baseball title. Having picked up a few extra dollars, the Joe Alpert' Giants now became the Denver White Elephants as the team hurried off to Wichita, Kansas, where the National Baseball Conference Tournament was starting. Tagging along, the Texas Spudders also went to Kansas and, along the way, renamed themselves the Texas Centennials.

O'Neil's White Elephants were listed as a "new and surprise entry from the Denver Post tourney."[60] Interestingly, the National Baseball Congress Tournament was fixed so that African American teams would eliminate each other in the early rounds. In that arrangement, Bismarck, a predominately African American team, played the Monroe Monarchs, and the Memphis Red Sox battled the San Angelo Black Sheepherders. O'Neil's team was the only African American team to be pitted against a white team in the opening round.

Game one, on August 16, 1935, saw O'Neil's revamped Miami Giants/Denver White Elephants crush the New Orleans Holy Name baseball club 13-7. Having gone 2-for-6 at-bat, O'Neil also stole a base, scored once, and knocked in one of his team's runs.[61] O'Neil's team was finally eliminated on August 24, when they were slaughtered 17-1 by the Cleveland Cloths team, which represented Shelby, North Carolina. In winning, Shelby set a tournament record for one inning scoring, with thirteen runs in the fifth.[62] The win brought Shelby's record to 4 and 1, but Bismarck, with Leroy "Satchel" Paige's infectious personality drawing record-breaking crowds, was leading the tournament with a perfect record of 5 and 0.

As one of baseball's leading pitchers, Paige was having a fabulous season in 1935. "Backed by a mixed team [of African American and Caucasian ballplayers], probably the fastest club ever organized outside pro leagues," Paige was well on his way to his first summer of five-hundred batters whiffed.[63] In the tournament opener, Paige struck out sixteen members of the Monroe Monarchs. In his second appearance, he struck out seven in two and two-thirds innings against Wichita Water Works. In the championship game, Paige struck out fourteen members of the Duncan, Oklahoma, team, winning 5-2. He finished the tournament with sixty strikeouts and won four games, establishing records that still stand.

Although his team was eliminated from the tournament, O'Neil made new friendships-- valuable relationships--which would last a lifetime. He met Homer "Goose" Curry and Harry Else who were with the Monroe, Louisiana team. Curry became O'Neil's manager in 1937, and Else his teammate in 1938. He also met Hilton Smith, and John Lyles, who performed with the Memphis Red Sox. Lyles and O'Neil would reacquaint themselves in 1938 when Kansas City visited St. Louis to face that city's Giants. Lyles also played with Indianapolis in 1938. Smith became O'Neil's lifelong friend when both were teammates in Kansas City. O'Neil also met Satchel Paige, one of the most publicized African Americans in baseball.

Unfortunately, their financial woes continued. O'Neil received "twenty-five dollars" from the tournament.[64] With one additional game scheduled in Western Kansas at Goodland, it was hoped that their bad fortune would keep changing for the better. However, there was no such change. An early-season snowstorm blew into Goodland just as the team reached town. Because there were no opportunities for games, the Miami Giants broke up, and everyone went their separate ways.

Stranded in Kansas, unable to pay train fare home, O'Neil and Major hoboed back to Wichita and eventually made it back to Florida after O'Neil's parents wired one-way train passage for two. "We thought they were going to send us a little [extra] money, too, but they didn't," O'Neil stated, "We got on the train with seventy-five cents between us and three days of traveling ahead."[65]

By the end of that summer, his nerves were frayed. O'Neil admitted, "I slept for two straight days, and when I woke up, I said, 'Mama, that's all! I'm not going anywhere ever again.'"[66] He hadn't lied to his mother, at least not on purpose. He believed he was through with the substandard life that barnstorming baseball provided and hadn't intended to go traveling again. Not now, not ever. It turned out to be a false promise and a repentant mood that lasted a mere matter of months. It took one letter, one important piece of mail traveling with a three cents stamp on Acme Giants stationery for him to leave the comfort of Mama's outstretched arms.

"Last Season, the Acme team toured Canada and the northern states, winning 120 games while losing but twenty. 'Foots' O'Neil, first sacker is the clown of the visitors."

Rockford, Illinois Star, May 17, 1936

Buck O'Neil says...

"One thing about it is, during the season we played a lot of local teams, especially in the mid-west, they had some good local baseball teams in the mid-west, this was the people who had the teams like the oil companies had teams, the packing houses had teams, and we would play them, and we took most of the money."

From Dunseith To Memphis, And Back Again

Having already received an offer during mid-winter from Winfield Welch, by April of 1936, O'Neil sought to become a full-fledged member of the touring Shreveport Acme Giants. Welch, the team's manager, was a good friend of Kansas City's, J. L. Wilkinson. They had established a loosely formed working agreement that allowed Welch to furnish players to the Monarchs in exchange for mid-west bookings and cash considerations. The relationship took root in 1935 when Welch dealt

Floyd Kranson, Willard Brown, Harry Else, and Eldridge Mayweather to Kansas City. In addition

to O'Neil, who landed with the Monarchs in 1938, Welch was responsible for two of Buck's 1936

teammates, catcher Lionel Decuir and pitcher Eugene Bremer, coming to Kansas City. Despite

significant achievements by African American athletes in boxing, track, and other sports, very little

of the national recognition poured into the circuits where O'Neil was playing the best baseball of his

life.

When Welch formed his 1936 team, he needed to replace his first baseman. A

correspondence to O'Neil, the young Floridian's response over the winter, and his eventual

agreement guaranteed a summer of play and pay up north. Welch's Acme Giants, eager to abandon

the uncertainties of the barnstorming trail, made plans to relocate to Dunseith, North Dakota, where

they began playing in a series of lucrative tournaments as the Dunseith Acme Giants at the request

of two local entrepreneurs. Arnold T. Lilleby, owner of a local bowling alley, and George F.

Gottbreht, a buyer of livestock seeking to cash in on their talent, earnestly awaited their arrival in

Rolette County. The *Brandon Daily Sun* stated,

> The Acme Giants a traveling organization all the way from Louisiana, will be
>
> stationed in North Dakota all season. They were up in these parts last summer
>
> and made a good showing wherever they played. This season they will come
>
> north with a club rated as strong as Bismarck, a standard that will win them a lot
>
> of attention when they meet their opponents.[67]

On the way up, they played across Illinois, stopping in Peoria on Sunday, May 10, and Rock

Island on Friday, May 15, and Sunday, May 17 in Rockford. In Rock Island, the Acme team was

thumped in a 4-3 final[68] Bremer lost a five-hit eight strikeout game when the Illinois pitcher tossed a

4-hit six strikeout game. Winfield Welch, Bennett, and William Horne were the only Shreveport players to hit safely. At Rockford, John Markham struck out ten batters and captured the victory when William Horne banged a home run in a 5-2 win.[69]

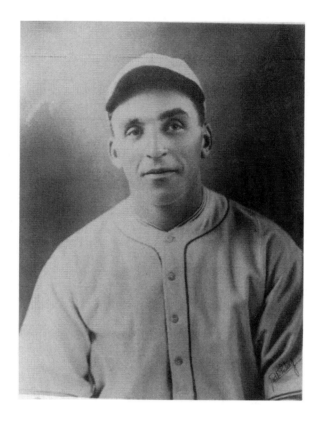

Larry Bettencourt. *Playing with the Texas League All-Stars, Bettencourt was a former St. Louis Browns' outfielder and a 1936 .308 hitter in 141 games for San Antonio of the Texas League who didn't recognize O'Neil, but Buck remembered him from their fall 1936 series in San Antonio.*

Their arrival in the tiny town of Dunseith was well received, but it was hardly the place to stage many games. The city's population of 484 in the 1930 census jumped up to 719 in the 1940 census, an increase of 48% in ten years. While the established Negro Baseball Leagues was struggling in the lower forty-eight states, there was some loose change to be made in North Dakota and across the Canadian border.

Dunseith's proximity to the twenty-four-hour International Peace Garden Border Crossing Station made it easy for the Acme Giants to cross into Canada.[70] Thus, they played as many games in Canada as they did in America. Up north African Americans had discovered they were a desirable commodity as their numbers were small. The 1930 North Dakota Census indicates there were only 377 Black residents in the state, down from 467 in 1920 with nearly a 50% down from the 617 residents they had in 1910. In 1930 Black residents constituted far less than 1/10 of one percent of the state's total population in a state that was slightly larger in square miles than Missouri and Oklahoma.[71] O'Neil was a witness at many of these games as his Acme Giants, labeled as one of the four best teams in North Dakota, positioned the town's name on a regional marque. Their arch-rivals were teams from Valley City, Bismarck, and Page.[72] Their living quarters was an abandoned creamery on the north side of town.[73] O'Neil was quick to say they were treated "Royally,"

> The town fathers gave us this big house of our own to live in, and we had a ball
>
> there. We did our own cooking and everything, and the best thing was that we
>
> had a nice big bathtub with hot running water to soak in. That was no common
>
> thing back then.[74]

With his relocation, O'Neil's salary increased to a guaranteed $30 a month as the team entered as many regional tournaments as could be booked. His Acme Giants' teammates were a good ball club, who readied themselves to play rain or shine. Their appearance in Dunseith, however distant from Louisiana, was no walk in the park. Some of the most talented African American athletes in the country had moved up North for the 1936 season.

Bismarck was easily the most dominant team in the region. Having won the National Baseball Congress Tournament in 1935, they were seeking to return to that stature with remnants of the previous year's squad. Pitcher Hilton Smith had returned, as had catcher Quincy Trouppe pitcher Barney Morris, and outfielder "Red" Haley. Valley City signed five African American players to its Hi-Liners team, which included three pitchers. W. H. Foster, a southpaw pitcher, Dan Thomas, formerly of the Chicago American Giants, Charlie Justice, formerly of the Detroit Colored Giants, along with Wilson, a catcher, and "Steel Arm" Davis were the new members of this team.[75] Page had Lefty Gaines before he jumped to Bismarck in June, along with Johnnie Lyles, formerly of the Memphis Red Sox. In addition to Welch, who pitched and played multiple positions, they came north lacking pitchers for the competition the Acme Giants were about to face. The ace of the Acme Giants pitching staff was John "Buster" Markham.

Markham, born October 12, 1908, in Shreveport, Louisiana, was the Acme's best hurler. Three years older than O'Neil, Markham had broken into professional play in 1929 with the Shreveport Black Sports of the Texas Oklahoma Louisiana League. He was a prominent force wherever he pitched. At times he could be downright dominant. When he wasn't pitching, he played on the infield. In 1930 he came to the Kansas City Monarchs and was a prominent pitcher in their pioneering effort to promote Night baseball.

The Acme Giants participated in a series of one-day tournaments across Canada upon reaching North Dakota. First-place money in these tournaments was $1,000. Two teams would play at 1:00 p.m., two teams would play at 3:00 p.m. The losers of the 1:00 and 3:00 p.m. game played at 5:00 p.m., and the winners of the earlier games played in the finals at 7 o'clock. Admission for the entire day was a whopping 75 cents, with a special 50 cents admission after 5 p.m. Children entered the park for a quarter.

On June 18, the Acme Giants finished horribly in a tournament at Brandon, Manitoba, and took fourth place money, losing to Valley City 1-0 and to Page 8-4. Bismarck took the first-place money.[76] The following day, June 19, they took third place money in a tournament at Page, North Dakota, losing to Bismarck, who took second place money after downing the Giants 15-8. Valley City took the first-place money in that tournament.[77] This day was memorable for other reasons, and every baseball player in the North was watching. It was the night that Joe Louis was defeated by Max Schmeling in front of a reported $547,531 gate at New York's Yankee Stadium.

The night pitted an undefeated 22-year-old Joe Louis against Germany's veteran and former champion Max Schmeling, age 30. The German, backed by an Aryan supremacy ideology which in many ways was a cousin to white supremacy in America, ruled the night. Louis hailed as unbeatable before the fight, lost his battle with two minutes and 29 seconds gone in the twelfth round before a crowd that numbered 40,000 at the stadium. He represented an entire race of marginalized people, who like himself, were fighting against racial stigmatism worldwide. On the next day, stories about the fight were front-page news all over the world.

Allan Gould's *Associated Press* article, which was carried over the nationwide wire, was loaded with racial overtones. He referred to Schmeling as the German but never referred to Louis as an American. Gould went on to use the word "Negro" as if the readers didn't already know, over a dozen times and tossed in words like "Chocolate" for added insult. One of the worst openings to any article came out of New York on the *Associated Press* wire, and it appeared in a Greensboro, North Carolina newspaper which stated,

> Many of the experts, who seized yards of loose rope and hanged themselves by forecasting Joe Louis could name his round and winning punch against Max Schmeling stubbornly stuck by their judgment today as they dangled from their self-made nooses.[78]

The baseball tournaments continued on June 24 in Virden, Manitoba, where Welch's Acme crew squeaked by Page in a 10-9 final before losing to Bismarck, who won the tournament. Hilton Smith held them scoreless in the final seven innings for the win.[79] The next day, June 25, the Acme team took fourth place money at Portage La Prairie, Manitoba, where they lost to Page 14-4 and 14-11 to Valley City.[80] O'Neil and his Acme teammates should have been discouraged after allowing twenty-eight runs on a single afternoon, but they weren't. They rebounded on June 26 to take second place money at the tournament in Russell, Manitoba, Canada. They defeated Bismarck 1-0 in the opener, then lost in the finals. An article in the *Russell Banner* wrote about the excitement that was aroused when Dunseith staged a batting rally in the ninth, almost tying the score against Valley City, winner of the tournament's final game by a 7-5 score.[81] The Acme team ventured into Canada, making appearances in Edmonton, Alberta, to battle the Calgarians and Shastas, then headed for Saskatchewan.

While the Acme Giants were playing their hearts out in upper north-western states like Montana, Idaho, and Washington, making visits to towns in near-obscurity, Jesse Owens was making United States Olympic history in Germany. On August 3, 1936, Owens captured his first Olympic medal in the 100-meter dash. That same afternoon the Acme Giants were in Regina, Saskatchewan, capturing a 3-1 win over the National team. Markham finished the game with fourteen strikeouts yet received little to no fanfare. Owens, after winning the long jump with a record leap on August 4, returned on August 5 to win his third Olympic Gold medal in the 200- meter sprint. On that same afternoon, the Acme Giants were in Broadview, Manitoba beating the local Red Sox team in an 11-1 final. The Giants returned to Regina on August 9 and lost a 6-1 game to the Nationals on the very same day Owens won gold medal number four in the 4 x 100 sprint relay. It was a week to remember in two foreign nations. Owens' feats were given national recognition; the Acme Giants' achievements are long forgotten. As the summer of 1936 progressed, they left Dunseith in their rearview mirror. After a stop in Drumheller, Alberta, on August 11, they began playing their way back to the south stopping for an appearance in Blair, Nebraska. Other games were scheduled in the Iowa cities of

Mason, Forest City, Pilot Mound, Charles City, and Waverly. Along the way, they participated in a tournament in Arlington, Nebraska, and took third place money.

The Acmes beat Sioux City Stockyards in the opener on September 2, when Welch picked up four of his team's seven hits in a 5-1 win.[82] The win pitted the Acmes against a rival African American opponent in the Texas Black Spiders for their next game. Against the Black Spiders, a game which included a pair of doubles, a pair of runs scored, and a stolen base in the Acme's 8-7 semi-finals loss.[83] As a unit, the Acme Giants made quite an impression on the Spiders manager Ruben Jones. So, after the closing of the season, O'Neil and a few of his Acme Giants teammates signed on with the Manager Ruben Jones' Black Spiders playing games in Texas before heading to Mexico. With a combined team of Black Spiders and Acme Giants that was made up of mostly Acme players, they now began calling themselves the Barnstorming Negro All-Stars team said to be representing Waverly, Iowa, O'Neil made quite an impression. He had three hits,

Playing as the Black Spiders of Iowa, they split a doubleheader at San Antonio against Bell Furniture, Markham losing the opener 8-7 to a crafty lefty named Ernest Nelson. The Spider/Acme team returned in the second game to log a 5-2 victory.[84] In the opening game, O'Neil picked up a trio of hits and scored a pair of runs. They made a quick jog over to Beaumont, Texas, for a game, then returned to San Antonio for a doubleheader against the Texas League All-Stars.

The Spiders/Acme All-Stars swept both games from a group of Texan League All-Star that included among its members were former big-league pitcher Hal Wiltse who had pitched 166 innings for the Fort Worth Cats in 1936, along with first baseman Lee Stebbins also of the Fort Worth Cats, a .293 batter in 139 games during the summer of 1936. At second base, the All-Stars had Charlie English a .301 batter in 122 Texas League games for the Fort Worth Cats. Larry Bettencourt, a former member of the St. Louis Browns and a 1936 .308 hitter in 141 games for the

47

San Antonio Missions of the Texas League, failed to add the punch that was anticipated. The white All-Stars lost both ends of the doubleheader. In the first game, O'Neil went 2-for-5 as he and his teammates belted Wiltse into dreamland in a 9-2 final. Eleven of their total twelve hits were obtained off the former big-league star. Markham won game two, a night shorten five-innings affair, 1-0, and pitched a three-hitter.[85] Keeping their winning momentum, the Spiders/Acme team crossed over into Mexico.

In Mexico, the team played well enough to receive an offer to join a Mexican League for the winter and remain in the country. There was one condition; they had to win an important exhibition game to get long-term I.D. Cards. But the Spiders lost and were told to go home. They were dropped off at the Lerado, Texas border crossing. "You know it's a tough league when they deport you for losing," O'Neil bemoaned.[86] They were unwelcomed visitors and thus asked to leave, which wasn't surprising. For Buck, it was an endless summer and unforgettable autumn with memories that would last until his dying day.

There were other reasons why the Black Spiders were expelled from Mexico. Lots of unethical activities were happening on the border between the United States and Mexico. An article titled "*Negroes Pay Before Entering Mexico*," which appeared in the *Detroit Tribune*, an article that also ran on the *Associated Negro Press* wire, told of the injustice African American people faced when trying to enter the country. Two men, Dr. R. C. Barbour, editor of *The Voice*, a national Baptist publication, and Dr. H. M. Smith, dean of the School of Religion at Bishop College in Marshall, Texas, brought these activities to light after they were stopped at the Laredo, Texas entry,

> While Mexico requires no deposit on [the] bond of American citizens who enter
>
> Mexico as tourists, yet she demands that all American citizens who happen to be
>
> Negroes deposit $150.00 (U.S. currency) before being allowed to enter Mexico.

We applied to Mexican Consuls at Galveston, Houston, and San Antonio with absolutely identical results. As soon as they discovered we were Negroes they refused to grant us the tourist identification cards which white Americans receive as a mere formality in 2 or 3 minutes at any Mexican Consulate.[87]

With the 1936 season behind them, O'Neil and Markham, now fast friends, roomed together in Shreveport until spring training started for 1937. As roomies, they were an odd duo, O'Neil, a rookie new to the game, and Markham, a veteran since the late 1920s. Their quest for a tomorrow that was better than days past helped them to co-exist in the most unlikely of unions, an underfinanced barnstorming baseball team.

The next year Markham was reacquired by Wilkinson for his Kansas City Monarchs. O'Neil anticipated he would also receive a contract. Welch's Acme Giants trained with Wilkinson's Kansas City Monarchs in Shreveport during April 1937.[88] Wilkinson was anxiously looking over Welch's pool of players when he spotted O'Neil and beamed approvingly. O'Neil recalled,

He [Wilkinson] liked the way [I] played and [said] that he would give me a job," "I thought I was going with the Monarchs because they left here [Shreveport] going to Mexico, but he [Wilkinson] didn't send for me, and I was surprised he didn't. I thought for sure that he would. I soon heard from him, and he told me that he couldn't because I was one of the guy's better ballplayers, and he didn't want to take me from the ball club. He did tell me that a guy was going to come through there and take me to the Memphis Red Sox, but I would be [the] property of the Kansas City Monarchs.[89]

The *Shreveport Times* confirmed that the Monarchs had indeed "Left Sunday night for an exhibition tour of Texas and Mexico."[90] Memphis, a charter member of the newly formed Negro American League, gave O'Neil his first league berth. Ironically, O'Neil wasn't the only person trying to leave Shreveport. Monarchs' trainer, Frank "Jewbaby" Floyd, arrested, and treated to some narrow-minded Southern justice, was also stuck in Shreveport, where Jim Crow laws made a mockery of the American justice system and tramped on every African American's freedom. His crime was taking baseballs from the local sheriff's son, who was hired to return them to the Monarchs. It was a clear example of two justice systems in American Society, one for African Americans and another for everyone else.

Delighted to be heading somewhere besides bigoted Shreveport, O'Neil looked forward to uniting with Homer "Goose" Curry the Red Sox manager. Going to the Negro American League, it seemed, was a wonderful opportunity. It was, after all, what O'Neil had wanted since childhood. Yet he wasn't quite sure if it served his long-range purpose to sign the first league contract waved his way. The thought of getting to Kansas City remained his goal.

O'Neil joined Memphis in 1937 with the assignment of beating out veteran Granville Lyons for the first base position. Unsuccessful in cracking Memphis' starting lineup, while feeling inadequate for riding the pines for his ninety dollars a month, O'Neil, too unhappy to be embarrassed, jumped to the Zulu Cannibal Giants.

If printed, the Zulus' box score stood out. With a roster that featured such delectable names as: "Kankel, Wahee, Limpepe, Rufigi, Taklooie, Tanna, Kalahare, Aber, Pembra, Impe, and Yip-Yaying," the fictitious labels made it nearly impossible to know who was actually on the squad. O'Neil confessed that he never could recall all of his teammates by their full names.[91] What O'Neil did recall was the Zulus' impact on African American society, "They upset a lot of folks."[92]

Promoted nationally by Abe Saperstein, the 1937 Zulu Cannibal Giants were based in Chicago. Much more than pure entertainment, the team was formed to mock Haile Selassie's resistance to Benito Mussolini's fascist take over in Ethiopia. In their ignorance and arrogance, American promoters named the team after the Zulu Kingdom, which was nearly 4,000 miles from Ethiopia in South Africa, an area where there was no known cannibalism.

Saperstein's "Cannibals" feasted on the competition. In 1935 the team reportedly won "133 out of 174 games played, tying 3."[93] The team's record in 1936 was "121 games won and only 20 lost."[94] Playing a high class of baseball, "A crowd of 30,000 witnessed the Zulus during a two-game set in Montreal, Canada. The club also drew large crowds to Chicago's Mills Park, Parkway Field in Louisville, and Detroit's Hamtramck Stadium."[95] The gimmickry was simple. Team members were adorned in grass skirts, instead of regulation uniforms, jungle headwear instead of baseball caps, painted faces, and some played without shoes. O'Neil's Zulu name was Limpope. Late in the season, O'Neil's and his Cannibals teammates visited Louisville, Kentucky, to play his former team, the Memphis Red Sox.

According to O'Neil, Red Sox owner, Dr. J. B. Martin told Curry, "Don't come back to Memphis unless you bring O'Neil. So 'Goose' offered me a raise, up to ten dollars from the ninety dollars a month I was making with them before, and I played with the Sox for the last month of the [1937] season."[96]

In 1938, Curry was released as Red Sox manager and replaced by Ted "Double Duty" Radcliffe, who took over as field general for Martin's Memphis Red Sox. Radcliffe went about the business of changing the team's roster. He brought Olan "Jelly" Taylor, a first baseman from the defunct Cincinnati Tigers, to Memphis. O'Neil, now free to leave, headed off to spring training with J. L. Wilkinson and the Kansas City Monarchs.

With a letter of commitment firmly in hand, O'Neil veered onto his divine path, a mission of sorts, through which the Negro American League would become the road, and Wilkinson's Kansas City Monarchs his vehicle to a legacy in baseball. "When I got to the Monarchs," O'Neil proudly evoked, "that was just like going to the Yankees for a white boy. The Monarchs were first class."[97]

"We were like the Yankees. We had a winning attitude, a sense of pride. We stayed in the best black-owned hotels and restaurants, and we played before 40,000 people, sometimes 50,000."

Charlie Huiskey, Sarasota Herald-Tribune, March 5, 1995

Buck O'Neil *says...*

"I guess the greatest thrill I got out of baseball is when I went to the Kansas City Monarchs. Because I had played ball just about all over the country, but I was playing on those little teams going hand to hand trying to make it. But to me, when I went to the Monarchs it was like a White boy from Georgia going to the Yankees. I was going to see and play with the best."

Kansas City, My Kind Of Town

Kansas City was jumping in 1938 when O'Neil arrived for his first season with the Monarchs!

Bryce B. Smith was mayor of the city, but the Tom Pendergast political machine ran Jackson County

Kansas City was a robust Midwestern city, the prairies' version of New York or Paris in the 1930s

with wide-open gambling and other socially prohibited activities. It was also an oasis for ethnic

extracurricular activities such as sports, theater, jazz, social clubs, and a continued indoctrination for

Southerners moving north. Sunday was an important day for baseball, the day when local fans stepped out to support the American Association Blues or the Negro American League Monarchs at Ruppert Stadium, and most on that day, came directly from church to watch a doubleheader. Musical entertainment in a city with many venues was an all-day, all-night affair. African American entertainers came to Kansas City in record numbers. Among the more chronicled to visit in 1938 were Jimmie Lunceford, Cab Calloway, Andy Kirk, Noble Sissle, Count Basie, and Stepin Fetchit. Segregation and discrimination continued to be widely practiced. The often hidden and unspoken institution of racism restricting where you lived, went to school, or purchased a home could not be overlooked. Segregation, though, was not without some benefits if you were connected to the "right" people. For O'Neil, a first-year Monarch, life in the big city transformed him from a rookie to a man – as an individual that easily adapted to his surroundings in a world that was full of adversity and adventure.

Tom Pendergast. *In 1938 he was the political boss controlling Kansas City. His reign over the wide-open city was about to end. In 1939 Pendergast was convicted of tax evasion and subsequently served over a year in prison. (Authors collection)*

Kansas City boasted a broad socioeconomic status for African Americans. It was a city to see and a place to be seen. For the more affluent, there was the Penrod Country Club in Bethel, Kansas, a small community in western Wyandotte County. Nestled in the country, in later years, it was Satchel Paige's hideaway. If a person needed a taxi service, they could telephone Victor-9765 to catch a Monarch Cab. Owned and operated by Newt Joseph, a former Monarchs' infielder, Monarch taxi stands were located at Eighteenth and Vine and Twenty-third and Olive. When Jazz legend Jay McShann left his hometown of Muskogee, Oklahoma, headed for Kansas City, the first words out of his mother's mouth was, "Look up your homeboy, Newt Joseph."[98] Since most people walked or rode the streetcars nearly everywhere, they went, being chauffeured around Kansas City's urban district to attend local theaters was a fashionable activity. For those who worked long hours in the packing houses of the west bottoms, it was impossible to attend most of the events, but they could listen to them on the radio if they had one. WHB radio broadcast an All-Negro Show on Saturday afternoons from 3 to 4 p.m., live from Lincoln Theater on Vine Street. There were local musicians and bands basking in local prominence like a young Charlie Parker who would go on to international fame as an alto saxophonist. Harlan Leonard's Kansas City Rockets were not yet a national item when they were booked by the Sans Pariel Club to play for the annual Valentine Dance on February 14, 1938.[99] Locally there was a battle of the bands in a big Labor Day Celebration and Musicians Ball at the Roseland Ball Room, which pitted Nat Towles and His Great Orchestra of 14 Southern Gentlemen against Leonard's K.C. Rockets, and five other Big Bands.[100] Admission to the event was 75 cents if tickets were purchased at the Monarch Taxi stand on Vine Street. The Monrovian Club was putting on its 4th annual Fashion show to present the latest in "Fashion Features."[101]

Getting dressed to attend these events was not without its problems. There was, as you might expect, discrimination against African American shoppers at many of Kansas City's well-known retail outlets, located at Tenth and Main, would not allow African Americans to try on clothing. Harzfeld's, another well-established Kansas City retailer, did not allow black customers to try on the clothing either, nor could you leave the store carrying your purchase in their "signature box" -- as they felt it would lower the value of their goods--they would much rather mail the items to their Black customers. The Leader retail outlet, with locations in Kansas City, Missouri, and Kansas City, Kansas, allowed African American men to try on their suits, but not their hats.[102] Every aspect of community life was restricted by race.

Education was a way to uplift one's self. Yet, segregation of African Americans in metropolitan Kansas City forced students into four areas junior high and high schools. In Kansas City, Missouri, most Black students attended Lincoln High School or R. T. Coles Vocational School. In Kansas City, Kansas, Sumner High School and Northeast Junior High were designated as Black schools. Corrupt city governments on both sides of the river had created an unseen boundary of limitations in urban education based on racism. There was one intuition of upper learning, Western University across the Missouri River in Kansas City, Kansas. It was an all-Black college that was responsible for bringing the Wilberforce Jubilee Singers to Memorial Hall in Kansas City, Kansas, on February 14, 1938.[103] Knapper's, a black-owned Book Store, provided everything from music to the latest books and novels on almost every topic.

Kansas City's abundance of Black wage-earning packing houses, factory, and domestic workers made it a familiar jumping-off point for African American entertainers as they headed west to California. As a consequence, Kansas City was inundated with an abundance of entertainment. Playing on a sports "chitlin" tour, so to speak, O'Neil offered, "We played that circuit just like the entertainers played that circuit."[104] African American singers, dances, and Big Bands were branded as "race artists." Baseball players were categorized as Negro Leaguers. In 1938, before he arrived in Kansas City to fill an engagement on March 8, Jimmie Lunceford stated publicly,

> There is no city in the world I would rather play in than Kansas City, where everyone is my friend, and before I leave on my next tour of Europe in [the] spring, I want to play again in the Paseo Hall and bring to my friends the greatest attraction they ever saw or heard."[105]

Stump and Stumpy. Their birth names were Edward "Eddie" Hartman and James "Jimmy" Cross. They traveled the country as part of Cab Calloway's show which arrived in Kansas City on June 10, 1938. (Authors collection)

Cab Calloway's itinerary included Kansas City and other Midwestern stops. Appearing nightly on the stage of the Mainstreet, a downtown theater and movie house, Calloway's orchestra opened their five-day Kansas City engagement on June 10.[3] The 3,000-plus seat Mainstreet Theatre opened in October of 1921, on the corner of 1400 Main Street. Its interior design was French Baroque, and the exterior a blend of the neoclassical and French Empire.[106] It was a beautiful facility. Featured in Calloway's touring show were such illustrious acts as Stump and Stumpy and the Six Cotton Club Boys. Ironically, African Americans were forced into overcrowded balconies to an area they referred to as the peanut gallery, as they crowded in to see Calloway's show. They were refused admission to the best seats in the house though charged identical fees for entry. House rules forced them into the balcony to an exclusively reserved area.

Originally booked into New York's Cotton Club, by 1938, Calloway's Orchestra had achieved international fame. Always appearing in a white silk suit, with top hat and tails, Calloway took his admiring public by storm with such songs as "Minnie the Moocher," recorded December 23, 1930, and "Kickin' the Gong Around" recorded October 21, 1931. In 1932 he made the first of many films, which included such classics as the *Big Broadcast* and *Stormy Weather*. In addition to 1938's Kansas City visit, Calloway appeared in a movie with the Ritz Brothers entitled *Straight Place and Show*, released September 30, 1938. It was also in 1938 that the first edition of Calloway's hipster's dictionary, the language of jive talk, was published.[107] Kansas City also hosted Andy Kirk's Clouds of Joy, a renowned orchestra that was popular on the radio. Kirk's Clouds of Joy made two Kansas City appearances in 1938.

---

[3] According to http://cinematreasures.org/theater/4866/. The 3,000-plus seat Mainstreet Theatre opened in October 1921 on the corner of 1400 Main Street.

Featured nationally on NBC radio affiliates, Andy Kirk's Clouds of Joy was led by Andrew Dewey Kirk. Born May 28, 1898, in Newport, Kentucky, and given the stage name Kirk, he had taken leadership of Terrence Holder's orchestra in 1928, renaming it Andy Kirk and his Dark Clouds of Joy. The orchestra's name eventually changed to Andy Kirk and his Twelve Clouds of Joy and featured pianist Mary Lou Williams. In 1936 the band hit it big with the record "Until The Real Thing Comes Along." On September 9, 1938, Kirk's band recorded another hit, "Bless You, My Dear," for New York-based Decca records. The orchestra appeared at Kansas City's Fairyland Park on June 15. Fairyland Park exercised its regular exclusionary practices of keeping African Americans from entering the park during the engagement.[108] In response, Kirk scheduled two concerts at Kansas City's Lincoln Theater, an African American venue, on May 20, 1938. Although Fairyland Park continued to operate under its segregationist rules and regulations, park personnel opted to book long-established race acts such as Noble Sissle.

Sissle, born July 10, 1889, in Indianapolis, Indiana, was an American jazz composer, lyricist, bandleader, singer, and playwright. He was noted for his collaborations with songwriter Eubie Blake. Sissle joined forces with performer Blake to form a vaudeville act, the "Dixie Duo." The duo began work on a musical revue, *Shuffle Along*, in 1921, which incorporated many songs they had written. When it premiered, *Shuffle Along* became Broadway's first hit musical written by and about African Americans. The musical introduced both "I'm Just Wild About Harry" and "Love Will Find a Way." Municipal Auditorium was another familiar Kansas City spot where African American entertainers performed in O'Neil's rookie season.

Count Basie's orchestra, featuring Jimmy Rushing, appeared at Municipal Auditorium on April 11, 1938, and Horace Henderson performed at this same location on April 19. The auditorium was a public venue, partially paid for with the taxes of African Americans, but segregation reigned supreme at all events. In 1936, Gus Greenlee, owner of the Pittsburgh Crawfords baseball team and manager of boxing's John Henry Lewis, came to Kansas City to watch his boxer in a scheduled 10-round interracial bout against Jack Kranz. According to an article in the Kansas City *Call*,

When his [Greenlee's] request for tickets was met with the reply, 'are they for colored or white?' Mr. Greenlee, immediately understanding what the statement meant, refused to buy the tickets, and walked away from the window, thoroughly disgusted.[109]

Count Basie. *His orchestra featuring Jimmy Rushing appeared at Kansas City's Municipal Auditorium on April 11, 1938. (Authors collection)*

Henderson performed at Municipal Auditorium, appearing before approximately three thousand people in an appearance that coincided with the Wheatley Hospital's annual fashion show. Of all the entertainers performing in Kansas City, none proved more controversial than motion picture actor Stepin Fetchit.

Armed with an array of egregious stereotypes, comedian-actor Theodore Perry, born May 30, 1902, and better known as Stepin Fetchit, provoked strong African American disapproval for his minstrel show antics. Portraying a lazy, whining, clown-like character with broken linguistics, Fetchit appeared in numerous 1930s and 1940s films and was a favorite with white radio audiences. In 1938, he appeared in two musical comedies, *Twenty Girls and a Band* and *Country Chairman,* a motion picture that starred actor Will Rogers. Fetchit's long history of racial characterizations moved from live minstrel shows through vaudeville into movies, radio and, unfortunately, onto television.[110] In 1938, others were in the early stages of their legendary Hollywood careers, though forced to struggle past the stereotypical roles for which they were routinely cast. Dorothy Dandridge appeared as a maid in the 1938 version of *Going Places,* along with fog-throated Louis Armstrong, Eddie "Rochester" Anderson, and Maxine Sullivan.

Edgar "Blue" Washington, a former Monarchs' first baseman, appeared in numerous movies in 1938. Washington's movie credits included *Kentucky* and *Charlie Chan in Honolulu* as well as *The Cowboy and The Lady.* If you missed him in those movies, he could also be seen in *Too Hot to Handle* and a movie directed by Frank McDonald titled, *Over the Wall* along with *Tarzan's Revenge.* Washington was cast as a native, stable hand, seaman, dockworker, and a convict in the movies in which he appeared.[111] Most of these actors, and many of the musicians, had gotten their start in churches, and nearly everyone in the African American community attended a church. Most ballplayers attended church regardless of their hectic Sunday schedules. Hilton Smith and Eldridge

"Chili" Mayweather attended St. Stephens Baptist Church. O'Neil attended Bethel African Methodist Episcopal Church. Wilber "Bullet" Rogan attended Centennial Methodist Church. Years later, Monarchs Jesse Williams and Connie Johnson joined Bethel A.M.E. Church, where O'Neil attended. State Public Accommodations Laws and restrictive covenants in deeds of homes assured that the unseen boundaries of social uplift wouldn't be changing anytime soon. White supremacy was already embedded in Kansas City culture, and it manifested itself at all the cities big-time events.

(L to R) Maxine Sullivan, Etta Jones, the Dandridge sisters, Vivian and Dorothy, and trumpeter Louis Armstrong. Black actors were routinely forced into stereotypical roles as Butlers, Maids, Porters, Musicians, and jitterbug dancers. Cast from "Going Places," a 1938 Warner Brothers movie. (Authors collection)

In Kansas City's theaters, night clubs and auditoriums, and in the stands at Blues' minor league baseball games, segregation was an everyday activity. Nonetheless, it was not the case at Monarchs' home games. As a rule, Monarchs' fans sat wherever they pleased, with little regard to race. Additionally, baseball games were viewed as a dress-up affair, much like a Cab Calloway or Clouds of Joy concert or church. Therefore, it was customary for everyone to be dressed in their Sunday best or nightlife fashionable apparel. In 1938, with zoot suits emerging as a fashion rage, nearly all the men were dressed for the occasion.

The zoot suit was a brightly colored suit with a belted waistline that was pulled up to the chest, broad-legged, cuffed trousers, and a long, three-quarter length coat accented with wide lapels and large padded shoulders. Zoot-suiters wore matching fedora-styled hats with a long feather and pointed-toed French-style shoes. First popularized by African American teenagers, labeled "Hepcats" by Cab Calloway, the apparel was popularized just as O'Neil was cutting his teeth in the Negro American League. In addition to professional athletes, it was popular among the early 1940's "jitterbug" crowd and Mexican-Americans. The style became so widely recognized that entertainers such as Frank Sinatra began wearing them in movies. Fading as abruptly as it began, the zoot suit craze nearly disappeared when World War II's Production Board regulators restricted the amount of material that could be used in men's clothing. Wartime rationing effectively banned zoot suits for their supposed waste of fabric, labeling it in direct conflict with American patriotism.[112] In California, the clothing provoked a brawl between whites and Mexican Americans, rightly titled the "Zoot Suit Riots" during the summer of 1943.

Inside and outside of Kansas City, manipulation of non-white customers at ballparks, auditoriums, and public facilities remained an ugly and unjust part of American culture. There were drug stores, retail outlets, restaurants, and hotels that openly refused to permit African Americans to enter the premises except as a messenger or servant, but not as a customer. On May 4, 1938, Representative Arthur Mitchell, an Illinois Democrat, and the only African American member of Congress, saw his case against discrimination on trains dismissed by the United States Interstate Commerce Commission. Mitchell had sued the Rock Island and Pacific Railway Company in 1937, after a train in which he was riding left Memphis and entered Arkansas. The conductor compelled Mitchell--over the congressman's protest and finally under threat of arrest--to move into the Jim Crow car with other members of his race. Mitchell refused to move and was immediately detained. In ruling against Mitchell, the United States examiner, William A. Disque, gave this simple statement, "The present-colored coach met the requirements of the law."[113] Discrimination at baseball parks was seldom as subtly approached.

In 1938, Ernest L. Brown, writing in the *Kansas City Call*, praised owner Jacob Ruppert for taking down the "Colored Section" seating signs inside Ruppert Stadium. Although removed, ushers persistently asked Negro patrons at American Association games to sit in the bleachers after they had paid the grandstand admission price.[114] Ruppert, the owner of the Kansas City Blues American Association team, also owned the New York Yankees. He received more criticism for the signs after Jake Powell's suspension from the Yankees for making insensitive remarks about African Americans over the radio in July of 1938. This same form of segregation was practiced in Topeka, the capital city of Kansas.

On August 11, 1938, during Buck O'Neil's first game inside Topeka' Ripley Park, the *Daily Capital* of Kansas advised African Americans to direct their feet toward the distinct Jim Crow section, where seats were reserved for "Topeka's colored fans."[115] Although Topeka was approximately sixty-five miles west of Kansas City, long forgotten was the Bloody Kansas history that fought to eliminate slavery and segregation based on race. In Dallas, as expected, the local *Times Herald* newspaper advertised half the stands as being "set aside for white patrons."[116] Clarifying how the segregation would be achieved, the writer added, "There will be both reserved and unreserved sections set aside for white patrons and Negroes." If for a moment players thought that Southern racism would be limited to seating--they were whistling Dixie. In Greenville, Mississippi, during a Monarchs' visit to that city, one unrestrained fan was singled out by the *Delta Democrat-Times* for being "the poorest sport." The article added, "He [the white fan] punctuated every yell with the word 'nigger.' It was 'Hit that ball, nigger,' and 'You ain't any good, nigger,' and so on, for several innings." The article added,

> There was no reason for this. No one else, white or colored, found it necessary
>
> to use a word that is especially resented in such a context and on such an occasion
>
> like last night. It takes a pretty small white man to believe that his statue is added
>
> to by such unprovoked gibes, and we didn't like it any more than did the self-
>
> respecting colored men and women who went to the ballpark to enjoy a ball game
>
> by skilled players of their own race.[117]

In addition to verbal attacks, traveling to and from cities, lodging and eating remained a grueling and very humiliating experience. African American baseball players, musicians, and entertainers traveled the same Midwestern highways as all other Americans, though denied many of the privileges along the way. Their buses filled with talent passed each other as ships do on the sea at night. Like the Monarchs, musicians traveled Highway 66 across the panhandle of Texas into Springfield and Joplin, Highway 270 up from McAlester, and Highway 81 into Enid, Oklahoma, and over to Highway 64 from Fort Smith, Arkansas, Highways 40, and 50 through Jefferson City, and Columbia to Kansas City, and over to Highway 65 Springfield to Sedalia. Former Monarchs' first baseman George Giles offered,

Accommodations were bad. Very bad! We [would] come to Manhattan [Kansas] to play, and two had to stay in somebody's house--two had to stay over here and two over there. Sometimes they'd fix meals for us at the Baptist church, or we'd go to the grocery store because we couldn't go to town to eat.[118]

Using restrooms was equally challenging. You needed a good Blatter to hold that urine. In some cities, it was lawful to bar African Americans from public facilities used by whites. Often, when the Monarchs' bus pulled into restaurants, gas stations, and rest areas, the "Out of Order" sign was immediately posted on restrooms.

When the Monarchs traveled to nearby St. Joseph or Topeka, they packed meals called "Dutch Lunches," and usually, they returned to Kansas City without the luxury of an overnight rest or a post-game shower. The traditional "Dutch Lunch" consisted of a sandwich, a soda, and a pastry. The snack was designed as temporary relief only. On longer trips, appetites usually went unfulfilled as O'Neil and his teammates routinely faced discrimination at hotels and restaurants where they could not register for rooms or order meals in the cafe. This was the case when four Pacific Coast athletes tried to stay at the Sovereign Hotel on the Northside of Chicago.

While awaiting their track meet with a Big Ten squad at Northwestern University's stadium, former Olympian Mack Robinson, Bill Lacefield, Leonard Spencer, and Tom Berkeley were instructed not to use the front entrance to enter the hotel. When informed of a wedding party that was scheduled at the hotel, they were told they could not eat in the dining room with their white squad members but would be served in their rooms. Angered, they packed their bags and moved to the Southside.[119] I'm almost certain that Robinson told his younger brother Jackie about the treatment they received in the Midwest.

Barred and prohibited from entering most white-owned hotels, motels, and restaurants, Monarchs players ate irregularly and often sought alternative accommodations in Black communities. Many times, they faced a subtle rejection when hotels posted "No Vacancy" signs. As a result, minority-owned boarding houses served as reliable alternatives. The team frequently bunked in large homes called rooming houses. Giles stated: "We [would] stay in a lot of rooming houses. You had to leave the light on while you slept. Bedbugs wouldn't move in the light."[120] Each player had a roommate, and there was usually one bed in the room, and both players shared that bed. In some rare cases where there were two beds in a room, four players would share the room, sleeping two to a bed. One of O'Neil's regular roommates was Norman "Turkey" Stearnes. O'Neil elicited one story that characteristically described his teammate who would get distraught if he failed to hit in key situations,

Turkey was a perfectionist, good outfielder, great hitter, could run that ball, [and] throw it. He carried two bats, all the time, to the ballgame. After the ballgame, that bat you never touched, you never touched Turkey's bats. He would take them up to his room with him. One day we were playing in Cleveland [at] the old city park. We could have won the game; we lost the ball game by one run. Turkey had two men on base, we needed three runs, and Turkey hit the ball [and] it [the hit] was about that far from going over the fence. And he hit the ball with the 34-inch bat--the other bat was the 35-inch bat. So that night [when] we were finished, we had food and stuff. I went up to the room, and Turkey was sitting in the middle of the bed [talking] with the two bats. And he said, 'Now I used you,' that was the 34-inch bat, 'but if I'd used you [the 35-inch bat], we would have won the game.[121]

In cities where there were no boarding houses for African Americans, teams kept traveling, often sleeping, and eating on the bus or the side of the road. Regardless of the negativity and other obstacles blocking their path, the men, the league, the Negro American League fans wisely thought positive, eagerly seeking the day when all would be received as full-fledged American citizens.

"First, the salaries of the players aren't very high. Men like Satchel Paige, Josh Gibson make $300 a month, with Satchel making a couple of thousand in bonuses, but the players who play all the games make from $200 a month DOWN, and they play in every game. The average salary is $150 a month. A player pays his own expenses while the team is at home and on the road; the club pays the room and board. I don't know just how much the various clubs pay now since food is so high, but a dollar a day was considered tops for board a couple of years ago, and some teams were allotted 75 cents a day."

Halley Harding, Los Angeles Tribune, October 4, 1943

Buck O'Neil says...

"I tell you what we did. We reinterpreted the way the game could be played, bringing a new dimension to competitive expression--we could play! We were the grandfathers of the [Michael] Jordans. The grandfathers of the great athletes you see now, or the great-grandfathers. We'd been playing that kind of baseball. It was so much faster than the game that they were playing in the major league because everyone was that much quicker."

The Negro American League

In 1938, the Negro American League was a six-team circuit that included the Kansas City Monarchs, Atlanta Black Crackers, Memphis Red Sox, Birmingham Black Barons, Indianapolis ABCs and Chicago American Giants. The Jacksonville Red Caps were an associate member of the league, although some sources list them as an official second-half league participant. The season was split into two halves. If a single team captured both halves, they have automatically declared league champions. If there were different winners of both halves, the winner of the first half would play the winner of the second half for the Negro American League championship. Since the most important thing was to keep the turnstiles clicking, many games, although played against rival Negro American League opponents, were not counted in the league standings. They were filed in the exhibition bin. Sagging attendance at league games, and a demand for their talent outside of circuit cities, forced every team to function with a regional exhibition schedule to show profitability. This was a barnstorming league, a league unlike any other in America except for the Negro National League. A league where players with nicknames like Jelly, Ankle Ball, Candy Jim, Bubba, Sug, and Buck thrived.

George Mitchell. He was manager of the leagues' 1938 Indianapolis ABCs. In 1924, he joined the St. Louis Stars and made sports history when teaming with twin brother Robert, a catcher, to form the Negro Leagues' first twin battery. (Authors collection)

Negro American League president, Robert R. Jackson of Chicago, Illinois, published no batting champions, nor did he document home run kings, stolen base leaders, or league-leading pitchers. No such league leader charts were ever printed--they do not exist. There was, however, a pennant race that most fans could follow. Still, it is difficult to know which games counted, or did not count, in the league standings. This was how the Negro Leagues functioned. Attendance totals were loosely kept and not recorded on most occasions.

Attendance totals for Negro American League contests were seldom published, and seldom did they reach expectation in this period where terms like "a big crowd" were commonplace. In many cities, attendance figures were in decline. Such was the case in Kansas City, where the Monarchs, who drew large crowds during the 1920s, were hit hard by the Depression. On August 1, 1920, the Monarchs drew 20,000 people for a game at Kansas City's Association Park against the American Giants. By 1938, crowds that previously averaged five thousand or more were down to three and two thousand people, and there appeared to be no end to the downward spiral. The league also suffered greatly from a lack of national publicity.

National articles, commentary printed primarily in the east failed to celebrate teams in the western Negro American League. When *The Crisis* magazine wrote its article on the state of Negro baseball in May of 1938, it leaned heavily towards teams and players in the eastern Negro National League. When speaking of western stars, the *Crisis* article spoke sparingly of Newt Allen, Andy Cooper, Henry Milton Floyd Kranson, Ted Strong, Turkey Stearnes, Alex Radcliffe, and Wilson Redus. They were the western players mentioned.[122] White sportswriters like Hugh Bradley of the *New York Post,* Jimmy Powers of the New York *Daily News,* and Murray Robinson of the *Newark Star-Eagle* were just as partial. They knew next to nothing about players in the western Negro American League. Most everyone had heard of the Kansas City Monarchs due in part to their success in the original Negro National League, their pioneering legacy with night baseball, and constant barnstorming during the early 1930s.

The Kansas City Monarchs' ownership consisted of two men, J. L. Wilkinson and T. Y. Baird. They were the Negro American League's only white owners. Wilkinson's partnership with booking agent/promoter Baird solidified Buck's 1938 employment in Kansas City. Andy Cooper was the team's manager. Their home field, as it had been since 1923, was Kansas City's Muehlebach Field, which changed its name to Ruppert Stadium to honor its new owner Jacob Ruppert in 1938. Ruppert also owned the New York Yankees, a team he reportedly purchased for $365,000 in 1914, when they were known as the Highlanders. O'Neil offered conceitedly, [We had] an outstanding park, always had good groundskeepers, the grounds were always good, and you're playing at home. And when you say 'playing at home, in Kansas City it meant quite a bit to you because you always had a lot of people there; and these same people, after you got through playing ball, you were going to meet them at the Blue Room or [at] the Subway [Club], it was just a great feeling. All the ballplayers that played all over the country wanted to come to Kansas City. [They] liked the park, and they liked the city.[123]

Wilkinson won respect from his players by enduring the hardships of racism and bigotry with them. He enjoyed life as a traveling owner and regularly rode his team's bus instead of driving his car on barnstorming trips. Wilkinson recalled, "They [the Monarchs] never permit[ed] things to become dull, keeping the party lively with their spontaneous humor and wisecracks."[124] Giving a gesture of goodwill, George Giles referred to Wilkinson as a "Prince of a man."

Tom T. Y. Baird and wife. *Baird's mother, Japha Duncan, was the daughter of Sarah Ann "Sally" Younger Duncan, the sister of Cole Younger, a famous Missouri outlaw that rode with Jessie James. (Authors collection)*

Andrew Louis Cooper, nicknamed Andy, returned as Monarchs' manager in 1938--his third year guiding the team. He was a playing manager, not a bench leader. Not counting the years before he came into the Negro National League, Cooper, a left-hander, pitched professionally for seventeen seasons. Born April 24, 1898, in Waco, Texas, Cooper moved to Wichita, Kansas as a teenager and was soon playing baseball locally. The *Wichita Beacon* noted, "[Andy] Cooper [had] lived in Wichita for ten years."[125] In Wichita, he was employed and played baseball for Cudahy's. According to O'Neil, "Cooper's sister [also] lived in Wichita, Kansas. Cooper entered the Negro

National League with the Detroit Stars in 1920 and was a mainstay of the team through the 1927 season. The *Detroit Tribune* had much to say about Cooper during those years. His attributes are best described by the men who saw him. Julian Bell, a pitcher on Detroit's 1923 and 1924 teams, who came to the Stars by way of Tennessee State University, said, "Cooper was our Sunday pitcher. I admired Cooper the most because of his control. He could almost thread a needle."[126] Another writer noted,

[He] was one of the few southpaws who possessed good control. Cooper never had much powder on the ball, and his curveball was just a 'wrinkle' if one is to believe the batters who opposed him. Cooper was able to pitch the ball just where he wanted it to go. Many were the times when an opposing batter would fling his bat in the air after striking out and walk back to the bench and tell his teammates, 'He ain't got nothing on the ball.' But the batters could not hit it.[127]

In 1928, Detroit dealt Cooper to Kansas City in trade for three players: outfielder Hurley McNair, pitcher George Mitchell, and infielder Grady Orange. A well-traveled Kansan, Cooper, spent the 1933 season pitching for Arkansas City, Kansas but returned to Wilkinson's Monarchs in 1934. Kansas City bartender, Julia Mae Jones, conducted many bars side chats with the Monarch skipper. "Cooper pushed his authority and wouldn't take no for an answer," recalled Jones. He didn't want to be disputed."[128] As a strategist chipped from the old Rube Foster School of deliberation, there was little doubt as to who was in charge of a Cooper-led team. O'Neil, in full admiration of his one-time manager, offered, "He knew the game very well, and he was a good teacher, a good instructor, excellent, and he had a way of getting to a ballplayer. He was kind of strict in some things, but he had all of the ballplayers' respect."[129]

Few managers could out-strategize Cooper, especially when it came to handling pitchers. Cooper's prize move was changing pitchers, specifically in exhibition contest--many times using four hurlers to complete a regulation nine-inning game. Equally as interesting was Cooper's way of getting the next pitcher to the mound. He whistled. Over time, his pitchers learned to differentiate their manager's whistle from noises in the grandstands, bleachers, and on the field. Hilton Smith proclaimed, "Cooper was a smart manager, and he was a great teacher--great teacher! A student of baseball, he would take me aside and just sit there and talk to me, and I'd watch how he'd pitch." [130] Although Cooper was born in the South, he never played for a Southern team, and in 1938 there were three Southern teams in the Negro American League.

The Atlanta Black Crackers were new to the Negro National League in 1938. John Harding, an Atlanta businessman with a profitable string of gasoline stations, was the team's owner. Unknown by many was his other business interest. His Black Crackers franchise was often kept afloat with an infusion of cash from his policy book and numbers business. He was the undercover Boss of a gambling operation that functioned within the city's Black community. Many of the older residents tolerated his policy operations because they had no social security, and playing the numbers gave them a limited hope of a bonus. It was a job for the runners and local places of business where numbers were collected. W. B. Baker was hired as the Black Crackers business manager. Originally named the Atlanta Athletics, Harding secured ownership of the Crackers in 1937 from Mike Schaine, a Jew who owned two theaters, the Harlem and Lincoln, in Atlanta's African American section of town. A Morehouse graduate and former Baltimore Elite Giant, Vinicius "Nish" Williams, organized the Atlanta Black Crackers for the 1938 season but handed the reins to Morris Brown alumnus Gabby Kemp in June of 1938. [131] At age nineteen, Kemp was the Negro American League's youngest manager.

James "Gabby" Kemp enjoyed the distinction of being one of baseball's scholar-athletes. As a student attending Morris Brown College, he earned varsity letters in baseball, track, football, basketball, and debate to become the first person in Morris Brown's history to receive five varsity letters in one year. In 1940, he graduated with his undergraduate degree, and in 1941, he returned to obtain a Master's degree. As a professional athlete, Kemp joined Atlanta's Black Crackers in 1935 when they were a Negro Southern League member. Kemp's professional career, 1935-1947, was all spent with the Atlanta Black Crackers.[132]

Atlanta's 1938 roster included Oscar "Pap" Glenn, James "Red" Moore, Thomas "P. I." Butts, Spencer "Babe" Davis, Charlie Duncan, Felix "Chin" Evans, Tom "Preacher" Howard, Eddie "Bullet" Dixon, Jim Reece, Jim "Flash" Cooper, Joe Greene, "Nish" Williams, Donald "Rabbit" Reeves, Don Pelham, Red Hadley, Leo Simms, and Alonzo Mitchell. Under Kemp's astute guidance, Atlanta captured 1938's second-half pennant. The Memphis Red Sox, another Southern team, were declared first-half champions.

The Memphis Red Sox were owned by three brothers who were Doctors, W. S., J. B., and B. B. Martin. There was a fourth brother, A. T. Martin, also a doctor, who elected to pay his way into ballgames rather than enter on a pass and then be called upon to pay his share of the deficits that often-faced Negro League teams.[133] Dr. W. S. Martin was a surgeon and superintendent of Collins Chapel Hospital. Dr. J. B. Martin was the proprietor of the South's finest African American-owned drug store and employed eleven workers. Named on their behalf, Martin's Park, located on Crump Boulevard, was the Red Sox's home field and the only African American-owned ballpark in the entire Negro American League.

Managed by Ted "Double Duty" Radcliffe, 1938's Memphis Red Sox squad was organized from remnants of the 1937 Negro American League Cincinnati, Tigers. Radcliffe's famous

76

nickname came courtesy of Alfred Damon Runyon, who, after watching Radcliffe pitch in the first game of a doubleheader and then catch the second game, was instantly impressed. The next day he tagged Radcliffe as Double Duty, and the nickname stuck and became one of baseball's all-time best. Runyon was known for creating colorful nicknames.[134] One of his most celebrated creations was the name he gave heavyweight boxing champion James J. Braddock whom he tagged the "Cinderella Man."[135] In December of 1937, Radcliffe, both a pitcher and a catcher, signed as the team's new manager. The Cincinnati Tigers, a team he managed in 1937, disbanded, which allowed Radcliffe to bring most of his former squad to Memphis. Lloyd "Ducky" Davenport, Cowan "Bubba" Hyde, Neil Robinson, Olan "Jelly" Taylor Marlin Carter, Porter "Ankle Ball" Moss, Eugene Bremer, Willie Jefferson, and Jess Houston all followed Radcliffe to Memphis. Added to these players were Nat Rogers, Woodrow Wilson, Larry Brown, Bob Madison, Clifford Allen, and Wayman "Red" Longley. Brown started the 1938 season with the Philadelphia Stars before coming back to Memphis. Bremer began the 1938 season under Manager Radcliffe of the Red Sox but ended it with Manager Andy Cooper of the Kansas City Monarchs.

A Southerner by birth, Radcliffe was educated at Mobile, Alabama's Booker T. Washington High School. He was accustomed to being in segregated spacious while living in one of the most segregated cities in the nation. Ted started his semi-professional baseball career there with the Brooklyn Giants. In 1919, Radcliffe relocated to the North, to Chicago, and found employment with the Illinois Giants before joining Gilkerson's Union Giants. In 1927, he entered Negro National League play with the Detroit Stars.

Manager Radcliffe had great admiration for other players within the circuit. He once boasted with assured confidence, "Give me Ducky Davenport, Willard Brown, and Turkey Stearnes in the outfield, and I wouldn't lose a game."[136] The other Southern team in the Negro American League was the Birmingham Black Barons.

William "Dizzy" Dismukes was manager of Birmingham's 1938 Black Barons and A. M. Walker its owner. Barons' team members included David Whatley, Fred Bankhead Parnell Woods, Bert Johnson, Henry "Butch" McCall, Harry Barnes, Armand Tyson, Dewitt Owens, Goldie Cephas, Alonzo "Hooks" Mitchell, Clifford Blackman, and "Nish" Williams, who came in midseason from the Atlanta Black Crackers.[137] Dismukes' career was long and distinguished, and it covered every phase from player to administrator.

Dismukes, a submarine-style pitcher in his heyday, was born and educated in the South. He was born March 15, 1890, in Birmingham, Alabama, and he was educated at Birmingham's Miles College. Ironically his first chance to turn professional came with his 1908 signing with St. Louis, Missouri, Tigers. He would log many outstanding feats in the years to come. In 1911, Dismukes defeated the National League's Pittsburgh Pirates by a 2-to-1 score in an exhibition game. Although starting 1912 with Indiana's West Baden Sprudels, he jumped to the St. Louis Giants later that season and pitched a no-hitter against Rube Foster's American Giants of Chicago, winning 1-0. Returning to Indianapolis to join the ABCs on May 9, 1915, he pitched yet another no-hit game against the Chicago Giants. As an administrator, he managed the Pittsburgh Keystones in 1922, the Indianapolis ABCs in 1924, and the Memphis Red Sox in 1925, and he was appointed manager of the St. Louis Stars, succeeding Branch Russell in 1926. In 1932, he led Cumberland Posey's Detroit Wolves in the short-lived East-West League. James "Candy Jim" Taylor, born February 1, 1884, in Anderson, South Carolina, was the only Negro American League manager older than Dismukes. Taylor's years in baseball were many.

The Chicago American Giants were owned by Horace G. Hall and managed by Taylor. Seeking veteran leadership, Taylor, one of two Negro American League bench managers, was also newly hired by the Giants, a team started by Andrew "Rube" Foster in 1911. Although the American Giants' ownership often changed after Foster's death, Hall, a former insurance executive, purchased the team from its previous owners and began forming a championship aggregation with stability.

Manager Taylor wanted everything to be first-class. He lived in Chicago's prestigious Hotel Brookmont, one of the finest "colored hotels" in the world, when not traveling the country by bus. He was rounding out a professional career that started in 1904 with the Birmingham Giants. His family legacy is one worth further examination.

As one of four famous brothers who played professional baseball, Candy came to Chicago with a reputation for developing young talent. Bert Gholston, a former Negro National League umpire, called Candy Jim, "A man of strong personality blunt and frank, of fine training, great ability, and organizing capacity. His most important asset is his keen and intense interest in all young players. His handling of young players under fire has received words of commendation from baseball men of note and sportswriters who know the game from every angle."[138]

As a manager with the second-longest tenure in Negro baseball, teams under Taylor's leadership dated back to 1920 when the Dayton Marcos of the original Negro National League offered him a circuit managerial job. In 1928, Taylor's young and talented St. Louis Stars won the Negro National League pennant. Superstition, it was rumored, ruled Taylor's life, and therefore, he rode herd over his players. According to infielder Marlin Carter,

Taylor chewed tobacco and would spit it on you [for good luck]. He thought that peanuts were brain food and bad luck. You couldn't eat peanuts on his bench. When Fred Bankhead played against Taylor's teams, he would save [everyone's] peanut hulls and drop them in front of Taylor's dugout, [before making a mad dash to the field]. [139]

Taylor was equally as contemptuous about being late and ordered his players to arrive on time. "Be on time!" He abruptly declared, "I wouldn't wait on my mother if she were late [for the bus], so why would I wait on you?" [140]

Giants' home games were played at Thirty-Fifth Street and Shields Avenue, where they performed for nearly a quarter of a century. The field was formerly named Schorling Park. In 1910, an unexpected alliance with the owner of White Sox, Charles Comiskey, who reportedly ordered the grandstands torn down and the lumber sold to keep out competitors, gave John M. Schorling complete control of his former American League grounds. Schorling, a saloonkeeper who dabbled as a baseball promoter, opened his initial Chicago Park ballpark at Seventy-Ninth Street and Vincennes Avenue in the 1890s. He later operated Auburn Park, home to Frank Leland's Leland Giants. Schorling and Andrew "Rube" Foster formed a partnership in 1910, and the new park opened for business in 1911. Foster, the owner of the team, and Schorling, owner of the park, shook hands on a deal that lasted until Schorling's retirement. After Foster was forced by illness to step down in 1926, the team and park were put in Schorling's possession. In 1929 Schorling sold both the park and the team to W. E. Trimble of Princeton, Illinois, at which time the park hosted other events.

Dog racing enthusiasts leased the park in 1932, but the sport was never legalized in Cook County. The park sat idle, and the American Giants started to barnstorm. Giants' manager, Dave Marlarcher, kept the American Giants going by turning it into a barnstorming outfit until 1935 when Robert A. Cole--a local funeral home owner--secured lease of the grounds and put the American

Giants back into the park. When Cole's other dealings prevented him from engaging actively in baseball, H. G. Hall, an official of Chicago's Metropolitan Assurance Company, purchased the club and renamed Schorling Park to Giants Park. While the Giants' home field situation was stable and secure, the Indianapolis ABCs were strictly a road club.

The new Indianapolis ABCs were owned by Allan "Memphis" Johnson and managed by George F. Mitchell. They were based in Mounds, Illinois. The Mounds Blues were organized in 1935 as a semi-professional aggregation representing southern Illinois. By 1936 they had become one of the best drawing cards in Illinois.[141] Johnson, owner of Mounds' Southern Illinois Night Club, and sponsor of the Mounds, Illinois, Blues baseball club, decided to enter the professional baseball arena in 1937. Like Hardin of the Atlanta Black Crackers, Johnson was a policy book and numbers banker in Illinois. His money was being made outside of baseball. The Mounds Blues represented Indianapolis in the Negro American League, with players from St. Louis, Chicago, and other Illinois communities

Manager George Mitchell, born March 31, 1900, in Sparta, Illinois, formerly pitched in the Negro National and Negro American Leagues. Beginning in 1924, when Mitchell joined the St. Louis Stars, he made sports history when teaming with twin brother Robert, a catcher, to form the Negro Leagues' first twin battery. Mitchell also pitched for teams in Detroit, Kansas City, and Pittsburgh.

Indianapolis' 1938 squad featured John Lyles, Alfred "Buddy" Armour, Quincy Trouppe, Ted Strong, James Armstead, Marshal Riddle, Frank "Chip" McAllister, Robert Dean, Ted Alexander, and Walter Calhoun. Armour, a great young hitter, was said to have led the Provincial League in batting with a .348 average in 1949 with the Farnham Black Sox.[142] He could hit. Raymond

Taylor, an Indianapolis catcher, started the season with the Memphis Red Sox and ended it with the Kansas City Monarchs.

The Jacksonville, Florida Red Caps, signed as an associate league member, were among the least covered of the Negro American League teams. Although there were no printed standings of how well they finished in 1938, records from previous years established their competitiveness. It was reported that the Jacksonville Red Caps "played 89 games in 1935 and won 70 losing 16." A year later, the club won "77 and lost 26." Their 1937 reports displayed a record of "44 wins and 23 losses." [143] In one of the few league standings where the Red Caps name appeared, they were 1-1 to start the second half on July 23. [144] The Red Caps' roster included, among others; Herbert Barnhill, Albert "Cool Papa" Frazier, Leo "Preacher" Henry, Alonzo Mitchell, Willie Ferrell, Howard "Duke" Cleveland, Ernest Jones, John Williams, Joe Royal, Leroy Holmes, Marcelius D. Cox, Lacy Thomas, and Henry Turner.

Underfinanced, constantly on the road, and traveling with an itinerary that was as rigid as it was restrictive, O'Neil's Negro American League comrades endured the daily hardships of life in segregated baseball of the 1930s. Yet, and despite these obstacles, the Negro American League survived. They were riding a punctuated rhythm of success as the 1938 Negro American League campaign began. Their arrival was a highly anticipated event in communities all across America.

"Kansas City has shifted Mayweather from first base to the outfield because of his hitting, and John O'Neil, a youngster, will play first."

Chicago Defender, May 28, 1938

Buck O'Neil says...

"The majority of guys that were playing major league baseball at the time, [graduated] high school or didn't finish high school. This was the same in black baseball. Now, if we had gone into White baseball, a lot of the White guys that were playing baseball wouldn't have jobs. And, it was more or less a commercial thing. And they were thinking at the time, well, the people wouldn't come out to see a Black guy play ball with the White guy. That's what they were thinking at the time."

Help At The Initial Sack

John "Buck" O'Neil was a yearling seeking a second opportunity to break into the Negro American League at the start of the 1938 season. Having arrived in Kansas City, he was more curious than uneasy. He had the difficult task of winning the first base starting assignment. An outstanding player named Eldridge Mayweather already occupied the position. As current guardian of first base, he had no plans on relinquishing that space, a spot he had held since joining the Monarchs in 1935. Additionally, since Mayweather was a better hitter, it did not appear that he would voluntarily surrender the position either.

O'Neil joined a Kansas City team that was loaded with talent! Fleet-footed Henry Milton in left field and center fielder Willard Brown controlled the outer garden. Hilton Smith pitcher; Frank Duncan, catcher; Wilber "Bullet" Rogan at utility and Andy Cooper as manager formed the nucleus of that season's illustrious squad. When Kansas City acquired Norman "Turkey" Stearnes in August of 1938, O'Neil was bestowed with the honor of playing with five Hall of Famers during his rookie season with the Monarchs.

John "Buck" O'Neil. *Represented in the Negro American League were students, past and current from many historically Black Colleges and Universities. O'Neil's college was Edward Waters in Jacksonville, Florida. (Authors collection)*

All totaled, O'Neil played alongside Brown for twelve seasons (1938 to 1950), ten seasons with Smith (1938-1948), one with Rogan (1938), and three with Stearnes (1938-1940). X would manage O'Neil for three seasons (1938-1940). This does not include the years he played with Satchel Paige.

In O'Neil's first summer, his name was often misspelled. He was referred to as "O'Neal" by numerous media sources. Seldom, if ever, did the press mistake the name of Kansas City's veteran first basemen, Eldridge "Chili" Mayweather

Mayweather had captured first base with his arrival in 1935. Before 1935, there were only four everyday first basemen in Monarchs' history: Edgar "Blue" Washington (1920), Lemuel Hawkins (1921-1927), L. D. Livingston (1930), and George Giles (1927-1929) and (1931-1934). Having replaced Giles in 1935, Mayweather supplied more home run punch than all other Monarchs' first basemen. To earn a spot in the lineup, O'Neil's dethroning of Mayweather was the only option. Not such an easy task for a rookie, especially one hired for his defense rather than offense.

Mayweather was born November 24, 1909, in Shreveport, Louisiana, in Caddo Parish. His mother, Dalsie Anderson-Mayweather, was a 17-year-old homemaker from Shreveport, his father, Alva Mayweather, a 22-year-old laborer from Grand Cane, Louisiana.[145] His birth name of Alva Jr. was later changed to Eldridge, middle initial E. The date of the change is unknown. The spelling of his last name also changed. Some documents list his last name differently spelled, while most list it as Mayweather. His date of birth is alternated with November 26, 1909.[146] Standing five-foot-seven, weighing in at 188 pounds, Mayweather appeared much larger at first glance. When speaking to those who knew Mayweather, his friends and church members said he "never raised his voice and was very even-tempered and was a perfect gentleman off and on the field."[147]

Mayweather's whispering voice was a far cry from his aggressive slugging on the field where he helped Kansas City win with alarming regularity. He came to Kansas City as proprietor of baseball's sweetest long ball swats. By mid-July of 1935, the Kansas City's *Call* newspaper proclaimed, "The club has played 79 games to date, losing four."[148] The same article acknowledged that Mayweather "hit 20 home runs in 50 games." Big numbers despite the twenty games he missed with a sprained knee.

In 1936, when Kansas City signed slugger Pat Patterson, there was the hope of a three-way slugging bee by the team's other prolific long ball hitters--Mayweather and Willard Brown. That dream was dashed when Mayweather broke his leg in Borger, Texas, on May 12. "Mayweather pounded into home sliding feet first safely," pronounced Borger's *Daily Herald.* "As he hit the plate, his right leg twisted acutely, and he was carried from the field suffering from a broken bone in his ankle."[149] When Mayweather returned, his hitting appeared unaffected; however, in the field and on-base, it was a different story. With Mayweather slowed by injury and a real liability on defense, Manager Andy Cooper was seeking a logical successor. Buck O'Neil's 1938 appearance resurrected hope in a renaissance of the Monarchs' infield.

At six-foot-two-inches tall, O'Neil's body type comprised the physique, height, and reach needed for his infield position. He looked like an athlete. In addition to being three years younger than Mayweather, O'Neil, a stellar defensive first baseman, hoped to capitalize on Mayweather's two weaknesses--fielding and injuries. In coming west, O'Neil also sought to become more like his favorite first baseman, the man he initially patterned himself after. O'Neil wanted to be in the National American League what Walter "Buck" Leonard was to the Negro National League. O'Neil admired Leonard, first baseman of Pittsburgh's Homestead Grays. He recalled,

> I liked 'Buck' Leonard, I was playing right along there with him, but he was a
> little older than I was. I saw him play; I saw the way he carried himself; he could
> do it all as a first baseman.[150]

Homestead Grays. On Easter Sunday, April 17, 1938, in New Orleans, Louisiana, the Grays, and Monarchs split a doubleheader. A total of seven future Hall of Famers participated in the two games. (Authors collection)

White players were just as enamored by Leonard. Carlton Overton Tremper, who was once handed a $10,000 bonus to sign with the Brooklyn National League team, and who later played for the Brooklyn Bushwicks, said, "There are no better fielders in the majors. In smartness, speed, and throwing, he [Leonard] equals the best in the game."[151]

Emulating the things that he watched Leonard do while alternating between first base and right field, O'Neil worked assiduously for a starting spot. With interludes of outstanding fielding and hitting exhibited by both O'Neil and Mayweather, by May 15, the argument was settled--John "Buck" O'Neil was Kansas City's new first baseman. Help had finally arrived.

"New Orleans baseball fans will get a chance to see the outstanding Negro baseball players in the country in action this afternoon at Heinemann Park when the Homestead Grays, world champions, and the Kansas City Monarchs, winners of the Negro American League Pennant, clash in a doubleheader starting at 2:30 o'clock."

New Orleans Item, April 17, 1938

Buck O'Neil says...

"There are approximately 200 men in the Negro leagues now. They earn from $200 to $800 monthly for five months. Some 80-odd of these will draw this amount from Winter League baseball. These salaries, of course, will not compare to those of Williams or DiMaggio with their multi-thousand-dollar draws. But it beats the hell out of loafing on Central Avenue or Beal Street or Eighteenth and Vine."

Spring Training with The Champions

<u>April 9-Galveston</u>, <u>April 10-Houston</u>, April 12-Houston, <u>April 14-Houston</u>, <u>April 17-New Orleans</u> <u>(D.H.)</u>, April 19-Monroe

(NNL) O'Neil's Batting: G-2 AB-3 R-1 H-0 2B-0 3B-0 HR-0 SB-0 BA-0.00

O'Neil's Fielding: PO-13 A-0 E-0 DP-3 TC-13

Spring's summons to "Play Ball" was a ritual that conjured up athletes from all over America. It was a prideful action that brought together talented men who ceremoniously banded together during our nation's segregated and unequal past. Black men were eager to expel the long-standing belief that they were unqualified to perform in the National and America Leagues and minor leagues all over the nation. They took the field with a stalwart self-assuredness that few could miss or deny. Yet, while spring's blooming tulips announced the return of veterans and rookies, daily newspapers practically ignored them. Still, the new Negro American League, a league which the Monarchs helped form in 1937, assured that professional baseball as played by African Americans was more than pie in the sky--it was an actual organized structure playing with equality that rivaled the National and American League's brightest stars.

Philadelphia Stars. *In an April 10, 1938, exhibition win over the Philadelphia Stars in Houston, Texas Monarchs' pitchers John Marcum, Floyd Kranson, and Dick Bradley collectively struck out sixteen batters. (Authors collection)*

The year before, 1937, was the inaugural season of the new Negro American League. The Kansas City Monarchs and Chicago American Giants battled in a playoff for the first league championship. The championship series, in which Kansas City captured four games to one, included a seventeen-inning tie. The long and grueling extra-inning game played on September 12, 1937, in

Chicago, Illinois, ended in a 2-2 deadlock. Andy Cooper Monarchs' manager, performed the superhuman feat of pitching all seventeen frames.[152] It was only fitting, then, that these teams meet in the opening month of 1938. When the 1938 season started, there were certainly a lot of players in the new league that had played in the original Negro National League started in 1920. Every team had one or two players; the Kansas City Monarchs started the season with five.

Among the former Negro National League veterans on the Monarchs' roster were players like Newt Allen, Andy Cooper, Frank Duncan, Wilber "Bullet" Rogan, and Jack Marshall. The Atlanta Black Crackers had one holdover in "Nish" Williams. The ABCs of Indianapolis had three former Negro National League veterans in manager George Mitchell, Quincy Trouppe, and Bobby Robinson. Birmingham had two old-timers in Jabbo Andrews and manager "Dizzy" Dismukes. Memphis employed catcher Larry Brown and the always colorful "Double Duty" Radcliffe. The team with the most former Negro National League players also had the most colorful nicknames. The Chicago American Giants had on its roster "Turkey" Stearnes, "Sug" Cornelius, "Frog" Redus, "High Pockets" Ted Trent, and manager "Candy" Taylor. The original Negro National League disbanded after the 1931 season, but these veterans were still active in 1938. The availability of the name motivated the formation of a new Negro National League in the East in 1933. The eastern Negro National League circuit started the 1938 season with seven teams. Pittsburgh fielded two teams in the Crawfords and Homestead Grays. The remainder of the league included the Philadelphia Stars, Baltimore Elites, the Newark Eagles, New York Black Yankees, and Washington Black Senators. The Homestead Grays and Philadelphia Stars were added to Kansas City's spring training schedule for games to be played in the south.

While Wilkinson and Baird prepared their Monarchs' spring training itinerary, it was nearly impossible to overlook Kansas City's local news headlines. Two African American men, William

Wright, and John Brown, were to become the first and second men to be executed in the Missouri State Prison gas chamber since legislation, which passed in 1937, substituted gas for hanging in crimes of capital punishment. Both men received the state's ultimate punishment--a dose of hydrocyanic acid gas on March 4, 1938. Wright was originally convicted and sentenced to die for the murder of Dr. J. T. Mc Campbell, a druggist and former Washburn University baseball player, whom he gunned down during a holdup in March of 1933. Wright's punishment was historic as he became one of the first African Americans in Missouri's long and discriminatory history to receive capital punishment for killing another African American.

Assiduously formulating his spring agenda, Wilkinson, as he had done many times before, wisely re-signed Wilber "Bullet" Rogan, who was in the twilight of a great career. Once considered the world's greatest all-around baseball player, Rogan occupied the dual role of coach and utility player. In his prime, Rogan feared none of baseball's greatest hitters. James "Biz" Mackey enjoyed telling stories about Rogan. One of his favorites occurred when both were playing in Cuba during the winter of 1924-25,

> With [Esteban] Montalvo, one of the best hitters ever to step to the plate at-bat,
> Mackey said he gave Rogan a signal. Rogan shook his head. Mackey signaled for
> a curveball, and again Rogan shook his head. Mackey said he then walked out
> to the mound to try and find out what Rogan wanted to pitch. 'What's the matter,
> Bullet?' he asked. 'There's nothing wrong,' Rogan said. 'Only I'm going to throw
> those babies, Montalvo, [Alejandro] Oms and [Bernardo] Baro, some drop
> balls. 'Say, are you crazy,' I yelled. 'Don't you know those babies kill drop balls?'
> Mackey said he then called [Adolfo] Luque and explained to him what Rogan
> wanted to do. 'If Rogan throws Montalvo, Oms, and Baro a drop ball, they will

hit it out of the lot. They just love drops,' I said. 'Yes, but they haven't seen Rogan's drop ball,' Bullet countered. And he proceeded to throw nine drop balls past Montalvo, Oms, and Baro to retire the side. Mackey said it was one of the best-pitching feats he had ever witnessed.[153]

Two other longtime Monarchs, Newt Allen and Frank Duncan, were added to Wilkinson's list of players. Collectively the trio had forty-eight years of professional experience between them. Rogan joined the Monarchs in 1920, Duncan in 1921, and Allen in 1922. Jack Marshall, a veteran infielder with twelve seasons of professional experience, was also added to Wilkinson's stable of talented athletes. The remainder of the roster was formed of youngsters, youthful lads of age thirty and younger.

Henry Milton, Byron "Mex" Johnson, and William "Bill" Simms were both invited to camp. Milton, age 29 and an Indiana native, formerly played outfield with the East Chicago Grasselli Giants before joining Kansas City in 1935. Simms, a former Monroe Monarchs team member, age 30, signed on to play right field. Arkansas-born shortstop Byron "Mex" Johnson, age 26, was introduced to Kansas City audiences in 1937. The Monarchs carried a staff of seven to eight pitchers in 1938. John Markham, Hilton Smith, I. V. Barnes Andy Cooper Floyd Kranson, and Dick Bradley were the mainstays of the staff. Smith, Barnes, and Bradley were all strikeout pitchers with impressive totals. Additionally, Smith and Barnes were outstanding hitters and often filled in as outfielders. Bradley, a Benton, Louisiana native, was playing around Shreveport, Louisiana, when the Monarchs lured him westward late in 1937. His lively fastball was often compared to Bob Feller's speed, and Feller was a well-known American League strikeout pitcher. O'Neil recalled that Bradley's mother worked for some wealthy white folks in Benton."[154]

John "Buster" Markham age 29, was listed among the returning pitchers. Markham originally joined the Monarchs in 1930, left, then returned in 1937. Hilton Smith, age 26, was a 1937 returnee, as was 25-year-old I. V. Barnes. Smith joined from Bismarck, North Dakota. Barnes joined on a recommendation from Lee W. Payne Dean of Boys and Owen Smaulding, a one-time Monarchs' pitcher and baseball manager at Piney Woods College Country Life College in Mississippi.[155]

Isaac and Mary Barnes gave birth to I.V. on December 23, 1912, in Silver Creek, Mississippi. The son's name often appeared as Isaac, but this was not his real name; his name was initials only. His college team, Piney Woods, used baseball as a form of recruitment for students as they traveled under the banner of the name St. Louis Blues. Under Smaulding's guidance, the Blues traveled to the Pacific Coast in 1936. Barnes was scouted after a game in Jackson, Mississippi, during the 1936 season. Barnes endured the long bus tours and daily pitching assignments to win a spot on the Monarchs' roster in 1937, the year he graduated. Barnes captured regional attention after his memorable performance against Cleveland's Bob Feller in the fall of 1937. Battling Feller, Barnes was superb, striking out eleven. Hall of Famer "Big Cat" Johnny Mize, a first baseman who batted .364 and collected 204 hits for the St. Louis Cardinals in 1937, was held to a single hit. That night four pitchers, three for the All-Stars and Barnes for the Monarchs, struck out twenty-six batters. At least two of Barnes' college teammates, Howard Easterling of the 1937 Cincinnati Tigers and Herman Dunlap of the 1938 American Giants, also graduated to Negro League play.

New to the Monarchs were rookies, Roosevelt Cox and John O'Neil. Both were college men. Cox attended Wiley College in Texas. In the Negro American League, Cox and O'Neil were joined by many college men. Represented in the circuit were students and graduates of Prairie View A&M, Wiley College, Lincoln University of Jefferson City, Clark University, Morris Brown, Morehouse, Rust College, Daniel Payne, Wilberforce, Piney Woods, Morgan State, and Indiana State University.

There was the traditional purchasing of new equipment, endless packing of everyone's personal items, farewells at the Eighteenth Street Paseo YMCA, and finally, the departure south. Embarking toward Texas on Saturday, April 2, 1938, the Monarchs' bus hauled a cargo that would forever etch their names into baseball history. Wilkinson, together with the booking agent and co-owner, Baird, along with Duncan, Rogan, Allen, Mayweather, Cox, Brown, Markham, Milton, Marshall, and trainer Frank "Jew Baby" Floyd exited with the primary group from Kansas City. In Fort Smith, Arkansas, Manager Andy Cooper Johnson, Simms, Smith, Kranson, Bradley, Barnes, and O'Neil boarded, carrying all their worldly possessions in duffle bags and grips. Clamoring to see who was on board, O'Neil's broad smile could never be mistaken for a frown as he spotted his old roommate John Markham. Chaffing on old times, conversations, happy and energetic, continued as the drive and scenery changed from tedious to uneventful. As the bus veered into Houston, Texas, pitchers McLemore and Charlie Beverly, along with others that had aspirations of joining Kansas City's 1938 squad, united at the team's training headquarters.

Spring training was less than a week old when the Monarchs took the field in actual competition and started stirring the stew for what would become a gumbo of opponents. Negro baseball's bewildering economics dictated that when men touched dirt, they began playing games in front of paying crowds. Financially strapped for cash, Negro League ballplayers were not permitted to sweat themselves back into condition, as was the custom for National and American League players.

On April 9, in a 3:00 p.m. encounter at Galveston, Texas, situated within the affable surroundings of Moody Stadium, the Monarchs and Philadelphia Stars collided in what became the first of many spring training games. The Stars fielded five former Monarchs.

There were lots of former Monarchs on Philadelphia's 1938 roster: George Giles (1927-1934), Curtis "Moochie" Harris (1931-1936), Dewey Creacy (1922), Pat Patterson (1936), and Henry McHenry (1930 and 1937), had all served admirably with past Monarchs teams in the years indicated, before moving to other teams. The remainder of the Stars' roster included Manager Jud Wilson, Clyde Spearman, Jake Dunn, Larry Brown, Earnest "Spoon" Carter, Rocky Ellis, Alfred Harvey, Jim Missouri, and William G. "Bill" Perkins.

Kansas City lost its pre-season opener when Dunn's first-inning home run, with two mates on base, helped Philadelphia to a 6-0 victory. In addition, Spearman collected two safe blows and busted the game's second home run. Pitching was the contributing factor in Philadelphia's lopsided take-away. The Stars' pitching duo of Missouri, the lanky southpaw, and right-handed McHenry limited Kansas City to four hits. Kansas City countered with Beverly, Kranson, and Bradley, but the Philadelphians, led by hitters Dunn and Spearman, raked up eleven hits. Marshall, Allen, Simms, and Beverly picked up hits for Kansas City.

Marshall was in his first season with the Monarchs. Born August 8, 1908, in Montgomery, Alabama, William "Jack" Marshall turned in a splendid first game. Having worked his way through an assortment of Northern teams before joining the Monarchs in 1938, he was a man of higher education. He had attended an African Methodist Episcopal college in Ohio named Wilberforce.[156]

Henry McHenry. *A former Monarch himself, right-hander McHenry was in mid-season form when he defeated the Monarchs in his hometown of Houston, Texas on April 9, 1938. He had just returned from Winter League play with Marianao in the Cuban League. (Authors collection)*

Four of the Stars' first-inning runs were obtained off Monarchs' starter "Lefty" Charlie Beverly A native of Houston, Texas, only a few years prior, Beverly was considered one of baseball's preeminent left-handed strikeout artists. In 1931 he joined the Monarchs in midseason from the San Antonio Indians, and for the next two years, averaged three hundred strikeouts a season. Homestead Grays' owner, Cumberland Posey, earnestly selected Beverly to his "All-America Ball Club in 1931."[157] As a pitcher of extraordinary ability, Beverly tossed many memorable games in the fall of 1933. At least three of these games deserve special mention.

Listed among Beverly's 1933 conquests was a game of thirteen strikeouts against Dizzy Dean's All-Stars which highlighted a 5-4 Monarchs' win in Kansas City.[158] The Cardinals' famous outfielder, Pepper Martin, accounted for three of Beverly's total whiffs. Beverly followed that game with an October 11, 3-0 win, and fourteen batters struck out in Oklahoma City, Oklahoma, against Paul Waner's all-Star team.[159] In addition to Waner of the Pirates, the All-Star's lineup included Forrest Jensen, Pirates' outfielder; Glen Wright, Brooklyn Dodgers' shortstop; Larry French Pirates' left-hander and Hollis Thurston, a Dodgers' right-handed pitcher. To show this performance was no fluke, Beverly finished off Waner and his All-Stars for a second time with thirteen strikeouts on October 15, in a 3-2 win at Kansas City.[160] Slugger Buzz Arlett of the International League batted cleanup and was a strikeout victim three times. There was also the October 13, 1934 game against Dizzy Dean's All-Stars in Des Moines, Iowa, a game won 9-to-0 by Kansas City. In that game, Beverly's performance of nine innings pitched, five hits allowed, and fifteen strikeouts provided most of that day's highlights.[161] Beverly pitched so many great games it is impossible to list them all, but by1938, injuries had taken their toll on the outstanding lefty.

It was obvious that the once amazing Beverly, who allowed numerous early runs, was only a shell of his legendary self. The Saturday, April 9 game would be one of Beverly's last as a Monarch.

Ironically, this same game would be John "Buck" O'Neil's first in a Monarchs' uniform. O'Neil and Mayweather, rivaling for ownership of the initial sack, went hitless and scoreless in that Sunday's opener.

Lingering in Texas, where Negro National League opponents were in abundance, the Monarchs traveled to Houston and trounced the Philadelphia Stars on Sunday, April 10, by a 7-1 score.[162] Markham, Kranson, and Bradley combined for sixteen strikeouts, limiting Philadelphia Stars' batters to four hits. Bradley, in earning a spot on the roster, was throwing with veteran-like consistency. He was fast but frequently inaccurate. Being hit by one of his wild throws could surely inflict damage. One of Bradley's swift pellets once landed on "Sug" Cornelius' spine, sending the American Giants' pitcher to the hospital with spasms.[163]

In their second game in Houston, Kansas City batters pounded Philadelphia's pitchers for seventeen hits. Marshall, the Monarchs' third baseman, led all hitters with four safe blows. Getting off to a second-inning lead, when Milton, Simms, and Brown connected for a run, Kansas City returned in the third, scoring three additional times to take a 4-0 lead. Run number five resulted from Newt Allen's sixth-inning solo home run into left field. Philadelphia scored their lone run in the fourth with a barrage of singles by Harris, Perkins, and Harvey. O'Neil and Mayweather, Kansas City's competing first basemen, went hitless for a second consecutive game. Cheerful for having captured the season's first win, a day later, that celebration turned somber when news of Cristobal Torriente's death reached camp.[164] Although better known as a former American Giants outfielder, Torriente had also played with two of Wilkinson's Kansas City clubs, the 1916-1917 All-Nations, and the 1926 Monarchs. By hearsay news of the Cuban's death from Tuberculosis at age-44 was widely circulated.

A stocky Cuban of enormous flash, Torriente, ornately adorned with chain-link gold bracelets around his neck and bulky diamond rings on his huge fingers long before it was fashionable, was hard to overlook. In addition to his noted ability as a hitter, in pitcher Willie Foster's opinion, "You weren't going to find anybody that could play more outfield than Torriente."[165] Known for his intrepid play, in November of 1920, Torriente slammed three home runs in a game against the New York Giants. Babe Ruth pitched and held down first base for the Giants on that eventful afternoon but failed to hit a single homer. One newspaper surmised,

> If Torriente were a shade lighter in color, he might stand on the same pinnacle with [Tris] Speaker and [Ty] Cobb. Every ball he hits is a bullet, and among his other accomplishments, he can field, throw, and run.[166]

Though neither team stopped to mourn Torriente's sorrowful death, he remained in their subconscious. Richard "Subby" Byas an American Giants' catcher, remembered the exact date and place where he'd first heard of the great outfielder's demise.[167] A deciding game was played between the Monarchs and Philadelphia Giants on April 12, which the Monarchs won.[4] The results of the three-game series against the Philadelphia Stars are still up for debate.[5] The Monarchs remained in Houston for a third game on April 14.[168]

Remaining in Houston for additional training, the Monarchs were defeated in a 9-to-5 final by Manager Vic Harris' Pittsburgh Homestead Grays at West End Park on Thursday, April 14. Kansas City lost in typical fashion--on a Josh Gibson home run. Gibson's seventh-inning blast with

---

[4] No account of the series' final game between the Monarchs and Philadelphia Stars was printed in the *Houston Chronicle* newspaper. Another reference in the *Hutchinson, Kansas News*, said the Monarchs won, "two of three from the Philadelphia Stars of the Negro National League."

[5] A note on the series' final game appeared in the April 24, 1938, *Chattanooga Daily Times* where Manager Jud Wilson said they had triumphed over the Monarchs twice by 10-4 and 6-0 scores.

two men on lifted the Homesteaders into a distant lead. Gibson, born the same year, and a mere forty days before O'Neil, was already an established star, having entered the professional ranks as a teenager in 1930.

Gibson, Vic Harris, Chester Williams, and O'Neil's former Miami Giants' teammate Sylvester Sneed collected eight of Pittsburgh's ten hits while pitcher Roy Partlow tossed a four-hitter, allowing only Newt Allen, Willard Brown, Frank Duncan, and Roosevelt Cox to reach safely. Mayweather, Kansas City's first baseman on that day, went hitless and scoreless. O'Neil sat idly on the bench and was not penciled into the lineup. On Easter Sunday, April 17, the Monarchs reached New Orleans, Louisiana, for their first scheduled doubleheader of 1938 and another game versus the Grays. Kansas City split a holiday double-bill before three thousand spectators at Heinemann Park.

A crowd that numbered from 3,000 to 5,000 watched the Grays take the opener, a 4-3 win in ten innings. Players on Pittsburgh's roster looked to be in midseason form. In the second inning Buck Leonard, the Grays' first sacker, lined a shot into right with three men on to ignite the scoring. Willard Brown, hitting a ball that seemed to disregard gravity, clouted a beeline drive into the deepest part of center field for a homer to start the Monarchs' scoring. The New Orleans *Times-Picayune* described Brown's homerun drive as "one of the hardest hits ever produced in Heinemann Park."[169] Kansas City made a game of the festivities in the tenth, but Ray Brown, the Grays premier pitcher, fanned Willie Simms for the final out with a Monarchs' base runner stranded 90 feet from home.

Although Kansas City was bumped for the loss, it was a good day for the Monarchs' first baseman. Mayweather broke his string of hitless games, going 2-for-4 with a two-base hit and two runs batted in. O'Neil, unable to enter the contest, languishingly sat the bench for a second consecutive game. In his soul, he had to be thinking, I can beat this guy out of the position. I can beat this guy!

In the nightcap, Monarchs' batters shelled Partlow for a 6-3 win. O'Neil, taking over at first base, went 0-for-2 with a run scored, then participated in two lightning-quick double plays for the Monarchs. Unfortunately, though, O'Neil was still seeking his first hit when the team's bus rolled out of New Orleans. They motored to Monroe, Louisiana for the final game of their three-city tour versus the Homestead Grays. On April 19, the Monarchs' scheduled Tuesday night game at Monroe's Casino Park against the Grays was canceled because of wet conditions.[170]

"T.Y. Baird, [a] part-owner of the Monarchs, who booked the game here, reports he'll have one of the best ball clubs ever assembled anywhere this year, White or Black. Before the old Negro National League disbanded in 1931, his team won four pennants and three world's series in twelve years, and he predicts his 1938 nine may be the best he has ever had."

Dallas Morning News, April 17, 1938

Buck O'Neil says...

"As far as segregation...Now, we would have more problems North, I believe, than South. Because South was this...you knew, what you had to do. They had good black hotels, they had good black restaurants in the South, but when you pass the Mason Dixon line, now you're getting in the places that you didn't have it. Now, we wouldn't go into a white restaurant in Atlanta. But we just might go into a white restaurant when we got to Washington. But the guy wouldn't serve you."

Back To Texas, Headed North

April 20-Texarkana, April 21-Tyler (day), April 21-Longview, April 22-Marshall, April 24-Dallas, April 26-Waco, April 27-Enid, April 28-Hutchinson, April 29-Joplin, April 30-Bartlesville, May 1-Springfield

(NAL) O'Neil's Batting: G-1 AB-1 R-0 H-1 2B-0 3B-0 HR-0 SB-0 BA-1.000

O'Neil's Fielding: PO-0 A-0 E-0 DP-0 TC-0

(WA) O'Neil's Batting: G-3 AB-11 R-3 H-3 2B-0 3B-0 HR-0 SB-2 RBI-1 BA-2.73

O'Neil's Fielding: PO-1 A-0 E-2 DP-0 TC-1

Returning to Texas, Wilkinson slotted additional spring games against the Chicago American Giants at several East Texas League cities that included Texarkana, Tyler, Longview, Marshall, and Waco. In leaving Jacksonville and Daytona Beach, Florida, after playing spring training games with the Jacksonville Red Caps, the American Giants were working their way north for the season opener. They reunited with the Monarchs in Texas for additional spring games.

On Wednesday, April 20, Kansas City, a winner of three out of six exhibition games with one winning score unsubstantiated, lost a 9-4 game to Taylor's American Giants at Burnett Park in Texarkana, Texas. Few details of the game were listed in the *Texarkana Gazette,* which noted that both teams had scored in the first inning and that Chicago bunched six hits for the victory.[171]

Chicago continued their victorious romp at Tyler, Texas, where they thumped Kansas City by a 3-2 score on April 21. The Thursday game gave local fans their first opportunity to see the best of big-time baseball in a grandstand that was divided with the right field side of the grandstands revered for white fans.[172] Another local newspaper's cynicism announced, "The Monarchs have a charcoal edition of Joe Medwick in Willard (Home Run) Brown, a husky outfielder who clouted 45 home runs last season; for the Kansas City aggregation."[173]

*American Giants, 1938. Standing (L to R): Edward "Pep" Young, Norman "Turkey" Stearnes.
(Kneeling) Richard "Subby" Byas Alex Radcliffe. (Authors collection)*

Kansas City defeated Chicago 6-3 in Longview, Texas, as the daily travel grind continued.

Heading into Marshall, the local newspaper noted, "[Willard] Brown had four home runs and

[Turkey] Stearnes three in the prior three games.[174] Kansas City won a 9-to-1 ballgame in Marshall,

Texas, at an event tagged by Wiley College Alumni as "Henry Milton Night" on April 22 in a Friday

night encounter at segregated Matthewson Park where white fans were restricted to the grandstand along first base.[175] In getting the win, a trio of Monarchs' pitchers, Dick Bradley, John Markham and Hilton Smith, held Chicago to four hits.[176] Following that event, both teams motored toward Dallas, Texas, for a well-publicized Sunday encounter

No less than four newspapers covered the Monarchs versus American Giants April 24 appearance in Dallas. A hotbed for spring training excursions, Steer's Park had hosted the New York Yankees, the Chicago White Sox, the Pittsburgh Pirates, and St. Louis Cardinals in 1938 spring play. The Monarchs versus American Giants game at Steer's Park was the city's first Negro League spring encounter of 1938.

A pre-game report in the *Dallas Express* newspaper took delight in comparing various Monarchs to well-known big leaguers. Mayweather was called a "Stuffy McInnis type," and Newt Allen was rated in the same class as "Charlie Gehringer, Frankie Fritsch, and Eddie Collins."[177] Another article called Stearnes a "Babe Ruth and Tris Speaker rolled into one."[178]

Paced by Stearnes, who picked up three hits in four trips, which included a single, triple, and a home run, the American Giants, beat the Monarchs 9-to-2.[179] In addition to Stearnes' four runs batted in and three runs scored, other Giant hitters similarly rattled Kansas City's assortment of hurlers. O'Neil pinch-hit for shortstop Bryon Johnson in the ninth and singled. It was his only at-bat.

Four pitchers, Smith, Kranson, Markham, and McLemore, twirled for Kansas City. Tom Johnson and William "Sug" Cornelius divided hurling chores for the American Giants Smith was credited with the loss and Johnson the win--although Cornelius hurled more innings.

Right-hander Cornelius, Chicago's well-publicized ace, an alumnus of Clark University, was born in 1907 in Atlanta, Georgia. Cornelius broke into professional ball with Tom Wilson's

Nashville Elite Giants in 1929. He was signed by Memphis in 1930 and Birmingham in 1931 before securing an American Giants contract in 1933.

The Dallas crowd was estimated at "4,000 Negro fans and 1,000 whites," as reported in the *Dallas Express.*[180] The same newspaper labeled Stearnes' home run--a hit that hadn't snuck into the deep left-center bleachers as "the longest drive made in Steer Stadium this year."[181] The spring motorcade continued towards Waco, where both teams engaged in an 8:00 p.m. game at Katy Park.

Frank "Creepy" Crespi. On May 1, 1938, the Monarchs lost in Springfield, Missouri to that city's Cardinals in a 6-3 final. Crespi had one hit in four at-bats, a double with the bases loaded that drove in three runs. (Authors collection)

While pre-publicizing the game, the *Waco News-Tribune* suggested, "If it were possible to make several of the stars you will see tonight, white, they would not be here, but would be playing in the major leagues at this time."[182] Despite troublesome spring rains earlier that day, nearly three thousand fans, including among them a reported seven hundred whites, showed up at Waco's Katy Park. The Monarchs captured the game by a 6-to-5 tally, scoring the winning run in the final inning. The game also featured "Two roaring homers, one being far over the center-field wall," for which no player received credit.[183] Having completed their series, both teams continued spring training and barnstorming nightly.[184]

After the brief series, the American Giants remained in Texas for games in Galveston on April 28 against the Morgan Line Tigers.[185] The Monarchs motored towards Enid, Oklahoma, for an April 27 night game versus the Enid Oilers.

With their 1937 National Baseball Congress Tournament win in Wichita, Kansas, the Oilers were reigning national Semi-professional champions. Kansas City captured the Wednesday night encounter when Cooper and Markham combined for a one-hitter. The one hit, a home run by "Dutch" Prather, scored Enid's only run in the Monarchs' 5-1 victory.[186] In the Negro Leagues, there were no players nicknamed Dutch, Whitey, Hans, or Swede. There were, however, several players nicknamed "Buck."[6] Nicknames can say more about a man's ethnicity than is often intended.

The Enid encounter was followed by games in Hutchinson, Joplin, Bartlesville, and Springfield, as the Monarchs clashed with several Class C, Western Association League teams. O'Neil often remarked that coming to the Monarchs was just like a white boy going to the Yankees. At least two of the white boys they battled in the spring of 1938, Russ Derry and Frank "Creepy" Crespi, would experience that emotion. All along the way, O'Neil, and Mayweather battled for the

---

[6] The Enid *Daily Eagle* failed to print a box score or cover the game with much detail. Pitchers Cooper and Markham are the only Monarchs mentioned by name in the newspaper's very brief summary of the game.

starting position, although detailed accounts of their struggle rarely appeared in print. In Hutchinson, Kansas, where the Monarchs played often, they needed "no introduction," yet when the local newspaper cited members of the traveling squad, O'Neil's name was not listed.[187]

Joplin was a New York Yankees' farm club in 1938. In the pre-game publicity, the *Joplin Globe* reported that the Monarchs had a spring record of six wins and four losses in eleven spring contests.[188]

Manager Ted Mayer, a professional ballplayer since 1928, managed the Joplin Miners for the American League Yankees. Mayer's Miners were defeated in a landslide 12-2 final that was witnessed by 1,000 fans.[189] Willard Brown laced a pair of clutch triples and a single to drive across five important runs. Monarchs' pitchers; Cooper, Markham, and Smith, held Russ Derry, a future New York Yankee, to no hits in four at-bats. O'Neil, who was moved to left field, went 2-for-4 with a stolen base. Mayweather did not fare as well against Joplin, finishing 0-for-5 at- bat. The next day, the Monarchs returned to Oklahoma to meet the Bartlesville Chiefs in yet another night contest. Located between Joplin and Bartlesville was the little town of Baxter Springs, Kansas. The Monarchs chose to stay there because it was more accommodating.

The Bartlesville team was receiving players on options from the American League Browns and minor league Tulsa Oilers. The local minor leaguers themselves were coming off the road, having played in Fayetteville, Arkansas, Rogers, Arkansas, and Siloam Springs. It was aggressive travel for a minor league team, but small peanuts compared to the octave leaps and broad jumps Negro major league teams were making daily. Against the Monarchs, Bartlesville was defeated in an 8-7 final before what the local newspaper called the "biggest Municipal field crowd of the spring."[7]

---

[7] The local *Bartlesville Daily Enterprise* failed to print a box score from the game—only the score was given.

Almost as quickly as it ended, the Monarchs were back on the bus speeding towards Springfield, Missouri, for yet another interracial tussle. With successive victories over Enid, Hutchinson, Joplin, and Bartlesville, another win was virtually assured in Springfield, where Kansas City had not lost a game since 1928. Instead, it became a night when history did not repeat itself. [190] The Springfield franchise belonged to the St. Louis Cardinals, and they were out for revenge in their last exhibition match before the start of the Western Association campaign. [191] When the starting line-up was printed in the local newspaper, O'Neil was penciled in as the left fielder. [192]

Russ Derry. The Monarchs thumped the Joplin Missouri Miners, a New York Yankees minor league team winning 12-2 on April 29, 1938. Derry, a future Yankee went 0-for-4 that afternoon. O'Neil went 2-for-4 with a stolen base against his team's Western Association League foe. (Authors collection)

In Springfield, Kansas City was bumped in a 6-3 loss by Manager Clay Hopper's young Cardinals at White City Park. Right-handed throwing, Roland Van Slate held Monarch batters to eleven scattered hits.[193] Despite multiple hits by Milton, Brown, and Mayweather, no Monarch could deliver in the clutch. Kansas City squandered away numerous scoring opportunities early but gave their admirers a treat in the later innings. Fans were out of their seats, standing with hearts racing in the ninth after Kansas City loaded the bases with two outs. Wilber Rogan was coming to bat, and it looked like the game would be broken wide open. He had won the admiration of many with his hitting and pitching feats over the years, and many thought he was about to spoil the hometown's chances yet again. This, however, was not to be his day.

Rogan fanned for the game's final out. The mighty struggle was over. Kansas City had lost. In reviewing the box score O'Neil, in right field, that night went hitless in four official plate appearances. The same box score showed that Hooper, the Springfield manager, hit well. He got one hit in four at-bats. It was an impressive swat, a home run over the scoreboard in deep center field. Frank "Creepy" Crespi top recruit who later joined the National League Cardinals in St. Louis, had only one hit in four at-bats.[194] His hit, a double with the bases loaded, drove in three key runs.[195]

Meanwhile, reports of Monarchs' games were almost nonexistent in the Kansas City newspapers, where many eagerly awaited the results. There was a write-up in the April 18 edition of Kansas City's *Times* and another in the same newspaper on April 25--but little else. Other than these two instances, news of Monarchs' pre-season games reached Kansas City with an odd and unconcerned irregularity. As a result, much of John "Buck" O'Neil's first spring training--as it was for the entire Negro American League--was played in near anonymity. The whole story can never be told. With few exceptions, this is as good as the coverage may ever get.

"The Kansas City Boosters club has planned a big demonstration at the park. Due to the opening falling on Sunday, the usual parade through the downtown streets will not take place. The Wayne Miner post, American legion drum and bugle corps, the pride of Missouri, will march its 150 members to the flagpole and assist in the flag-raising. The Boosters club of more than 500 will follow."

Chicago Defender, May 14, 1938

Buck O'Neil says...

"I say, don't feel sorry for me because I played some of the best baseball that was ever played. The Negro Leagues was nothing like the 'Bingo Long Story,' nothing like 'Soul of The Game.' The Negro League was the third-largest business in this country. All you needed was a bus, a couple sets of uniforms, and you could have 20 of the best athletes that ever lived. That was Negro League baseball."

Ring Around The Circuit

May 7-Jonesboro, May 8-Memphis (DH), May 9-Memphis, May 10-Memphis (DH), May 11-Little Rock, May12-Springfield

O'Neil and his Kansas City teammates opened the 1938 Negro American League campaign in Jonesboro, Arkansas, and moved on to Memphis, Tennessee, for more games at Martin Stadium. After battling that city's Negro American League Red Sox, they continued to Kansas City, where on May 15, they began a home series with the Chicago American Giants. Wilkinson and Baird's Monarchs finished May with a series against a third Negro American League adversary, the Indianapolis ABCs. Listed among May's non-league exhibitions were contests in Enid, Mariana, Des Moines, and Peoria as the team toured into Oklahoma, Arkansas, Iowa, and Illinois.

As far back as 1900, Kansas City usually had two professional teams, one white, the other black. The Kansas City Blues, members of the segregated American Association, remained Kansas City's white professional team, whereas the black teams changed many times.

The Kansas City Jenkins team of 1906 was the first to bring regional honors to Kansas City's African American baseball teams, but they were strictly a semi-professional unit. Tobe Smith's 1907 Giants of nearby Kansas City, Kansas, became the city's first African American professional team. In subsequent years other teams prominently emerged. "Topeka" Jack Johnson's Royal Giants (1910-1911), the Royal Americans (1912-1915), and J. L. Wilkinson's All-Nations (1915-1917) were the leading Kansas City teams. Nearly all functioned with limited home success as they haphazardly scheduled their activities around Blues' home games. In 1920, the formation of Andrew "Rube" Foster's Negro National League fairly neutralized Kansas City's American Association Blues in popularity.

Porter "Ankle Ball" Moss. A right-hander, he was the superior of several underhanded pitchers appearing in the Negro American League. Born June 10, 1910, in Ohio, Moss was murdered in 1944 by an unknown assailant as he sat on a train with his teammates near Knoxville, Tennessee. (Authors collection)

Wilkinson's Monarchs, organized in 1920 as charter members of the Rube Foster-led Negro National League, were Kansas City's most successful sports franchise. Between 1923 and 1929, Wilkinson's Monarchs won two World Series and four Negro National League pennants. The winning continued into the 1930s, as the Monarchs barnstormed against the most renowned athletes and teams in baseball. In a half-decade of barnstorming, 1930-1936, Wilkinson's Monarchs won more than 800 games. The Negro National League disbanded in 1931, but the Monarchs had already started barnstorming with their night baseball. They optioned out of the league to make more money touring from city to city, getting lots of opportunities to play minor league teams while expanding their territory and brand recognition. Wilkinson enlisted the Monarchs into the new Negro American League in 1937 and won yet another pennant. It was his team's fifth Negro League pennant in twelve years of league play. In Kansas City, they played in prejudiced surroundings, which always made them appear second fiddle to Kansas City's all-white Blues. It was a double standard of major league proportion and a continued agitation, especially after the Blues were purchased by Jacob Ruppert in 1938. Ruppert, also the owner of New York's American League Yankees, increased fees paid by the Monarchs to rent Ruppert Stadium. Forced into a capricious payment arrangement by their shared use of the stadium, Wilkinson's Monarchs rarely surpassed twenty-five home games thereafter. Most of their home games were scheduled doubleheaders. Nonetheless, they were allowed to utilize dressing rooms and allowed to take post-game showers, something that was rather unique for most of the parks where Monarchs' games were played.

Buck O'Neil recalled, "When the Monarchs played in Kansas City, we changed at the stadium. In other cities, we might change in the same clubhouse as the [home] team. In parks that had no dressing rooms, we would dress at the hotel or change at the YMCA."[196] One of the first business orders of any new Monarch was to purchase a YMCA membership. The cost was $3. When changing at YMCAs across the country, before or after games, players would flash their membership cards to get access to rooms which allowed them to change clothes and take showers. In cities like St. Joseph, Missouri, there was an upcharge for dressing at the YMCA that reached $7.20. Kansas

114

City, the city the Monarchs represented, was an active participant when it came to segregation in public spaces.

By forcing African Americans to the east side of Kansas City an accepted separation enforced by law, coupled with the city's other segregationist policies in education and employment, and an overall bigoted disregard by Kansas City's four daily newspapers proved to be a promotional and financial boost for the minor-league Blues. The policies were a virtual wreck for the Negro American League, its owners, and fans. The hypocrisy could be witnessed in events such as opening day attendance.

On April 29, 1938, the Blues drew an opening day crowd of 16,206, which toppled all other American Association teams. In St. Paul, their nearest American Association rival for opening day league attendance, there were 10,169 paid admissions. By contrast, the Monarchs, despite having four future Hall of Fame inductees in their lineup, opened to a mere 6,000, nearly ten thousand fans fewer than the American Association Blues, who had no future Hall of Fame inductees on their roster. Black people were attending American Association games despite the Blues' roster and poor treatment they received at parks which were highlighted in the *Pittsburgh Courier*,

Listen! If any one of us wanted to talk to one of the ballplayers whom we've been spending our hard-earned dough on, screaming, and hollering, stamping our feet, and clapping our hands for, we'd probably be ignored. If he did speak to us, it would probably be a disrespectful salutation, such as 'Hello, George,' or 'what ya say, Sam.' Or maybe even worse than that. Oh, he wouldn't, eh! That's what you think. Don't forget that he comes from Mississippi, Georgia, Texas, or any other place you can think of below the Mason-Dixon Line. And he's white. He looks upon us as something the cat brought in. Even though he is playing ball in a

115

northern city, making northern money, he still looks upon us that way. He's a leopard, and you know what they say about their spots. You can't change 'em.'[197]

There were other reasons for the lackluster crowds at Monarchs' games. Much of the disparity came in newspaper coverage. During the 1920s, Kansas City's four daily newspapers prohibited photographs of Monarchs' baseball players in their publications. Instead, photographs of Babe Ruth, Ty Cobb, Lou Gehrig, Knute Rockne, Red Grange, Jack Dempsey, Gene Tunney, and others graced the sports pages. Only one photograph of a Kansas City Monarchs player appeared in a Kansas City, Missouri daily newspaper between 1920 and 1937, and that had been an image of Wilber Rogan during the Monarchs' first appearance in the "Colored" World Series in 1924. This means nearly 24,753 editions of Kansas City's four daily newspapers failed to elevate Monarchs' teams to a plateau of equality shown to the American Association Blues, for whom many photographs were published. In keeping with the daily newspapers twisted "more thrills than stills" agenda, all aspects of impartiality went awry.

Overemphasis on the Blues by reporters at the *Star, Times, Journal* and *Post,* didn't carry over outside the city where praise and admiration were given to Monarchs' players on many occasions. Outside Kansas City, many newspapers chose to illustrate their lengthy articles with printed images.

A team photograph of the Monarchs appeared in the Hutchinson, Kansas *News* on April 28, under the title, "To Play Larks Tomorrow Night."[198] There was another team photograph in the *Chanute Tribune* on May 13. That the Monarchs were featured in print with photographs was old news to local Chanute residents because minority baseball was traditionally saluted. Around the turn of the century, this Kansas town had the much-celebrated Chanute Black Diamonds, known as one of the fastest Colored ball teams in the state.

The *Chanute Tribune* added an image of Harry Else on August 15. Other newspapers also bucked the trend of the established Kansas City press. Newt Allen was pictured in a June 6 issue of the *Wichita Eagle* and a July 21 edition of Canada's *Estevan Mercury* newspaper. Manager Andy Cooper's image appeared in a July 18 issue of the *Bismarck Tribune*, as did Byron Johnson's on Thursday, July 21. The *Tribune* printed photographs of Hilton Smith, Floyd Kranson, and Dick Bradley in its July 23 edition of the newspaper. Cooper's picture appeared again in the *Junction City Union* on August 22. In Topeka, located sixty miles west of Kansas City, Bullet Rogan on August 11 and Harry Else on August 12 were pictured in the *Daily Capital*. One Southern newspaper, the *Kentucky Leader* of Louisville, printed a photograph of Byron Johnson in a September 10 edition. A June 22 edition of the *Banner-Journal* in Black River Falls, Wisconsin, featured a Monarchs' team picture promoting their appearance in that city.[199] And, there were others. The *Kansas City Kansan*, when promoting the Monarchs' game against the Memphis Red Sox on August 2, 1938, illustrated their article with a photograph of Manager Cooper. It was the only known Monarchs' photograph to appear in a greater metropolitan Kansas City daily for the whole year. Newspaper articles of the time, when printed in daily sports pages, contained their own unique brand of tenuous prejudice. That Kansas City was a prejudiced and segregated town is a heritage that cannot be denied.

Universally, as if the daily beat writers had attended the same prejudiced school of journalism, articles were flavored with subtle and not so subtle hints of racism. In many newspapers, African American athletes were referred to as "dusky," a term touted as a more acceptable reference than the more traditionally used "darky." Under this description, Joe Louis World Heavyweight champion, became the "Dusky Destroyer," and Henry Armstrong, World Feather, Light and Welterweight champion, the "Dusky Dynamiter." The so-called list of "dusky" athletes included Johnny Woodruff, a legendary mile and a half-mile runner at the University of Pittsburgh and

William Watson, a high jumper for the University of Michigan, and many, many baseball players. The word dusky always referred to something dark.

Dusky Maid, a horse at Charleston, West Virginia's Lincoln Fields racetrack, and Dusky Prince, a pony at Charleston's Fair Grounds, were two of the many black horses that ran under such titles simply because of their black coats. When referring to other leagues, leagues formed of players with Caucasian ancestry, further references to race, skin color, or ethnicity were eliminated. No one referred to the National or American leagues as the "all-white National League." Seemingly, African American athletes needed to be singled out by their race, thereby differentiating them from the rest of American society, and on occasion, the discourse took a hateful turn for the worst. Wichita, Kansas' *Eagle* newspaper took great delight in referring to Atlanta's Negro League entry as the "Burnt" Crackers.[200] In Viroqua, Wisconsin, the Vernon *County Censor* newspaper headline boasted, "Thousand see Coons whip the House of David."[201]

A day after the Monarchs' 1938 opener, the Kansas City *Journal Post* and *Kansas City Star* newspapers, two important newspapers, failed to print any photographs, the *Journal Post* didn't bother with a write-up about the games. Only a box score and a brief post-game description appeared in the morning edition of the Kansas City *Times*. There was a deeper reason as to why the local dailies ignored opening day festivities--two African American teams were playing. While the Black-owned Kansas City *Call* treated the event as an important lead story, Kansas City's daily newspapers treated it as they had in previous years--they simply ignored it. Therefore, very little publicity and low salaries were a sign of the times for African Americans in baseball--especially so when they were playing other African American teams. The league had no power or resources to fight these racial traditions. Thus, making something out of nothing became the struggle of everyday life in Negro baseball. Segregation, as O'Neil remembered, was not without its benefits. Reflecting on his rookie salary, O'Neil offered,

> I came here [Kansas City] making $100 a month. Let me tell you, they would
>
> give me a dollar a day for meal money. That's $30 came out of that $100. So, I
>
> got $70 [as my salary]. But even at that, I was able to kick some money home."[202]
>
> In those days, you could get breakfast for 25 cents and dinner for 35 cents. We
>
> didn't eat more than two meals a day. Cigarettes cost 15 cents, and I could go to
>
> a movie for 10 cents. So, you could operate out of a dollar.[203]

Wilkinson, an owner of the Monarchs, had lots to say about how he paid his players. In an interview published in a Springfield, Missouri newspaper, he went into detail about what he was paying members of the Monarchs without naming names. "Players in the Negro League [draw] from $150 to $300 a month...rookies [broke] in at $125," was the information he provided.[204]

On the whole, African American baseball players were vastly underpaid even by their own cultural standards. Jesse Owens, the African American track hero of the 1936 Berlin Olympics, turned professional in 1937 and ran exhibitions at baseball fields. Participating in a sport where professional opportunities were limited, Owens was earning a creditable living by 1938. "Ordinarily, I run three or four times a week," Owens stated, "and average about $400 a week, but when I am booked as solid as I am at present, I make about $750 a week."[205]

O'Neil's monthly salary of $100 a month may have worked for some rookies, but veterans with families required more income--increases they seldom received from team owners. Clarence "Fats" Jenkins of the New York Black Yankees had lots to say about the situation. According to Jenkins, "The average pay for Negro league ballplayers is about $175 per month, for a period of something like four months, beginning in May, and ending in September."[206] Jay H. Ferguson, the author of the article that published Jenkins' statement for the *Chicago Bee,* responded in shock, stating,

> I was not only astonished but astounded to discover that the boys who are called
>
> upon to give their best at all times in order to attract the fans through the
>
> turnstiles, were being paid an average salary of about $700 for the season, which,
>
> to them is a year's work at that profession.[207]

He questioned why the "Moguls of the Negro big leagues don't just give their hired hands a tin cup and a pair of dark goggles, and tell them to sign up in the panhandler's league where they may beg legitimately."[208] He was making a valid point when looking at what white American and National League players were earning. In startling comparison, outfielder Joe DiMaggio of the New York Yankees demanded $40,000 as compensation for the 1938 season but conceded to sign for $25,000. His teammate, Lou Gehrig, was pulling down a heaty $39,000 in annual compensation.[209] O'Neil was certainly no DiMaggio, but Willard Brown was, and his salary wasn't even in the same zip code with either of these baseball greats. The same could be said for Monarchs' Newton Henry Allen He was a star performer in every capacity of the word. Wilkinson was paying him a meager $150 a month.

Born in Austin, Texas, and raised in Kansas City, Allen attended Bruce Elementary and Lincoln High Schools. Allen's first baseball team was the Kansas City Tigers; however, he could never break into their starting lineup. Consequently, he shuffled to the Paseo Rats and the Swift's team in a local packinghouse league before turning professional with the Omaha, Nebraska Federals in 1921. The next year, 1922, Allen signed with J. L. Wilkinson's All-Nations, a Monarchs' second team. At the season's end, Allen was promoted to Wilkinson's Negro National League Monarchs, where he remained for many years.

Throughout the 1920s, Allen's hitting improved. "A line-drive hitter, with occasional power" is how O'Neil classified Allen.[210] "As far as I'm concerned," responded pitcher Doolittle Young, "Colt, we called Newt 'Colt,' was about the best second baseman the two years that I played in Kansas City that I had ever seen. He wasn't such a good hitter, and he didn't steal many bases, but he caught all the balls hit down that way.[211] He knew how to play second base very well." O'Neil thought the secret to Allen's defensive success was his "wrist." O'Neil pantomimed from a slightly bent-over position, then explained, "He could throw as hard from there, as I could rear up, and throw. [He had] lots on the ball and [threw] a strike!"[212] Jesse Williams, a Monarchs' shortstop, concluded, "Allen looked better missing a ball than most people looked catching it. And, I never saw him make a bad throw to first."[213] Frank Duncan was known to have said, "I used to get a thrill just knowing he was putting on a Monarchs' uniform."[214] When speaking of Allen, Wilkinson admitted, "In his prime, [Allen] never had an equal."[215] O'Neil added, "Newt had Hall of Fame credentials. He was the best I have ever seen, making the double play."[216]

Allen's blunt but straightforward actions on the field were the opposite of his unassuming and quiet ways that foreshadowed life off the field as one of his league's most popular players."[217] Allen recalled, "The women, they were lovely everywhere we went. If they didn't recognize me in my regular clothes, then I'd go up to them and tell them who I was. But sometimes they could be a worrisome deal."[218] Off the field, Monarchs players needed to keep a strict dress code. Precisely knowing what to wear, when, and how to wear it served as an index to each player's character. Allen's fastidious wardrobe was labeled one of the Negro Leagues' best-dressed players. All the ballplayers wore hats when they dressed up, but with space so limited on the Monarchs bus, there was also much borrowing and lending of clothing between team members. O'Neil boasted,

> During that time, all the athletes [and], musicians dressed. When we came to town, any town, we dressed. In Chicago, after the ball game, you got to come to town. If a ballplayer came here [Kansas City] and he didn't have a suit [Wilkinson] would send him to Meyers, the tailor, on Eighteenth Street. We couldn't wear a Monarch cap unless we had on the Monarchs' uniform. You could wear the jacket on the bus when it was cool, but when you come to town, no, no. At night when you got ready to come out, you had a collar and tie.[219]

Kansas City opened the regular season against Memphis in Jonesboro, Arkansas, where they were turned back by the Red Sox. The locals were as hot as their team's colors, having already taken three games from the Atlanta Black Crackers before the Monarchs' arrival. Evidently, O'Neil had a pretty good spring because Manager Cooper kept him with the club as a back-up at first base and a substitute in the outfield. O'Neil's recollection of Martin Park and its fans was positive,

> I shall never forget Martin Stadium because it was a Black [owned] park, and it was right in the middle of a Black neighborhood. Everything was Black. Good grounds-people. I guess the park seated around twelve thousand.[220]

The May 7 loss in Jonesboro was Kansas City's first of the season.[221] For game two, later that evening, the series moved into Memphis, Tennessee, a distance of 70 miles. The *Memphis Commercial Appeal* announced they were coming but gave few details on the team or that the Monarchs had won a 7-1 game in the Memphis opener.[222] The doubleheader that followed, on

Sunday, May 8, resulted in a sweep by the Memphis club, who captured a pair of games by identical 2-1 scores in a Sunday doubleheader at Martin Park.[223]

Game one was a pitchers' battle between Red Sox hurler "Ankle ball" Moss and Kansas City's Floyd Kranson. A bumpy start by Kranson allowed the Sox to score in inning one when Davenport stole second, then advanced to third when Cox, the Monarchs' catcher, threw wildly into centerfield. Davenport scored while second baseman Newt Allen was throwing out Cowan Hyde. Neil Robinson followed with a double against the left-field wall, just missing a home run by mere inches. Ted Radcliffe popped out for the third out. Kansas City tied the score in the second. O'Neil, first up, walked but was thrown out on an attempted steal of second by Radcliffe, the Memphis catcher. Jack Marshall whiffed for out two. Byron Johnson, the next batter, walked and came scampering home on Kranson's double over Hyde's head into right field.

Game two was another pitchers' battle between Kansas City's Buster Markham and Willie Jefferson of the Red Sox. Both pitchers fired four-hitters. The Monarchs' lone run came in the second on the double by Buck O'Neil that was followed by another double by Frank Duncan. Trailing 1-to-0 going into the seventh, Neil Robinson opened with a double to the left. Radcliffe, on an attempted sacrificed bunt, was safe when Newt Allen, covered at first base but failed to touch the bag before the runner. Red Longley was safe on a fielder's choice as Robinson scored. Raymond Taylor, pinch-hitting for Clifford Allen, was hit by a pitched ball, filling the bases. Eugene Bremer pinch-ran for Taylor, and the next batter Zearlee Maxwell sacrificed. Bremer raced around to third on a wild pitch and scored while Mayweather was racing Moss to first base after momentarily fumbling his grounder.[224]

The Red Sox scored the winning run in the seventh, an inning in which they never hit safely. Kranson pitched a six-hitter and lasted eight innings before being yanked for a pinch-hitter. Hilton Smith finished the contest for Kansas City. Moss gave up four hits in getting the 2-1 win.

On Monday, May 9, the Red Sox beat the Monarchs in an 8-7 final for their third consecutive win. Kansas City broke their losing streak with a victory in Memphis on Tuesday, May 10, but it hadn't come against the Red Sox. In a three-team doubleheader that included the Chicago American Giants, Kansas City beat the American Giants 4-0 in game one but lost their fourth consecutive game to Memphis in the nightcap by a 7-6 score.[225] Having lost five of six games to the Memphis Red Sox set a precedent for the 1938 first-half pennant race. The Red Sox were every bit as competitive at the beginning of the season, but they weren't deep enough with the talent to keep the pace over the long, hot, and exhausting summer, and it hurt them badly.

On the morning of May 11, the team reached Little Rock, Arkansas, where they began a touring series against the American Giants. Both teams were working their way to Kansas City for the 1938 season opener. The game was a Wednesday night encounter at Travelers' Field. When the *Arkansas Gazette* penned the Monarchs "claim the National Negro baseball championship," it was providing subtle wordplay used routinely by daily newspapers to discredit and bring doubt as to which teams' pennants were legitimate.[226] Kansas City hadn't claimed the title. They won it by defeating the Chicago American Giants. On this night, Kansas City tore into Chicago's pitching for 12 hits and won by a margin of 10-2, before what the *Gazette* called "One of the largest crowds ever to see a Negro baseball game here."[227]

Hundreds of fans, mostly Black people, packed Travelers' Field and were rewarded by shortstop, "Mex" Johnson, a hometown favorite, who contributed mightily with a pair of triples, and a single in five at-bats. With little time to celebrate, they boarded the team bus for another night of being jerked around as they raced down numerous back roads and highways.

The following morning, they woke up early, but only God, their owners, and the bus driver knew where they were headed. Games had been scheduled in Kansas, Oklahoma, and Arkansas. In Chanute, Kansas, approximately one hundred miles into the road trip, local officials were already pondering the possibility of not playing Monday's game, as the field was wet from a previous night's thunderstorm. Rainfall was also threatening their return to Springfield, Missouri.[228]

As the Monarchs motored towards Springfield for a May 12 night game at that town's White City Park, both local dailies sleeplessly proclaimed "a section along the first baseline will be reserved for the Negro fans," which assured there was segregation at the park. Fans were being reminded in print that segregation in the Ozarks wouldn't change anytime soon. The highly segregated White City Park, as was noted in the local Springfield *Leader and Press,* who revised the statement to read that there would be "special seating for Colored People," assured all that this practice was an acceptable business practice.[229] It was a familiar refrain that teams from the Negro American League repeatedly witnessed, although not always printed. The same newspaper referred to the Monarchs' pre-season loss to the Cardinals' minor league team on May 1. The Monarchs were scheduled to battle the American Giants in an 8:15 night game, but a combination of damp grounds and cold weather caused a cancellation of the exhibition. They were finally headed home to Kansas City. By starting the home portion of their schedule, they began their shared arrangement at Ruppert Stadium with the American Association Blues, Kansas City's white minor league professional team.

"Negro baseball is distinguished principally by dexterous ball handling, fluent fielding, and daring base running. Both afield and on the runways, he capitalizes his natural speed and coordination. He goes into the bases recklessly, spikes flashing, and arms widely outspread in a manner that suggests a huge eagle swooping to perch on a narrow ledge. He's a master of the art."

Cleon Walfoort, Milwaukee Journal Sentinel, August 28, 1938

Buck O'Neil says...

"I think baseball makes a mistake when it doesn't find office positions for so many of its standouts after they retire, and I mean both Blacks and Whites."

Winning, It's What We Do

<u>May 15-Kansas City (DH)</u>, May 16-Chanute, <u>May 17-Enid</u>, May 18-Enid, <u>May 19-Shawnee</u>, May 20-Mariana

(NAL) O'Neil's Batting: G-2 AB-6 R-0 H-2 2B-0 3B-0 HR-0 SB-0 BA-3.33

O'Neil's Fielding: PO-5 A-0 E-0 DP-0 TC-5

(E) O'Neil's Batting: G-2 AB-6 R-2 H-3 2B-2 3B-0 HR-0 SB-1 RBI-0 BA-3.33

O'Neil's Fielding: PO-21 A-1 E-0 DP-2 TC-21

Winning was the name of the game, and consequently, on Sunday, May 15, 1938, John "Buck" O'Neil played his first home game as a member of the Kansas City Monarchs at Kansas City's Ruppert Stadium. The event, a doubleheader versus the American Giants, was scheduled for an after church 1:15 p.m. start time. The historic opening day events were attended by Kansas City business, church, and civic leaders. Two key players were missing from the Monarchs' lineup during the opening day festivities. Infielder Jack Marshall and outfielder William "Bill" Simms were no longer on the roster. Although both played well during spring training, neither was in uniform when Kansas City made their home debut. Having found employment elsewhere, Marshall landed a better-paying opportunity in Elgin, Illinois, as one of four African American members of the Tri-State League's Elgin Stars. Simms was shipped to the American Giants, where "Candy" Taylor was in desperate need of outfielders.

Jack Marshall. He was the Monarchs' most consistent spring training hitter but jumped for a better-paying opportunity in Elgin, Illinois, where he participated in the Abe Saperstein promoted Tri-State League. (Authors collection)

Since opening day fell on a Sunday, the usual three-mile parade from Eighteenth Street and Vine Street to the park at Twenty-Fourth Street and Brooklyn Avenue was postponed. Instead, inside the park, Roy Dorsey, Monarchs' Boosters club organizer, gave a reception for both the Monarchs and American Giants that preceded the game.

At the park, T. B. Watkins, owner of the community's largest mortuary, threw out the ceremonial first ball, and Elmore Williams, a prominent banker and Elk member received the first ball. Led by Wayne Minor's 150-piece American Legion Drum and Bugle Corps, the dignitaries concluded their procession around the warning track with a pennant flag-raising ceremony. Ruppert Stadium's admission fee was 25 cents for bleachers and 65 cents for box seats. Still, at that low price, many seats were unsold at game time.

Coming off a doubleheader sweep of the Black Barons on Sunday, May 8, at Birmingham's Rickwood Field, the Chicago team was seeking to add to their win streak. Unable to duplicate that feat in Kansas City, the Giants were forced to settle for a split of the twin-bill, winning the opener 4-2 and losing 3-0 in the nightcap.

Smith, Kansas City's ace, started the home opener, leaving in the seventh with the score tied 2-to-2. Buster Markham, who replaced Smith, yielded only two hits during his two innings. However, a bad throw by first baseman Eldridge Mayweather blew a custom-made twin-killing and put runners in scoring positions. Chicago's Ormand Sampson hit safely and chased the base runners home for the victory.

Playing an error-plagued game, Mayweather's miscue and three others by Byron Johnson marred the Monarchs' defensive efforts as Chicago capitalized on three unearned runs. Jess Houston, hurling all nine frames for Chicago, ended with an eight-hitter, and allowed only one extra-base hit, a triple to Willard Brown in gaining the home-opening victory. Mayweather's error was partially responsible for the Monarchs' loss. Eagerly awaiting his opportunity to replace the struggling first baseman, Buck O'Neil, the Monarchs starting right fielder, earned one hit in four at-bats. That performance prompted manager Cooper to position O'Neil at first base in game two.

Theodore "Ted" Trent. *On opening day, May 15, 1938, O'Neil of Florida's Edward Waters College got one of his two hits off Trent a former college student from Florida's Bethune-Cookman College. (Authors collection)*

In the second game, Floyd Kranson's four-hitter helped Kansas City to a 3-0 win. All of Kansas City's scoring occurred in the fourth, when Wilson Redus's error in left field, a two-base hit by Allen, and successive singles by Brown and O'Neil accounted for all of the Monarchs runs. In driving Brown home, O'Neil collected his first run batted in at Kansas City's Ruppert Stadium. O'Neil finished 1-for-2 in the abbreviated nightcap, gaining his hit off another Floridian, Ted Trent, who struck out five Monarchs in his seven-inning stint.

Right-hander Ted Trent could not hit very well, but on the mound, he would curveball the opposition into submission.[230] Trent's curveball was considered among the Negro American League's best and was repeatedly advertised to the public. Secured from New York's Black Yankees, he had also played with the St. Louis Stars. Trent missed most of the 1935 campaign due to an injury yet returned to form in 1936.

Scheduled to perform in a night exhibition on May 16, a *Chanute Tribune* advertisement showed a city that was anxiously anticipating their arrival. An announcement in the *Tribune* offered, "For the dusky-skinned lads Monday, he [manager Alf Krone] is saving [pitcher] Claude Willoughby."[231] Local promoters had signed Willoughby, a one-time member of the Philadelphia Phillies, to pitch the game. The right-handed dart-throwing mound artist was born in nearby Buffalo, Kansas. His big-league resume included six years in the National League and a 38-58 career record.

On the morning of May 16, the *Chanute Tribune* noted, "Officials of the city team were undecided at noon today whether or not the game with the Kansas City Monarchs scheduled for tonight could be played or not because of the soggy condition of the diamond after a night of rain. Manager Krone said a decision would be made early this afternoon."[232] Consequently, the event was postponed and rescheduled for August 24. Perhaps they would face Willoughby on the next visit.

Returning to the bus, the team steered westward for a 230-mile excursion back to Enid, Oklahoma, where they were scheduled for a two-game set.

On a damp and cool spring, May 17, Tuesday night in Enid, Dick Bradley's five-hit pitching gave the Monarchs a 3-1 decision over Enid's Eason Oilers.[233] Throwing wildly enough to keep opposition batters loose, Bradley forced pop-outs and vain whiffs as five batters struck out and many others swung aimlessly at pitches they could barely see and couldn't hit. Bradley also registered four wild pitches, which paved the way for the lone Oilers' run. The game was a challenge throughout as Enid went ahead early.

Kansas City tied the score in inning two when a single and a two-base hit forced in a tally. In inning six, the Monarchs scored on an error and a single by Rogan to add some needed cushion. Frank Duncan's seventh-inning home run, a hit that eclipsed the top of the scoreboard, resulted in Kansas City's third and final run. The Monarchs threatened in the eighth when a hit and two walks loaded the paths, but after two out, the threat was dissolved when Johnson was retired by Enid's second baseman. Dallas Patton, the Oilers' right fielder, revived fans' hopes in the home ninth when he banked a two-bagger off the right-field wall and advanced to third on a wild pitch. Bradley tightened after that and forced the final three batters to retire in order. In winning, Bradley hurled his first complete game of the season.

Native American hurler Milt Perry surrendered nine hits and went the full route for Enid's Oilers, striking out eight Monarchs. Three costly errors behind him proved too much to overcome. Before his 1938 loss, Perry had defeated the Monarchs twice, helping Enid to wins over the Monarchs in four of their past six battles. On May 18, inclement weather caused the postponement of a second game in Enid.[234]

After Enid, the Monarchs won a 7-6 game in Shawnee, Oklahoma over the Phillips "66" Gassers. The night featured 21 hits, 10 for the Monarchs and 11 for Shawnee. Eleven of the hits went for extra bases, the Monarchs getting eight of those hits. Barnes, Markham and Smith pitched for the Monarchs, Smith getting the win. In the seventh, a single by Milton, a double by Cox, and a triple by Allen produced three runs and the victory. Allen finished the evening with a trio of runs driven in on what would have been his 37th birthday.

The winning continued with 4-2 victory in Marianna, Arkansas, on Friday night against the Buffalo Aces. The Buffalo team, an associate member of the Negro National League, was actually from New York State. In coming to Arkansas, they were taking spring training and playing games in Marianna, a small town about fifty miles south of Memphis, Tennessee. Owned by Jack Singer, a well-known sports promoter of Buffalo, this team caused considerable waves among league officials by hiring three members of the Memphis Red Sox.[235] After Marianna, the Monarchs returned to Kansas City for a May 22 double-bill against Indianapolis in games three and four of the 1938 home schedule.

(L to R) Candy Jim Taylor, J. B. Martin, William Little, Frank "Fay" Young, and Arthur Tony.
(Authors collection)

"The Monarchs jumped into the league lead at the expense of the Indianapolis ABCs who dropped both ends of the double bill at Ruppert field in Kansas City, MO., on Sunday while the Memphis Red Sox was plastering the Giants with two whitewashes."

Chicago Defender, May 28, 1938

Buck O'Neil *says...*

"I got my big thrills playing with men like Satchel Paige. I got my greatest kicks being with them than from anything else I've ever done."

Double For Your Trouble

May 22-Kansas City (DH), May 23-DesMoines, May 24-Peoria, May 25-Peoria, May 27-Chicago, May 28-Chicago, May 29-Chicago (DH), May 30-Chicago

(NAL) O'Neil's Batting: G-5 AB-18 R-2 H-5 2B-0 3B-1 HR-0 SB-1 BA-2.78

O'Neil's Fielding: PO-54 A-0 E-0 DP-1 TC-37

(E) O'Neil's Batting: G-2 AB-8 R-3 H-3 2B-0 3B-0 HR-1 SB-1 RBI-1 BA-3.75

O'Neil's Fielding: PO-21 A-0 E-1 DP-1 TC-22

Kansas City returned to their home field on May 22, where they were to meet Indianapolis in the fourth doubleheader of the month and the second on their home field. The homestand would be brief as the Monarchs were headed to Iowa and Illinois. In Chicago, they were scheduled for yet another doubleheader against the American Giants, but first, they needed to dispose of the up-and-coming ABCs in a league where multiple twin-bills and young talented players proliferated.

134

Andy Cooper. *As player/manager of the 1937 Monarchs, Cooper pitched all seventeen innings of a game against the Chicago American Giants in the Negro American League playoffs. He was the manager of the Monarchs in 1938. (Authors collection)*

In the opening game of the May 22 doubleheader, ABC's manager, George Mitchell, decided to match his rookie pitcher Ted Alexander against Monarchs' veteran Hilton Smith. The first-year pitcher, Theodore Roosevelt Alexander, had one of the longest names in baseball but one of the shortest outings of the day. He struck out three in his brief appearance but was quickly relieved of his duties after the Monarchs scored seven runs in three innings. J. Brown, Walter Calhoun, and James Armstead followed him to the mound with limited success.

Smith held Indianapolis to five hits in a 16-1 dispensing of the ABCs. Two of Indianapolis' five hits belonged to Ted Strong. Alexander, Marshall L. Riddle, and Armstead also hit safely. Kansas won by capitalizing on the ABCs' lack of experience. The team was loaded with rookies. Riddle, age-20, born April 22, 1918, was a rookie from Carbondale, Illinois. Left-handed hitting Armstead, age-20, born September 8, 1919, a student at Louisville, Kentucky's Municipal College for Negroes, was taking his first crack in professional ball. He was born in Birmingham, lived for a while in Louisville, Kentucky, and eventually moved to St. Louis, Missouri, where he was recruited by the ABCs.[236] Like many of the ABCs he had ties to St. Louis and Quincy Trouppe.

Eldridge Mayweather, reluctantly having handed over his first base position, was moved over to the right side of the field. Avenging himself for the previous week's errors, Mayweather slammed a home run, a double, and two singles. In addition to scoring his first runs at Kansas City's Ruppert Stadium, O'Neil fielded flawlessly and contributed to a rapid-fire double play that included Johnson and Allen. O'Neil went 2-for-4 at-bat which highlighted his first multi-hit game inside Ruppert Stadium. Smith, having pitched a complete game, was also perfect at-bat. He went 5-for-5 with a pair of two-baggers and a trio of singles.

Game two resulted in a brilliantly pitched 1-0 Monarchs victory, as pitcher Alfred Marvin allowed three hits and hurled the full route of the seven-inning encounter. Frank McAlester nicknamed "Chip," another 20-year-old pitcher, was equally effective for the ABCs. For seven innings, he yielded two hits. McAlester's one mistake resulted in a fifth-inning home run by Willard

Brown that gave Kansas City a win. Marvin finished with four strikeouts compared to McAlester's eight. Marvin is a mystery, as this was the only game that he pitched for the Monarchs in the entire 1938 season. The writer at the *Kansas City Call* seemed to know him well as they listed both his first and last name in their accompanying article while gloating on the fact that Smith and Marvin had held Indianapolis to eight hits in the doubleheader.[237] The unknown Monarchs' pitcher must have been good because he held Strong and Trouppe, the fourth and fifth batters in the Indianapolis line-up, hitless in six at-bats.

According to the Kansas City *Call* Sunday's doubleheader crowd dipped below 1,700, while a reference in the Kansas City *Times* estimated the crowd at "1,400, a difference of 300 people."[238] Nonetheless, the victory ran the Monarchs' record to three and one in games played at Ruppert Stadium, where their differential was 22 runs to 5. Monarchs' pitchers had flung two home shutouts, much to the small crowd's delight.

With these wins, the Monarchs went into first place in the Negro American League pennant race. The American Association Kansas City Blues were scheduled for home games on May 24-25 against the St. Paul Saints and May 26-28 versus the Minneapolis Millers. The minor leaguers were to remain in the city until May 31, concluding their lengthy star versus the Milwaukee Brewers. Forced onto the road, the Monarchs scheduled a May 23 appearance in Des Moines, Iowa, and a two-game series in Peoria, Illinois, beginning May 24. Moving on to Chicago, they were scheduled to engage the Chicago Mills semi-professional team at Shewbridge Field on May 27. On May 28, the Monarchs were to open a five-game series with the American Giants.[239]

After driving two hundred miles to Des Moines, Iowa, upon arrival, Monarchs' management was informed that their nighttime game against league rival Indianapolis was canceled. The weather was not, according to local newspapers, "beautiful."[240] During the daytime, local temperatures climbed to 64 degrees, but by 8:00 p.m., temperatures dropped to 58 degrees and continuously fell. Because of Des Moines' diminutive advance sales, a decision was made to cancel that night's event, freeing the Monarchs to motor the distance of 250 miles to Peoria's Woodruff Field where Scully Jones' All-Stars awaited their arrival. The bus rolled swift and furious as dawn turned to dusk.

Jones' Peoria All-Stars were managed by a famous Peorian, Eddie Saurs. Its roster was a combination of local Sunday Morning Baseball League All-Stars. Anxiously awaiting the Monarchs, the Peoria team was making their 1938 debut. Both games had late 8:00 p.m. starts, and with admission being 25 cents for bleachers and 40 cents for grandstand seats, sizable crowds were anticipated.

Hits were as prevalent at Peoria's Woodruff Field as bugs in the lights. The hits allowed the Monarchs to gallop to an easy 10-4 victory over the local All-Stars.[241] Brown's and Rogan's hitting was most prolific, as both banged out three solid hits. Two of Brown's hits were homers, and they accounted for five of his teams' scores. The colorful writer at the *Peoria Journal-Transcript* advised that Monarchs' hits were as "Prevalent as fleas in a dog kennel."[242]

All-Stars' Elmer Ambrose, pitcher, a former member of Grover Cleveland Alexander's House of David, and a veteran of minor league play, which included six seasons in the American Association, lost a bittersweet contest. He gave up only four hits in the first five innings but was nicked for that many more in the sixth. One of those hits was Brown's homer with two men on. In that inning, Kansas City romped around the bases five times. The Monarchs scored twice in the seventh, taking advantage of one hit and two errors. In inning nine, Brown hammered one of Lefty Towers' slants for his second homer, with a man on, and the Monarchs tallied another counter besides.

Kansas City worked three pitchers against Peoria in Bradley, Kranson, and Barnes. Bradley allowed two hits in three innings, Kranson four in four innings, and Barnes issued no hits or runs and finished the game.

The Peoria All-Stars suffered a second loss the following day, on a Wednesday night, May 25, going down to a 6-2 defeat. As he had done the day before, the writer at the *Journal-Transcript* began his follow-up article with something catchy. "The guy that said yuh gotta get hits to win ball games," he wrote, "must have written all the schoolbooks the Kansas City Monarchs ever studied."[243] Eddie Reynolds, Peoria's starter, was belted for twelve hits in seven innings, after which Lefty Newell halted the scoring. O'Neil and Mayweather both homered in the game. Mayweather went 2-for-4 at-bat, with a double and a home run. O'Neil went 3-for-5, with a homer and a stolen base. O'Neil's home run, as history would record, was his first known four-ply blast as a member of the Kansas City Monarchs. Kansas City exited Peoria riding a modest five-game winning streak. After reaching Chicago, they set up residence at the well-known Vincennes Hotel.

Taking a day off, something they rarely did, allowed the players an evening of entertainment which they used to dance in the Vincennes' Platinum Lounge ballroom. It was during one of Kansas City's visits to Chicago that Willard Brown met his wife, Dorothy, at the Vincennes Hotel. The hotel was located on the corners of Thirty-Sixth Street and South Vincennes Avenue. Lots of people made money when the Monarchs came to town. Not only were they talented ballplayers, but they were also first-class tippers. They knew when to drop a dime. They tipped janitors at the YMCA, the boys shagging foul balls, batboys, attendants at service stations, and waitresses at hotels. Tipping was a hallmark of their generosity and all-American charm.

A day later, on May 27, Kansas City's Monarchs stepped into Chicago's Shewbridge Field, a spacious urban ball diamond located at Seventy-Fourth and Aberdeen Streets where they were billed to play Chicago Mills. Scheduled for a 9:00 p.m. start, Friday's encounter was sponsored by Fort Dearborn's Athletic Club, financers of the field's recently installed $10,000 lighting plant that generated 125,000 watts of power.[244] Seeking to profit from their venture, Association heads sought membership in the Tri-State League and contracted with Negro American League teams for their open dates. The Monarchs responded with an appearance--their first at Shewbridge Field in six seasons.

Tri-State League teams included: the Madison Blues, Fort Wayne Harvesters, the Chicago Mills, Sheboygan Chairs, Elgin Stars, the Indianapolis Kingans, Spencer Coals of Chicago, and Indiana's South Bend Studebakers. Abe Saperstein was the league's president. Many of the Monarchs' games against Tri-State opponents were booked by Saperstein and Willard "Dutch" Witte of Beloit, Wisconsin. During the summer of 1938, Wilkinson's Monarchs would battle nearly every team in the league. In addition to contracting former Monarchs infielder Jack Marshall, the Elgin's Stars suited up three additional African American athletes in pitchers Willie Foster, Norman Cross, and infielder Ormand Sampson, who joined from the American Giants. The Tri-State League was one of the few interracial leagues in the Midwest.

On Friday night, the Kansas City Monarchs defeated Chicago Mills 10-to-0.[245] A total of eighteen Mills' batters struck out to highlight the combined efforts of Hilton Smith and I. V. Barnes. Mills' pitchers, Connie Mack Berry and Ray Malstrom we're unable to halt Kansas City's scoring. The 6-foot-3-inch Berry, a Southerner by birth, had been the center for North Carolina State University basketball team before turning to baseball. He would eventually play basketball for the Oshkosh All-Stars from 1939 to 1946. He also played professional football in 1939 with the Detroit Lions and other National Football League teams. His career in athletics was far better documented than that of men wearing Negro League uniforms, who were equally as gifted at playing more than one sport.

Following the Monarchs' preliminary win over Chicago's Mills, they began a series of five games against the American Giants. Holiday festivities dictated the series' arrangement of Negro American League games. A single game was played on Saturday, May 28, and a doubleheader on Sunday, May 29. There was another doubleheader scheduled on Memorial Day, May 30. That final doubleheader was the fifth twin-bill played by the Monarchs in May. All of the Chicago games were played at Giants Park. Jack Marshall rejoined the Monarchs as the third baseman for the Chicago series.

An oddity in the scoring gave Kansas City a 3-1 win in the opener.[246] Leading by two runs in the ninth, Kansas City added five additional runs. Then the rain fell, and it rained so severely that the Giants, the home team, were prohibited from going to bat in their half of the ninth. Therefore, Kansas City's runs went into the discard bin, and the score reverted to the last half of the eighth inning. Kansas City, having taken an early lead, therefore, preserved the win.

Kansas City defeated the American Giants 5-0 and 6-1 on Sunday, as Kranson whirled a three-hit shutout in the opener and Smith a nine-hitter in the nightcap. Kranson held Giant batters without a hit for seven innings. Alex Radcliffe spoiled the Monarchs 'no-hit, no-run contest by smacking a single in the eighth. In inning nine, Bibbs and Sampson added singles. Outfielder Henry Milton robbed another would-be American Giant batter with a running catch in which he lunged, dived, and rolled but held onto the ball.[247]

During Monday's scheduled doubleheader on May 30, the American Giants snapped a five-game losing streak in game one, beating the Monarchs 6-5 in thirteen innings. Chicago pummeled three Kansas City pitchers, Markham, Barnes, and Kranson, for fifteen hits to gain the victory. Rain washed out the second game after three innings were played. Kansas City was leading 3-1 when the proceedings were halted. Manager Candy Jim Taylor had delayed and slowed up the game and was finally ejected for his abuse towards the umpires.[248] Where box scores were available, Marshall failed to produce as he had during spring training. In the three games where information is available, he went 1-for-3, 0-for-4, and 0-for-5 with a run scored and a stolen base. This performance effectively ended his season with the Monarchs for 1938.

Leaving Illinois with six wins in seven tries, and with one day sandwiched between for travel, the Monarchs crossed into Wisconsin and headed towards Madison, the Capital City. Unable to gain much national attention for themselves, they relaxed and read about other teams in the national news. That day's baseball news was centered on New York Yankees' first baseman, Lou Gehrig, who during a Yankees 12-5 thumping of Boston's Red Sox, reached number 2,000 in consecutive games played in a major league career.

"John O'Neil, giant first sacker, played great ball around the initial sack, his long reach saving several errors."

Davenport Democrat, August 2, 1938

Buck O'Neil *says...*

"We stayed at the best hotels in the world. In New City, we got the Theresa, the Woodside, the Braddock, and Detroit the Gotham, Chicago, the Persian. So actually, we were staying at the best hotels in the world; they just happen to be Black owned. We were eating at the best restaurants in the world. I know we were eating the best food because, at that time, the best cooks in the world were Black."

The Streak

<u>June 1-Madison, June 2-Madison, June 5-Kansas City (DH), June 6-Wichita,</u> June 7-Oklahoma City

(NAL) O'Neil's Batting: G-3 AB-10 R-0 H-1 2B-0 3B-0 HR-0 SB-1 BA-.100

O'Neil's Fielding: PO-30 A-0 E-0 DP-1 TC-30

(E) O'Neil's Batting: G-2 AB-4 R-2 H-1 2B-0 3B-0 HR-0 SB-0 RBI-1 BA-2.50

O'Neil's Fielding: PO-20 A-1 E-0 DP-0 TC-21

By resuming operations on the barnstorming trail, Kansas City began with two exhibition encounters in Madison, the Wisconsin state capital. The barnstorming continued with additional appearances in Missouri, Oklahoma, and Kansas. They were winning quite often. Setting their exhibition opponents aside, the Monarchs returned to Kansas City for games against the Atlanta Black Crackers at Ruppert Stadium. In the process, the Monarchs began a consecutive winning streak of thirteen in a row. It was an impressive streak that was quietly usurped by other national historical events. The American Association Kansas City Blues also hit the highway for games in Louisville, Kentucky, before going on to Indianapolis. While the Monarchs were winning on the road, Kansas City was also getting more than its fill of African American entertainment in an appearance by Hollywood's "Stepin Fetchit" and his Harlem Hit Parade with the Erskine Hawkins' big band.

(L to R) Newt Allen, T. J. Young, Norman "Turkey" Stearnes, Eddie Dwight, "Dink" Mothell and Wilber Rogan, 1934. Travel was complicated. Players were routinely prohibited as customers in hotels and restaurants and routinely denied their equal rights as provided in the constitution in public facilities. (Authors collection)

On a Wednesday night in Madison, Wisconsin, the Monarchs started the first of a two-game series. Madison's team was a hard-nosed semi-professional opponent. They were, always, a worthy foe who could give a creditable contest. The Monarchs first visited Madison's Breese Stevens Field in 1930. An impressive crowd of 3,500 fans watched in awe as the Monarchs annihilated Madison in an exemplary 19-to-8 win in that initial visit. Some of the smaller towns pulled larger crowds than those in Kansas City, and this popularity kept the Monarchs returning to towns like Madison year after year. In 1934, the Monarchs returned to Madison for a two-game series. That year, Kansas City captured 8-4 and 7-3 victories. They returned the following year, 1935, and lost for the first time in a 10-to-6 setback. Visiting Wisconsin again in 1936, the Monarchs defeated Madison twice, but their winning was halted in 1937 when Kansas City lost three of a five-game series. Two of Madison's wins came in extra innings, while the other was an exciting 1-0 pitchers' battle. In returning to Breese Stevens Field, Kansas City cautiously confronted their worthy adversary, one of the leading teams in that region.

Realizing the enormity at hand, manager Andy Cooper pulled Bradley, his starter, after just three innings when Madison touched him for two scores in inning one. Kansas City rallied in the second on O'Neil's walk, Duncan's infield out, and Bradley's sharp single to right field. In inning four, Kansas City knotted the score when Johnson scored on Markham's single into right field. In the home half of that same frame, with Markham pitching, Madison scored the game's winning tally. Unable to mount a rally, Kansas City was upset by a 3-2 score.

Despite the evening's cool breeze, Madison's Ralph "Lefty" Blatz pitched in midseason form. Holding Monarchs' batters to six singles, Blatz walked away with a well-earned victory, having allowed three hits in the last five innings. After the fourth, Kansas City failed to advance a man past second base. Blatz's control was excellent, and "in a pinch," as the *Wisconsin State Journal* noted, "He was able to put the ball pretty much where he wanted."[249]

Impatiently waiting for the game on the afternoon that followed, the Monarchs gained an even break by thumping Madison 4-to-0. The much-touted Smith versus Walter Zuehls match-up favored Hilton, who limited Madison batters to five hits. Smith whiffed ten batters to earn his first game of ten-plus strikeouts for 1938. Madison was unable to get a runner beyond second base the entire game. Zuehls, a former University of Wisconsin Badgers' pitcher, allowed eight hits and fanned nine. Monarchs' right fielder, Chili Mayweather, took an immense liking to Zuehls' offerings and went 3-for-4, registering a double and a stolen base. Kansas City, having resumed their winning ways, would not taste another defeat until nineteen days later.

As the Monarchs returned home to Kansas City from Wisconsin, Stepin Fetchit's Harlem Hit Parade was opening at Kansas City's Newman Theater. Fetchit, whose real name was Lincoln Theodore Monroe Andrew Perry, was accompanied by trumpeter Erskine Hawkins' twenty-two-piece orchestra in what was called an All-Negro revue. Fetchit, who was billed as "Hollywood's lazy laughable star," performed five stereotypic stage shows daily between the photoplay movie *Little Miss Thoroughbred*. As an actor/comedian, Perry operated within a period of intense motion picture racism. He took lemons and made lemonade out of a career that would make him Hollywood's first Black millionaire. He was working hard for the money he earned. During his stay in Kansas City, a mere 25 cents gave white fans the best seat in the house of this segregated theater where a division of the races was strictly enforced. Perry practically lived in the theater during his Kansas City visit. Hawkins would record the jazz classic "After Hours" in 1940 and was the first to release "Tuxedo Junction" for RCA Records in 1939. Glenn Miller, a white artist, covered the song and took it to Number 1 on the Billboard charts. Miller's slower version of the same song sold 115,000 records in its first week on the market.

The Monarchs returned west to Ruppert Stadium for games five and six in the home portion of their Negro American League schedule. Since the Blues were out of town in Columbus, Ohio, an opening in the schedule allowed J. L. Wilkinson to slot a doubleheader at the Stadium. Catching an evening when the temperature was 85 degrees--outstanding baseball weather--the Kansas City Monarchs snatched two games from the Atlanta Black Crackers, winning, 6-3 and 6-5.

In the first game of the June 5 doubleheader, Monarch base runners combined for four early scores, adding two more in inning four. That initial scoring started with a walk to Milton, a triple by Cox, and singles by Allen, Duncan, and Johnson. Atlanta scored two in the third and another in the fourth, but the scoring ceased as Monarchs' pitcher Dick Bradley tossed a five-hitter and struck out twelve bewildered Crackers. Alonzo Mitchell, Atlanta's losing hurler, lasted two innings, having allowed four hits and five runs before his exit.

Donald Reeves, the Crackers' right fielder, made one of the game's best plays. After catching Mayweather's long foul ball, Reeves, still running in full sprint, collided with the outfield's stationary barrier, injuring his arm and leg. What made the play spectacular was Reeves' care of the ball after the collision--he held it! Concerned with Reeves' health, hardly anyone noticed that Allen scored after the catch. Unable to recover from his injuries, Reeves was carried from the field by his teammates. His injuries kept him out of game two, which the Monarchs also won.

Playing seven abbreviated innings, Mitchell, the Atlanta pitcher of record in game one, returned for game two and lost--two losses on the same day. Mitchell allowed eight hits and six runs in four, and one-third innings pitched. In inning four, a single by Allen, a double by Mayweather, and Willard Brown's home run hastened the pitcher's exit. Hilton Smith, who captured the win, along with outfielder Brown, finished with two hits each to pace the Monarchs' sweep. Brown's home run blast got special recognition in the press. The *Kansas City Call* noted, "[His] was one of the longest homers ever hit in the park. It cleared both fences now surrounding the left-field wall and went about 15 feet past the car tracks on the other side of the outer fence."[250]

In Brown, Monarchs' management had discovered an unfinished baseball gem. Originally signed as a shortstop, Brown rapidly developed into one of baseball's truly exceptional outfielders. Additionally, after a steady diet of curveballs from teammate Chet Brewer, Brown began to hit many home runs. He recalled,

They could get me out on the curveball when I came to the Monarchs. Chet Brewer, he was one of the best curveball pitchers in the league. Every day he would throw me nothing but curveballs. He'd throw a fastball to move me back and then throw the curveball. He'd say, 'That's the way they [are] going to pitch you. They know you're going to hit the fastball. The only thing you're weak on is the curveball.' He had one of the best curveballs, so when I learned how to hit it, that made me a finished ballplayer.[251]

Born on June 26, 1913, a date which is rarely publicized, Brown told the author that the majors changed his date of birth to make him appear younger when he signed in 1947. Several different dates have been publicized since. What they can't deny is that Willard Brown blossomed into five feet-eleven inches of pure exhilaration. Though blessed with tremendous "natural" ability, "Brown prospered early on because he took instruction well," recalled O'Neil. O'Neil added, "Willard [Brown] was just about the most natural athlete that I have ever seen. Willard was so natural, really, that you always thought Willard could do a little more than he was doing. He could turn it on and off; this is the reason he played so long and so well. He was the most relaxed guy I have ever seen playing baseball."[252]

By contrast, it was Taylor, manager of the American Giants, who encouraged Brown to use a heavier 36-inch, 40-ounce bat. Brown eventually settled into a patented 36-36 medium handle rod. Brown stated that he attempted to pattern himself after his idol, Oscar Charleston, his favorite hitter.[253] Although Brown was never recognized for his speed, the only Monarchs who ran faster were Eddie Dwight and Henry Milton. Brown recalled a meeting he had with the Monarchs owner during the winter of 1934,

> Wilkinson came down [to Louisiana] and offered me $250 and a contract of $125 a month and a dollar a day to eat. I wasn't making but $10 a week, so you know I'm going to take that.[254]

Brown accepted the money and made it pay long-term dividends. In just his first season, according to one source, Brown led in long balls, "hitting forty-three home runs."[255] Another source credited Brown with "fifty-four home runs in 160 games." In 1936, Brown exceeded forty home runs for a second consecutive season. Then in 1937, it was reported that Brown slammed "forty-two home runs."[256] An additional source credited his 1937 home run total to be fifty-two.[257] His home run totals dipped in 1938, but he hit lots of triples and doubles.

Regardless of the totals, it was no subtle fact that Brown was one of baseball's most prolific long-ball threats. Look at what he accomplished after the major leagues integrated in 1947. On August 13, 1947, while playing for the St. Louis Browns, Willard Brown became the first African American to hit a home run in American League play. He went on to hit ninety-five home runs in five years of minor league play, 1950-1956.[258] He added another 101 home runs in the Puerto Rican Winter League, which included a league record of twenty-seven in a single season.

For Atlanta, James "Red" Moore, who went 2-for-3 that day, was also having a grand season. Moore, an Atlanta native, joined Mike Schaine's Atlanta Black Crackers in 1935, at age 17. He formerly played with an Atlanta team named the Oakland City Cubs. In the fall of 1935, his superior play in the annual North-South Game caught the watchful eye of Effa Manley, which eventually led to his signing with the Newark Eagles in June of 1936, where he remained through 1937. In 1938 he returned south in search of winter employment. Having taken a job at one of Schaine's theaters, Moore stayed in Atlanta to fortify the newly formed Negro American League entry when the Crackers were sold to Harden.[259]

Kansas City and Atlanta continued their series with nocturnal events in Wichita on Monday, June 6, and Oklahoma City on Tuesday, June 7.

In coming to Wichita, the Atlanta Black Crackers were attempting to disturb Kansas City's stellar winning record. Monarchs' teams had won forty-one games with only three losses dating back to 1920. The crowds were always large in Wichita, and some believed the Monarchs to be nearly invincible. As the Monarchs moved swiftly down Kellogg Street, Wichita's main drag, O'Neil sat silently, reflecting on the day in 1935, when Doby, Major, and he humbly caught a train at the local depot with scarcely a dollar between them and headed for Florida.

The 8:30 p.m. scheduled start provided sufficient advertisement to draw twelve-hundred in paid attendance to Wichita's Lawrence Stadium, as the Monarchs attempted to defend their won/loss record in a timely fashion.

I.V. Barnes hurling a game that lasted an hour and thirty-eight minutes, held Cracker batters to three hits. Ironically, it was the same number of hits he clouted as a batter. Holding the opposition to equal or fewer hits as a pitcher while getting as many or more as a batter was indeed rare. This unique feat, though seldom seen in other leagues, often happened in the Negro Leagues because pitchers were traditionally among the better athletes on a particular team.

For six innings, it was a hurlers' battle between six-feet-six-inch Charles "Slim" Duncan and Barnes Duncan, who was in his first year with Atlanta, utilized both an overhand and submarine

150

delivery. Each pitcher bore down, although Duncan was forced into some extraordinary throwing, pulling out of several tough spots. Kansas City eventually bounced Duncan for ten hits, although he struck out nine Monarchs. Barnes finished with eight strikeouts and gained the victory. As a hitter, Barnes showed great tenacity by collecting three hits.

Barnes' first hit was a rousing third-inning double, which might have been a homer if not for the wire that draped ball fields in the crude electrical wiring configurations of early night-lighting systems. Barnes promptly scored on Milton's inside-the-park home run. Spencer "Babe" Davis, an Atlanta outfielder from Winston Salem, North Carolina, misjudged Milton's dying duck, which rolled to the fence. Milton nearly stripped his gears as he circled the paths, hot on Barnes' heels. Barnes later added another double and a single to notch three hits. In clinching this contest, Monarchs' base runners erupted for four scores in innings seven and eight. The *Wichita Eagle's* glowing wrap-up reported that "Shortstop Johnson, in particular, flashed some brilliant fielding and throwing."[260]

In the Tuesday night game at Oklahoma City's Holland Field, Kansas City won another exciting 3-1 contest when Markham and Kranson combined for an eight-hitter.[261] Atlanta's Tom "Preacher" Howard was bumped for the loss. Howard, a native of Macon, Georgia, was a recent addition to the Crackers, having joined from the Jacksonville Red Caps. Wilber "Bullet" Rogan, playing in the city of his birth, paced Monarchs batters with a single, a double, and two runs scored. Surrounded by a busload of talented teammates, an aging Rogan was lucky if he played at all. Yet, and despite the competition, Rogan was in the lineup often.

Surprisingly, Rogan remained with the Monarchs in 1938, although Detroit had become an important bidder for his services. He nearly changed teams in early January when James Titus, owner of the Detroit Stars, made overtures to Wilkinson, the Monarchs' owner, to acquire Rogan and

Duncan in a two-for-one trade for catcher Shirley Petway. Titus hinted, "If Rogan comes to Detroit, he will probably be given managerial reins."[262] Wilkinson countered by asking for Roosevelt Cox, an infielder/catcher from Detroit's 1937 team.[263] The deal ultimately crumbled when Detroit was not offered a Negro American League franchise. Wilkinson intuitively acquired Cox, who was now a free agent, without trading Duncan or Rogan.

O'Neil recollected, "Rogan could [still] throw the ball by you, and he had one of the greatest curves too."[264] Although Rogan rarely pitched in 1938, he took the mound at least once. In Houston, Rogan's arm helped defeat the Philadelphia Stars.[265] By 1938 he was specializing in pinch-hitting and utility roles, which helped prolong his career, and the highlights were many.

During the Monarchs' mid-May visit to Enid, Oklahoma, Rogan's three hits, a stolen base, and an RBI defeated Monarchs' nemesis pitcher, the Native American Milt Perry. Rogan collected a trio of hits and runs in Peoria, Illinois, when the Monarchs thumped a local All-Star team on May 24.[266] Pinch-hitting for Andy Cooper on July 3, Rogan mounted a rally to tie the score in a win over Memphis' league-leading Red Sox. A day later, on July 4, Rogan went 2-for-5 with a double against this same Red Sox team. Playing in Manhattan, Kansas, Rogan collected one of eight Monarchs' hits and drove in a run against the Black Barons.[267] In a July 30 game against the American Giants, Rogan pinch-hit safely for Cox.

The wins in Wichita and Oklahoma City gave the Monarchs a four-game sweep over the Atlanta Black Crackers. In those four contests, Kansas City outscored Atlanta twenty-one runs to nine.

"Besides his powerful hurling staff, Manager [Andy] Cooper of the Kansas City nine is blessed with an array of sluggers that would make a few ball clubs of the higher classifications weak by comparison. Roundy, the famous Madison sports columnist, says that the Monarchs have three sluggers on their team that would do credit to a big-league team. Of the pitching staff, Roundy says that the three leading hurlers would be able to win 20 games each in the big leagues."

Sheboygan Press, June 15, 1938

Buck O'Neil *says...*

"We had wonderful times out there; we most certainly did. Don't feel sorry for nobody you see here. They could play the game as well as anyone who ever played. I don't care how far they go today. However high George Brett goes, or however far Reggie Jackson hits the ball, these fellows have all been there."

More Exhibitions, Less League

June 12-Kansas City (DH), June 13-East St. Louis, June 14-Belleville, June 16-Sheboygan

(NAL) O'Neil's Batting: G-2 AB-5 R-0 H-1 2B-0 3B-0 HR-0 SB-1 RBI-1 BA-2.00

O'Neil's Fielding: PO-20 A-0 E-1 DP-1 TC-21

(E) O'Neil's Batting: G-3 AB-13 R-1 H-2 2B-0 3B-0 HR-0 SB-0 RBI-0 BA-1.54

O'Neil's Fielding: PO-29 A-1 E-0 DP-2 TC-30

Having won four consecutive games from the Crackers prompted a return home to Kansas City's Ruppert Stadium for games seven and eight of the Monarchs' 1938 home schedule. On tap was the coming of William Dismukes' troublesome Negro American League Black Barons of Alabama. Kansas City returned home with a modest five-game home winning streak, a total of wins that was destined to increase against the Barons.

Joe Hauser. *With 63 home runs in 1930 and 69 in 1933, he was highly regarded as the only player to twice hit 60 or more home runs in a professional career. In 1938 he homered off Andy Cooper during the Monarchs' June 16, exhibition game at Sheboygan, Wisconsin. (Author Collection)*

Barnes got the better of Birmingham's Clifford Blackman, winning 5-1 in the opener. In the second game, Kranson, with O'Neil factoring into the results, completed Kansas City's sweep of the twin-bill with a 2-1 win.[268]

Barnes outdrew Blackman in the opener, although each allowed only four hits.[269] It was Blackman's wildness in the sixth inning that aided mightily in the Barons' defeat. Barnes struck out seven batters compared to four by Blackman. Barnes also had a better afternoon with the walks finishing with one, compared to seven by Blackman. The Monarchs punched out numerous hits, along with a trio of free passes and an error for four tallies in the sixth. Kansas City stole lots of bases. Cox, Brown, and O'Neil swiped bases for the Monarchs. Fred Bankhead, who would end the 1938 season with the Memphis Red Sox, also stole a base. Henry Milton was the Monarchs' hitting star in the game, with a double and triple in four at-bats.

Birmingham's lone tally came when Henry "Butch" McCall scored after hitting a triple.[270] McCall, a native of Laurel, Mississippi, was a highly sought-after player. Having joined Chicago's American Giants in 1936, McCall began his professional career a year earlier with the Hattiesburg, Mississippi, city team. He was said to be 6 feet 4, barefooted, and was rated as one of the most powerful men in the Negro American League, as well as a mighty swat man.[271]

In the second game, Barons' batters nicked Monarchs' pitchers for six hits in an abbreviated seven-inning game. But with only five hits of their own, Kansas City was unable to take the lead until late in the game. Trailing in the fourth, Allen led off with a walk and went to third on Mayweather's right-field single. Allen scored on O'Neil's sacrifice fly to center field for run number one. The Monarchs did not score again until inning six when Allen's double and O'Neil's single drove home the game's winning run. Floyd Kranson got the better of Julius Osley on the mound. The Monarchs' mounds man pitched a six-hitter, struck out three, and allowed no free passes. Osley tossed a five-hitter, struck out three, walked four, and balked once in his losing effort.

Kansas City's double spanking of Birmingham brought their record to seven wins and one loss in eight home games. The three thousand fans that attended Sunday's game was an improved Sabbath day crowd, one that was greater than most that assembled at other Negro American League games in this same period. In Chicago, the American Giants' low turnout was embarrassing. A mere

155

168 fans paid their way into Giants' Park on that same afternoon. "Baseball games are NOT being supported by our group," was the passionate plea of sports editor Frank A. Young in the *Chicago Defender*. "The depression may have had something to do with it. The recession may have something to do with it now. Neither the depression nor the recession has anything to do with the young Negro who prefers to spend his money to see two all-white teams play in a major league which draws the color line."[272] Crowds for Negro American League events remained sparse as the Monarchs headed out for twenty days on the road. While touring, they played two league teams, the Indianapolis ABCs and Chicago American Giants. They also swept into Illinois for exhibition games in East St. Louis and Belleville before heading to Sheboygan, Wisconsin.

Cab Calloway. His band and show arrived in Kansas City on June 10, 1938, for a five-day engagement at the downtown Mainstreet Theater. (Authors collection)

As the Monarchs continued their roadshow, Kansas City's reputation as an entertainment Mecca was nonstop with Cab Calloway's appearance at Kansas City's Mainstreet Theater. He was in town for multiple shows on five consecutive days. Calloway's band played between the movie photoplay, *The Adventures of Robin Hood*. The American Association Blues also returned for an extended homestay. Taking charge of Ruppert Stadium, the Blues entertained Louisville, Columbus, Toledo, Minneapolis, St. Paul, and Milwaukee with large and enthusiastic crowds. Performing outside Kansas City, on June 13, the Monarchs diverted from their Negro American League schedule to make an appearance at Edgemont Park in East St. Louis, where the local Blue Jays awaited their arrival. Kansas City showed up with a new third baseman in Packinghouse Adams.

The Monday night Edgemont Park crowd of over 1,100 was the largest of the season for the East St. Louis team. Art Wilson, a right-hander, and catcher Ray Besse were at the point for the Blue Jays.[273] "Buster" Markham and Frank Duncan were Kansas City's selection as that night's battery. Kansas City took an early two-run lead with tallies in the first and fourth innings. A double by Milton and a single by Adams started the Monarchs' scoring. East St. Louis scored a pair of runs in the sixth to tie the game at 2-2. Markham put the Monarchs back into the lead with a four-ply blast over the barrier in the right to start the seventh. That same inning, the Blue Jays scored three more runs, and suddenly Kansas City was on the short end of the scoring.

Late in the game, "Bullet" Rogan leaned against the wire netting inside the park to converse with a reporter from the *Belleville News Democrat.* "We're not so hot about beating these boys here," boasted Rogan, "but we do like to take those Stags because those guys have got a reputation, and a victory over them in our season's record book looks awfully nice."[274] Rogan added, "They're just getting a piece of us guys here tonight because we're saving the whole thing for the Stags."[275] Despite his smug comments, Rogan's teammates were losing the game.

Starting the ninth down by two runs, Hilton Smith, pinch-hitting for Buster Markham, singled. Henry Milton followed with a single, his third of the game. Roosevelt Cox was substituted as a pinch-runner for Smith. After two were out, local fans, presumptuous of a home win, started toward the exits. Mayweather grounded to the first baseman for what should have been the game's final out, but the pitcher covering first base missed the throw, allowing Cox to score and Milton to reach third. A double steal, with Milton scoring the tying run, shocked the residual crowd into staying.[276] Having tied the game in the tenth, Kansas City went on to capture another win. After two were out, Byron Johnson walked, and Cox followed with a double to push the winning run home. The Monarchs were ultimately 6-to-5 winners over the Blue Jays.[277] Manager Andy Cooper, who pitched innings nine and ten, received credit for Kansas City's victory. Sporting a winning streak of eight consecutive games, the Monarchs motored thru the industrial section of East St. Louis, Illinois, to nearby Belleville, Illinois, for a battle against the Stags Brewery team

On June 14, the Monarchs arrived in Belleville to face manager Clarence "Red" Hoffman's Stags. The baseball team was sponsored regionally by Stag Beer. The brew was well known to area beer drinkers. "Stag [was] the top-selling beer in metropolitan St. Louis, well ahead of Falstaff and Budweiser."[278] The National Prohibition Law, having been repealed in 1933, allowed United States alcohol consumption to grow at an alarming rate. The history of the National Prohibition Act, or simply Prohibition, dates to the period just after WWI.

Back in 1919, despite President Woodrow Wilson's veto, the United States Congress passed the Volstead Act Passage, which meant that the 18th Amendment accepted December 18, 1917, and ratified January 16, 1919, was now enforceable.[279] The manufacture, sale, and transportation of intoxicating liquor for drinking became illegal. Any beverage over 0.50 percent alcohol was considered as an alcoholic drink. When two court cases challenging the constitutionality of the Act were decided in favor of the government in 1920, breweries were left to contemplate survival strategies now that their primary product was illicit. The "noble experiment" was being viewed with increasing disfavor, and companies soon began scrambling for positions in the post-prohibition brewing industry.

Congress proposed a halt to the 18th Amendment with the passage of the 21st Amendment on February 20, 1933. Missouri ratified the Amendment on August 29, 1933, and on December 5, 1933, the 21st Amendment was fully ratified, and alcohol production in the United States resurrected itself.[280] Early in 1934, the Griesedieck Western Brewery, the company that produced Stag Beer, reopened for business.[281] "That first year, the company brewed nearly seventy-three thousand barrels."[282] Henry L. Griesedieck, Sr., the company's president, aimed to sell Stag beer to the man on the street at 10 cents a bottle. Griesedieck also believed in the concept of continuous advertising. "In 1939, approximately seventy newspapers carried Stag beer advertisements on a twelve-month basis. Those newspapers were located in Illinois (outside Cook County) and in Missouri, Oklahoma, Arkansas, Texas, western Tennessee, Kentucky, and eastern Kansas. The brewery also supplemented newspaper advertisements with billboards as a constant reminder of the selling story being told in newspapers."[283] Griesedieck Western also formed a baseball team to represent Belleville, Illinois, as another means of advertisement. The baseball team was also bringing recognition to Belleville.[284] On August 22, 1934, the St. Louis Cardinals, known as the Gas House Gang, who would go on to win a World Championship in October of that same year, also played an exhibition in Belleville.

Listed on the Stag's roster were many of the region's greatest non-league ballplayers. Billy Bayne, a one-time major league southpaw, Glenn Barthelme, a leading right-handed pitcher, Billy

Morris, Charlie Conners, Elmer Peters, Eddie Fischer, Art Weis, Wally Cookson, and Bob Campbell were all members of the Belleville team.[285]

Dick Bradley toed the rubber in the Monarchs 1938 visit to Belleville, a game that one Belleville newspaper summarized as "one of the most interesting ever played at Athletic Field."[286] Barthelme, pitching for the Stags, held Kansas City to nine hits. Bradley, a bit wild but steady enough to hurl a complete game, fast balled the Stags into submission, walking nine men––two more than he struck out. He did not allow a hit until the fifth inning and limited his opponents to four hits while tossing a complete game.

Kansas City scored two runs in the opening frame on a hit batsman, a single, and Willard Brown's double. For the next three innings, the hurlers engaged in a mound duel. The Monarchs added two more in the fifth when a Stags' outfielder dropped Mayweather's deep fly to center field. Three more Monarchs' runs were added in inning six and another in the seventh. In winning 8-to-3, only three of Kansas City's eight runs were earned. The victory, Kansas City's sixth consecutive victory without a loss in three years of games at Belleville's Athletic field, allowed for the Monarchs' return in August. A day later, baseball's biggest news was made by a National League rookie.

On June 15, 1938, lefty pitcher Johnny Vander Meer of the Cincinnati Reds tossed consecutive no-hitters. The first no-hitter was pitched on June 11, in a 3-0 win against Boston's Braves at Cincinnati's Crosley Field. The second was a 6-0 win over the Brooklyn Dodgers at Ebbets Field. The win at Ebbets Field had occurred in the first official National League night game with 38,748 watching. Riding the team bus in near obscurity, Monarchs' pitcher John Markham had also pitched himself into baseball's no-hit history. Back on May 15, 1930, in an 8-0 victory over the Waco Cardinals in Waco, Texas, he pitched night baseball's first-ever no-hitter. Additionally, the win was night baseball's first-ever perfect game. Unlike Vander Meer's feat, Markham's feat, a truly historic achievement, had gone unrecognized by baseball's elite because it occurred in a competition where at least one of the teams was Negro.

Hurrying like a bull leaving the stable, the Monarchs headed into Wisconsin where their next opponents, Joe Hauser's Chairmakers, were scheduled on June 16, in Sheboygan. There was no greater advertisement of Kansas City's arrival than the near ritualistic beatings they had given Sheboygan teams since 1936. Having never lost in Sheboygan, Kansas City boasted a perfect 2-0 record, an unblemished mark they were desirous of continuing. In 1937, the Monarchs embarrassed Sheboygan with a 20-to-4 win that highlighted home runs off the respective bats of Duncan, Brown, and Mayweather.[287] O'Neil's experiences were quite the opposite. The negative experience of his first Sheboygan visit still lingered.

In 1937, while a member of the Memphis, O'Neil and his Red Sox teammates suffered a humiliating 16-1 setback in Sheboygan.[288] Now that O'Neil was a Monarch, there was euphoria about returning to Wisconsin. Manager Cooper was not taking any chances, though, decided to utilize himself on the mound for a second time within the week. A wise move indeed, as Sheboygan's best player, Joe Hauser, was also its manager, and he hit from the left side of the plate. Sheboygan, having defeated Chicago's Colored All-Stars by a 5-3 score on June 12, was now well-positioned for the upset win.

Hauser, a journeyman player with Eastern, International, American Association, and American League experience, joined the Sheboygan's semi-professional team, the Chairmakers, in 1937. During his professional career, he appeared in 1,854 minor league games and 629 American League games. Hauser's greatest asset was his ability to hit home runs. He began 1938 as the "only player to [have] hit more than 60 homers in a [minor league] season twice."[289] In 1930, Hauser hit sixty-three home runs for Baltimore's International League team and a career-high of sixty-nine for Minneapolis of the American Association in 1933.

(L to R) John "Buck" O'Neil, William "Dizzy" Dismukes. *The Miles College graduate was manager of the 1938 Birmingham Black Barons. He later served as a big-league scout and died on June 30, 1961. (Authors collection)*

Cooper, making yet another atypical start, defeated Hauser's Tri-State League Chairmakers, winning 8-2. In thumping Hauser's mighty semi-professionals, Cooper's nine hits, eight strikeouts, and two walks over seven innings of hurling opened the gate for Barnes, who hurled innings eight and nine and allowed only one hit. Cooper's eight strikeouts were also his season's best. Ignoring the obvious good pitching offered by Cooper, the *Sheboygan Press* wrote, "The feature[s] of the game were the heavy-hitting and the brilliant fielding on the part of the Monarchs Johnson, shortstop, and Allen, second baseman."[290]

Johnson's one-handed stab of a Chairmakers smashing drive between third and short and his perfect throw to catch the runner at first received a thunderous ovation. Allen, at second base, with five putouts and two assists, also aroused the crowd's approval. Home runs by Willard Brown and a long-ball buffet of hits by Chili Mayweather were equally impressive.

Mayweather, stationed in right-field, went 3-for-4 with a triple and home run. Brown hit the hardest ball of the entire game, driving it far over the scoreboard in center field for a home run. Additionally, Hauser clouted a sixth-inning home run off Andy Cooper that eclipsed the right-field fence. Despite Hauser's feat, the Monarchs won their tenth consecutive game without a loss--a streak that continued into Illinois.

"O'Neil is a first baseman who is attracting much attention."

Chicago Defender, June 25, 1938

Buck O'Neil says...

"The thought used to be that a Black manager would have the White boys to contend with, that there would be disagreement. It's not so today, though. A Black manager couldn't afford to be an Uncle Tom. Many of the Black players are superstars; what would they think of a Black manager who bends over to appease White players?"

Chicago, A Great Baseball City

June 17-Chicago, June 18-Chicago, June 19-Chicago (DH), June 20-Chicago, June 21-Chicago, June 22-Flint, June 26-Chicago (DH), June 28-Milwaukee, June 29-Black River Falls, June 30-Charles City

(NAL) O'Neil's Batting: G-1 AB-3 R-0 H-0 2B-0 3B-0 HR-0 SB-0 BA-0.00

O'Neil's Fielding: PO-0 A-0 E-0 DP-0 TC-0

(E) O'Neil's Batting: G-2 AB-5 R-2 H-0 2B-0 3B-0 HR-0 SB-0 RBI-0 BA-0.00

O'Neil's Fielding: PO-6 A-0 E-1 DP-2 TC-7

Having worked their way into Illinois, it was only natural that a second visit to Chicago was imminent. While in the city, games had been scheduled with Chicago Mills, Spencer Coals, and league rival the American Giants.[291] They were in Chicago, the second-largest city in American, on the night of the heavily advertised Joe Louis versus Max Schmeling bout that was to take place at Yankee Stadium in the largest city in America. In finishing their late June schedule, the Monarchs took on new competition and saw their long streak of wins come to a screeching halt by a most unlikely candidate.

On June 17, 1938, the Kansas City Monarchs moved into Chicago, where they banged out a 7-2 win over Chicago Mills at Shewbridge Field. According to a report in the *Chicago Daily Tribune*, two Monarchs' pitchers, Bradley, and Ryan, combined for a three-hitter, with Roosevelt Cox making a rare appearance at catcher. Ryan, a new recruit, had gotten a tryout on this night, but he did not remain with the team after the game.[292] Chicago Mills was coming off a double win over the Fort Wayne International Harvesters in the Tri-State League competition before the loss.[293] Seeking revenge but getting none, it was the Mills' second loss without a win against the Monarchs in the 1938 season.[294]

The following afternoon, Kansas City opened a four-game set against the Chicago American Giants at Giants Park. Scheduling one game on June 18, a doubleheader on June 19, along with a single game on June 20, the Monarchs might decide the first-half pennant with a sweep of the series. Defeating the Giants 5-0 in game one, pitcher Hilton Smith hurled a seven-hitter.[295] With this victory, Kansas City's consecutive wins reached thirteen. They won and lost to the Giants in the middle of the series. In the series finale, Kansas City defeated Chicago by a 7-to-2 score to harness the series three games to one. The Monarchs were destined to lose another game before leaving the city.[296]

On June 20, in a night game versus Chicago's Spencer Coals, Kansas City lost a 5-to-4 game. Pitcher William "Lefty" Stevens stayed the entire route for his Coals team and drove in the winning run with a single in the ninth for the victory.[297] Two days later, Willard Brown went 3-for-4 in a big 6-4 win at Flint, Michigan's Athletic Park. It was a night where the future Hall of Fame outfielder hit a triple, stole a base, and drove in a pair of runs to aid Kranson and Cooper's nine-hit pitching victory.[298]

Regardless of the Monarchs' many achievements, on June 22, there would be no denying this historic day. Indeed, it was a day for African American sports achievement as Joe Louis, the celebrated "Brown Bomber," fought Germany's Max Schmeling in a historic rematch at Yankee Stadium.

As heavyweight champion, Joe Louis was called a perfect fighting machine. Louis, whose full name was Joseph Louis Barrow, burst upon the professional scene in 1931. At his peak, he appeared unbeatable. In a heavyweight career that lasted eleven years, Louis successfully defended his title twenty-five times. Co-managed by two African American men, John Roxborough and Julian Black, Louis was trained by Jack Blackburn, also African American.

In Louis's earlier fight with Schmeling on June 19, 1936, at Yankee Stadium, Louis was favored to win. Before that fight, Louis looked invincible. After an intense review of Louis's fight films, Schmeling insisted, "I see something." Indeed, he did. Schmeling repeatedly struck with rights over the top of Louis's left hand, and Louis dropped to the floor for the first time in round four. From there on, Louis absorbed a steady beating. By the twelfth, the left cheek of Joe Louis was swollen to almost twice its normal size by Schmeling's repetitive right-hand jabs. Louis, down for the count in round twelve, knelt against the ropes and took the ten-count for the loss. Schmeling's win was his greatest victory ever.

(L to R) Joe Louis and Bill "Bojangles" Robinson. On June 22, 1938, Louis overwhelmed Max Schmeling in two minutes and four seconds of the opening round as a Yankee Stadium crowd of seventy-thousand watched fistic history. Louis scored the quickest knockout ever registered in a heavyweight title engagement. (ACME Photo in Authors collection)

The 1938 Louis versus Schmeling rematch was fueled with controversy. In the wake of World War II, Schmeling's popularity with Hitler's Nazi Party caused considerable resentment against the champion fighter. When rescheduled against Louis, Adolf Hitler prophesied a glorious victory for Schmeling to underscore the superiority of Germany's Aryan race. However, an avenging Louis overwhelmed Schmeling in two minutes and four seconds of the opening round as a Yankee Stadium crowd of seventy thousand paying customers watched the big German get floored three times before referee Arthur Donovan gestured an end to the massacre.[299] Louis made boxing history that night, with the quickest knockout ever registered in a heavyweight title engagement.

Joe Louis' reign as heavyweight champion was celebrated as jubilantly by African Americans as any Aryan would have for Schmeling. Nonetheless, Louis's success was not celebrated by every American. Unable to harness a real-life title, white Americans readily accepted the fictionalized Joe Palooka. Created by Ham Fisher, Palooka's cartoon was intended to exemplify a politically correct sports hero--a standard that Louis' race prohibited him from achieving in America's prejudiced society. Thus, Palooka's mythical character symbolized to white Americans what Louis was for African Americans in real flesh and blood. He was Black America's all-American hero.

The Palooka cartoon found an audience in American daily newspapers. In print, he hobnobbed in high society, befriended well-known Hollywood celebrities, and most of all held the mythical heavyweight title of the world. In an age when African Americans were seldom celebrated nationally, Palooka's fictionalized image was designed to signify something other than good entertainment. Syndicated from 1930 to 1984, Palooka was also featured on radio and further popularized by movies. African Americans who were undoubtedly working hard to earn any celebrity status they might receive were unnerved by what they read. Members of the Monarchs, well-accustomed to media bias, kept on playing baseball despite the agitation they faced and felt within.

168

Yet, in their return to Chicago, the local "Semipro" teams were hoping to give the American League a run for their money.

On June 26, the Monarchs had scheduled a doubleheader in Chicago against Chicago Mills at Mills Stadium located at 4700 West Lake Street. Eldon McLean, formerly of Washington's American League Senators, was expected to pitch one of the games.[300] At the same time, Spencer Coals was scheduled to play a doubleheader against the barnstorming Piney Woods Collegians at Spencer Coals Field, 4200 North Central. A doubleheader between the sixth and seventh place Chicago White Sox and Philadelphia Athletics was scheduled at Comiskey Park on 35th and Shields. All three twin bills were scheduled to start at 1:30 p.m.[301]

The multi-team confrontation for fans never occurred as all three parks canceled their doubleheaders because of rain and soggy fields.[302] No baseball was played in Chicago. That day's biggest sporting news had nothing to do with Negro League teams, but it had included a Chicago team. In New York, Carl Hubbell of the Giants defeated the Chicago Cubs for his 200th career win.

The Monarchs remained in the region, reuniting with Taylor's American Giants, ninety miles from Chicago, with both teams anxious to display their talents during an open date at Milwaukee's Borchert Field on Tuesday, June 28.

Kansas City blasted American Giants' pitchers for fourteen safe blows, which accounted for a total of twenty bases in a 7-4 victory at the Milwaukee Brewer's American Association park.[303] Leading Kansas City's attack were Milton and Brown, both of whom connected for three hits. Every batter in the Monarchs' lineup, except for Cox, and O'Neil, hit safely. Smith allowed four hits in five innings for the win, which Kranson finished in relief.[304] After the game, they were back on the road for yet an overnight on the highway.

The Monarchs vacated the metropolis of Milwaukee, a city of some 587,472 people, for a Wednesday night game at Black River Falls, Wisconsin, a city of roughly 2,500 inhabitants, before moving on to play a Thursday night game in Charles City, Iowa, a city with an estimated population of 8,039.

At Black River Falls, the Monarchs won big when a mix of four passed balls, five errors, and a pair of wild pitches spoiled the local Merchants' big night of baseball. A local band that played before and during the game kept the Fair Grounds crowd entertained. Ernie Rudolph, one of the best mounds men in Wisconsin, pitched for the locals with ragged support. A walk, a passed ball, four errors, and two hits gave the Monarchs a four-run lead in the third. They added to the total in the seventh inning on a bit of heads-up baserunning by Henry Milton, who singled, stole second before going on to score when the catcher left home plate unoccupied while fielding Newt Allen's bunt. As a unit, Monarchs batters took great delight in Rudolph's pitching and landed on him for ten hits. Cox, Allen, Mayweather, and Brown picked up a pair of hits each. Dick Bradley and "Train" Jackson had full command of the Monarchs' pitching. They combined to toss a three-hitter with eighteen batters struck out, nine strikeouts for each pitcher. The *Banner Journal* newspaper stated, "Bradley possessed the fastest ball it has ever been our privilege to try to watch."[305] It is ironic then that Rudolph, who had won eleven games for Crookston in the Northern League in 1937, was later promoted to the major leagues. In 1945, at age 36, he broke into the National League as a pitcher for the Brooklyn Dodgers. Rudolph would enjoy the recognition he received for having a "Cup of Coffee" in the majors during an era when African American players were denied a sip from the same beaker. Like O'Neil, he ended up as a major league scout. After winning 10-0, the Monarchs crammed back into their bus and headed for Charles City, Iowa.

History had been made in Charles City in 1936 when O'Neil and Markham combined for a big Acme Giants' win at that city's Lions Field against the Texas Black Spiders. O'Neil went 3-for-5 with two stolen bases and chased home two RBIs in his team's big 14-3 win on that prior occasion.[306] Markham, with nine strikeouts, was credited with that night's win. In their return to Floyd County, they had hopes of achieving similar feats. They were to face an impressive local team. Charles City, a power in Northern Iowa semi-pro circles for over a dozen years, had become a hot spot for touring baseball teams.

O'Neil and Markham's return to Charles City pitted them against Glenn Smaha of Iowa State Teachers College, "Punk" Paine, Ken Reid, and the Finch family, Mully, Roger, and "Pickle."[307] Scores of that night's encounters have not been located, but it's safe to assume that the Monarchs won this game before heading back to Kansas City.

With the Kansas City Blues scheduled to conclude an American Association home stand O'Neil and his teammates were eager to make the 350-mile ride from Charles City to more familiar territory, with yet another extensive overnight ride on the thoroughfare.

"John O'Neil, at first base, is a newer man who is proving his worth. He is 6 feet 2 inches tall and has a long reach that saves his infielders many errors."

The Junction City Union, August 22, 1938

Buck O'Neil says...

"I guess [I wanted to play baseball] practically all of my life because I was raised in Sarasota, Florida, and the major league ball clubs trained in Florida. So, I had seen good baseball all of my life. I think most of the kids wanted to be professional baseball players. Now I had no idea about playing Black baseball. I was just thinking about professional baseball. Because I didn't realize that the major leagues were not for me at that time, I thought anybody could play before I realized the social situation."

Edged Out Of A Pennant

July 1-Storm Lake, July2-Chicago, July 3-Kansas City (DH), July 4-Kansas City (DH), July 5-Manhattan, July 6-Enid, July 7-Oklahoma City, July 8-Manhattan, July10-Kansas City (DH), July 11-Sioux City

(NAL) O'Neil's Batting: G-7 AB-26 R-5 H-5 2B-1 3B-0 HR-0 SB-4 BA-1.92

O'Neil's Fielding: PO-53 A-1 E-3 DP-1 TC-57

(E) O'Neil's Batting: G-3 AB-13 R-4 H-5 2B-2 3B-0 HR-0 SAC-1 SB-1 RBI-3 BA-3.85

O'Neil's Fielding: PO-39 A-2 E-0 DP-4 TC-41

The Monarchs returned to Ruppert Stadium in early July for back-to-back doubleheaders against Ted Radcliffe's Memphis Red Sox on July 3 and 4. Choreographing their way through the remainder of the month, home games were added against the fast-stepping Birmingham Black Barons and the always competitive Chicago American Giants. Included among July's non-league exhibitions were stops in Iowa, Kansas, and Oklahoma. July also included a two-week long hiatus from league play when the Monarchs and American Giants paired up to barnstorm into Minnesota, North Dakota, and Canada. Adding to their already potent lineup, Kansas City, in their search for younger talent to bolster their overall play, traded 37-year-old Frank Duncan to the American Giants.

Kansas City opened July, on a Friday evening, where they met the local White Caps team, champions of the 1937 Tri-State area. When the Monarch bus pulled into Storm Lake, it was raining. Rain delayed the game's start by 30 minutes. By the time the umpire yelled "play ball," a fairly large rain-soaked crowd had assembled. Monarch hitters went right to work on a local pitcher named Paul Messerly, who was buzzing them past most of the Kansas City team with remarkable ease. Henry Milton first up, struck out, but Roosevelt Cox reached on an error. Newt Allen followed and popped out. Two men were out when Eldridge Mayweather singled to score Cox. Mayweather stole second and went to third on an error when the catcher's throw bounced past second base. Willard Brown followed with a single to score Mayweather. Kansas City had two runs on the boards, and they wouldn't need anymore. I.V. Barnes was hurling sensationally and matching Messerly's best efforts. Brantley, a recruit pitcher eager for a longer stay with the Monarchs, followed Barnes to the mound and fanned six White Cap batters in the final three frames of a contest that lasted six innings. At the end of the sixth, the heavens burst, letting loose buckets of water to end the ballgame. Messerly had struck out many Monarchs, eight total but lost a 2-0 nail-biter on 5-hits. Two of the hits were credited to Brown. In their winning effort, Barnes and Brantley limited the White Caps to 5 well-scattered hits. After the weather-shortened game, the Monarchs took a sloppy ride to Chicago, where it also rained.

(L to R) Frank Duncan, Jesse "Hoss" Walker, and Andy Cooper. "I sure get a kick out of him [Duncan]," said St. Louis Cardinals' great Dizzy Dean. "He has a glove that makes that old ball pop, and he makes my pitch sound like a rifle shot, and he tells them, hitters, 'boy don't get near that plate, don't let that ball hit you or it kills you.'" (Authors collection)

After a brief stop in Chicago, where their doubleheader with Chicago Mills was completely rained out, they were back on the bus for yet another overnight drive towards Kansas City to begin a four-game series against Memphis, the start of five games in three days. The home games, numbers nine through twelve at the local field, were back-to-back doubleheaders with Manager Ted "Double Duty" Radcliffe's sizzling-hot Red Sox furnishing the opposition. In addition to being the longest homestay of the entire 1938 season, the series would also decide the league's first-half pennant. The July 4 games were part of a day-night doubleheader, the first game starting at 3:00 p.m., the second convening later that night at 8:00 p.m. Memphis had played gilt-edged ball all season. It was obvious that this was one of the best teams Memphis had ever assembled. "That 1938 team was as good as any I've ever seen," recalled Bubba Hyde, a member of the Red Sox squad.[308] They were winning with a regularity that was getting everyone's attention.

Following a 9-1 loss to the American Giants on May 21, Radcliffe's Red Sox quickly corrected themselves and disposed of the Giants 2-0 in each game of a two-game Sunday set on May 23. This proved to be the spark the Memphis club needed. They wouldn't lose another Negro American League contest until June 20, when the Black Barons squeaked out a 9-8 extra-inning win. Memphis compiled an enviable record of winning thirteen consecutive Sunday league games. Andy Cooper's red-hot Monarchs were winning just as often. They were nipping at the Red Sox's heels from the very start. This was very evident when both teams reached Kansas City, locked in a dead heat for the first-half pennant. To capture the pennant, Memphis needed two wins, the Monarchs three.

Kansas City won the July 3 opener by an 11-10 score in extra innings. Four Monarch pitchers labored through eleven innings to preserve the win. Smith began with his share of ineffectiveness and lasted a mere three and one-third innings. He retired after issuing eight hits and four runs. Floyd

Kranson followed with similarly poor results. Kranson lasted four and one-third innings surrendering four hits and three runs. Manager Andy Cooper, making his first mound appearance at Ruppert Stadium in 1938, was equally unproductive, yielding three hits, a wild pitch, and three runs in one-third of an inning. There were also lots of substitutions among Monarch batters. It was a game of checkers played like a chess match.

Marlin Theodore Carter and Olan "Jelly" Taylor. By age twenty-five, Carter had gone from team after team before reaching Memphis for the second time in 1938. Along the way, he had performed for the Shreveport Sports in 1931, the Monroe, Monarchs in 1932, and the 1933-1934 Memphis Red Sox. (Authors collection)

Harry Else pinch-hit for Mayweather in the eighth and reached safely as a hit batsman. Rogan, pinch-hitting for manager Cooper, intensified the rally with a run-scoring single. Kansas City was down by four runs. They scored additional runs on safeties by Milton, Cox, Brown, and O'Neil to tie the score at ten. In the Monarch eleventh, O'Neil reached safely on a Memphis error and scored the game's deciding run on singles by Duncan and Johnson. In the second game, loose fielding cost the Monarchs dearly in a 7-to-3 defeat. Barnes, Kansas City's starter, was momentarily blessed by Willard Brown's home run and a fleeting lead that quickly disappeared. By the sixth inning, the score was tied. Neil Robinson doubled to open the Memphis half of the frame. Ted Radcliffe followed with a walk, and Manager Andy Cooper called for a pitching change.

Enter Buster Markham as a reliever for Barnes. The first batter he faced, Zearlee Maxwell, flew a ball into right-center field. As Brown and Mayweather converged at top speed, neither called the other off, and neither saw the other coming. Slamming at full tilt, they collided with the forceful impact of two heavyweight contenders baring a knockout punch. Both were knocked unconscious, and before the side retired, four runs had tallied. With that collision, all hopes of winning the first-half pennant went out the window. It would take weeks for both men to fully recover from their injuries. Eugene Bremer disposed of Kansas City in the seventh to safeguard the Memphis victory.

With their victory in game two, Memphis ended Kansas City's record of eight consecutive wins at Ruppert Stadium and clinched a tie for the first-half title. For game three, Memphis paraded out a group of star players, and yet none stood more prominently than outfielder Nat Rogers.

William "Nat" Rogers, born June 7, 1893, in Spartanburg, South Carolina, was sort of a sports missing link. At age forty-four, playing in what others would have called the twilight of a long career, Rogers showed few obvious signs of aging though he was the oldest everyday player in the Negro American League. Rogers' career commingled the hard and glorious past of the 1920s with the optimism and hope of the 1940s rolled into one welterweight frame. Tipping the scales at a frivolous 150 pounds, he had performed for the American Giants and Kansas City Monarchs before 1938. In his recollection, which spanned several decades, Rogers played forty-five consecutive seasons without missing a year. His obscure baseball path started in 1911 and veered into the legacy of such long-forgotten teams as the Cincinnati Colored Browns, Williams' Giants, the Detroit Creamery, and the Illinois Giants.

On July 4, in the opening game of the second doubleheader, Kansas City Manager Andy Cooper utilized four pitchers, without success, to capture the series. Mayweather, still injured from his prior day's collision with Brown, did not appear in the game.

Smith, Jackson, Kranson, and Barnes proved ineffective to stop Memphis from scoring. Willie Jackson, the losing pitcher, lasted just two and one-third innings, during which time he surrendered six hits and allowed five runs. Memphis used two former Monarchs as pitchers, Bob Madison and Woodrow Wilson to subdue Kansas City. Madison was with the Monarchs in 1937, while Wilson, a native of Mexia, Texas, was a member of the Monarchs 1936 squad. He was the Negro American League's only left-handed submarine pitcher. Porter Moss, the league's premier right-handed submarine hurler, was also a member of the Memphis Red Sox. Wilson won his game at Kansas City, although it took a valiant effort to contain the nucleus of the Monarchs' potent lineup.

Allen with three hits, Cox, Brown, and Rogan with two, and O'Neil with one, accounted for all ten of Kansas City's hits in the losing effort. The remaining eight Monarchs on the scorecard proved inept. Neil Robinson, by contrast, sparked the Red Sox offensive effort, collecting three extra-base hits. Going 3-for-3, with a trio of runs scored, Robinson doubled twice and tripled.

Cornelius Randall "Neil" Robinson was an outstanding athlete who excelled at baseball and basketball. Abe Saperstein, the owner of the Harlem Globe Trotters basketball team, repeatedly tried to sign Robinson without success.[309] Around the league, players raved about his jaw-dropping power at the plate. Marlin Carter jokingly recalled, "Robinson hit one ball so hard and far that the owner of the field changed the name of the park from West End Park to Neil Robinson Park."[310] Cowan Hyde remembered, "Neil Robinson [as having] lived for a while in Gary, Indiana, although being born July 7, 1908, in Grand Rapids, Michigan."[311] Robinson came to Cincinnati in 1935, directly from Grand Rapids. "He played mostly in the outfield with the Cincinnati Tigers but was also a capable shortstop," touted Radcliffe.[312] Carter recalled, Robinson didn't hit many home runs in Cincinnati, "I betcha Neil he didn't hit two home runs in three years. He hit lots of doubles and triples. Then he came here [Memphis] in 1938. He must have hit 38 to 40 home runs right here, but he couldn't hit the home run in Cincinnati."[313] As one of the best players in the Negro American League, from 1938 to 1945, Robinson started in five of eight East-West games, including four straight from 1938 to 1941. He made it back to the East-West game in 1948 as the starting left fielder. Robinson dominated in those games, hitting .476, second only to Josh Gibson's .483. Robinson's lifetime .810 slugging percentage was second only to 'Mule' Suttles [in East-West play].[314] It was evident that Robinson's distance hitting was as important to Memphis as Willard Brown's was to Kansas City.

As a result, Kansas City, unable to receive more than an even break in the doubleheader, allowed Memphis to clinch the first-half pennant. Memphis Red Sox won the game 12-5. Memphis captured the Negro American League's first-half pennant with a winning percentage of .840 and posted a record of 21-4 to eliminate the Monarchs. Kansas City finished with 19 wins, 5 losses, and a winning percentage of .792. The ABCs with a .500 winning percentage, and a record of 6 wins against 6 losses, finished a distant third.

Although the pennant had slipped from their grasp, Kansas City was captivating in the nightcap's game two, winning by a 2-to-1 score. Dick Bradley's three-hitter overshadowed Memphis' Clifford Allen's five-hitter. A wild pitch in the eighth gave Memphis its only run.

While Brown and Mayweather recuperated from their injuries, the Monarchs resumed exhibition play approximately 130 miles away. On July 5, both players were missing from the Monarch lineup when the team reached Manhattan, Kansas, where members of the Chastains, a local Ban Johnson League team, anticipated their arrival. Adjusting for the missing outfielders, left fielder Milton shifted into center field, Rogan into left, and pitchers Markham and Smith patrolled right field.

Imported pitchers failed to give Manhattan enough momentum to match Kansas City's superior strength on the field. Ed Klimek, former Kansas State four-sport star, started and fared well until the fifth inning when Monarch batsmen collected five hits, one a home run by Milton, and scored four runs. Junior Purdy, who came on as Klimek's relief, held Monarchs batters to a lone single for a time, though he was cranked for four hits which accounted for five runs in the seventh.[315]

Even without the heavy hitting of Mayweather and Brown, Monarch batters rang out sixteen hits. Likewise, Cox and Allen finished with a trio of safe blows each. Milton, Else, and pitcher Willie "Big Train" Jackson banged out two hits each. Jackson, who issued ten hits, and struck out eight batters, was the Monarchs winning pitcher. Having whipped the Chastains 10-to-3, the Monarchs returned to the bus for another 250-mile swing into Oklahoma, where Enid's Eason Oilers were earnestly preparing for their arrival. Traveling rigorously across Oklahoma's barren prairie, a land broken and neglected, the Monarchs watched feebly as the landscape outside the window was transposed into a well-worn dust bowl. They were seeing lots of America but rarely were they in these towns longer than three or four hours. They had a routine. Arrive, stretch, play ball, wash up at the YMCA or a local school, change clothes, grab a sandwich with a soda, and board the bus for more travel. As they traveled across the Plains that were once inhabited by North American Indians, Monarchs' players experienced the Dust Bowl firsthand.

An unusually wet period, which increased settlement and cultivation in the Great Plains, ended rather abruptly in 1930 with a severe drought. Crops failed, leaving plowed fields exposed to wind erosion as topsoil was carried away by robust eastern windstorms. With their land stripped and barren, their homes seized in foreclosure, dirt-poor farmers were forced to leave the prairie states in record numbers. Migrants left farms in Kansas, Texas, and New Mexico, but all were generally referred to as "Okies." By 1940, two and one-half million people had moved out of the Great Plains; and of those numbers, 200,000 moved to California. The plight of "Dust Bowl" migrants was featured in John Steinbeck's 1939 novel *The Grapes of Wrath*.[316] Enid Oklahoma, because of its dependence on oil, remained an annual stop on the Monarch summer schedule.

On July 6, Oklahoma's Eason Oilers dropped a 13-5 contest to Kansas City at Easton Park. Monarch batters stung Eason's Gene Ledford for two second inning runs, succumbing to a steady barrage of base hits -- a lead which was never relinquished.

Rogan returned to left field, and Barnes, a pitcher, was slotted into right in an attempt to patch up Kansas City's lineup. The defensive shift never affected the offense as Byron Johnson and Hilton Smith slammed back-to-back second-inning home runs. The Monarchs added two important runs in the third on three hits, one a double by Rogan. In the seventh and eighth, Kansas City burst the game wide open. Five runs in those innings contributed to Kansas City's already top-heavy score.[317]

Both Smith and Markham pitched portions of the Enid game, but Smith, having struck out seven, received the win. At-bat, O'Neil, and Milton both registered a trio of hits--but Byron Johnson was hitting well also. In six games, four against Memphis, one at Manhattan, and one at Enid-- shortstop Byron "Mex" Johnson was batting .454 (10-for-22) with five runs scored. Without a moment's delay, the Monarchs were boarding their team bus in preparation for another one of those hundred-mile excursions to Oklahoma City. Kansas City caught up with the Birmingham team at Oklahoma City's Holland Field, where they were to start second-half league play. In the opening event of what was to be a four-game barnstorming series, Kansas City captured a 3-0 win.

Meeting in a Thursday evening league encounter, local promoters were forced to curtail the well-publicized event in the wake of rain and mud, playing five and a half innings before it became unbearable. Bradley pitched a hitless ball game over the short route while his teammates garnered three hits off Birmingham's Jack Burton. An error by David Whatley, which allowed Bryon Johnson to reach third base, and an outfield fly gave the Monarchs a run in their half of inning two. Milton's triple, along with an infield hit, and an error by DeWitt Owens, accounted for a pair of Monarch runs in the third and an eventual 3-0 victory.

As the series moved east, the Monarchs and Barons played a Friday twilight event in Kansas at Manhattan's Griffith Field. The field was situated at Fort Riley and South Manhattan streets and had been dedicated in 1936. Surrounded by 8-foot walls of stone, it looked more like a Federal Prison than a ballpark from far off. Kansas City won that July 8 game by a 12-3 score before a crowd of roughly eight hundred people, as batters on both teams struck out a collective twenty-seven times.

Combining for nineteen strikeouts, "lefty" Mose and Barnes tossed darts that went for bullseyes all evening. Mose started for Kansas City and struck out six in three innings, issuing two hits. Barnes, Mose's relief, whiffed thirteen additional batters and gave up six hits. Barnes's thirteen strikeouts were the second most for a Monarchs pitcher in 1938.[318] Birmingham's Clifford Blackman struck out nine and held Monarchs' batters to seven hits in the loss. Manager Andy Cooper was waving his scorecard from the dugout throughout the evening in an attempt to find ways for his team to capitalize on the Barons' mistakes. Blackman caught his attention. His performance left a lasting impression on the Monarch's manager, who sought to acquire Blackman for postseason play.

As the southerners from Birmingham motored around the mid-west and toward Kansas City, racial mayhem was breaking out in the Southern city of Cordele, Georgia, where a sixty-year-old African American named John Dukes was hung and his corpse set afire by a mob of angry citizens. The stench of Dukes' burning flesh should have rattled the crowd, but having already accomplished their distasteful deed, they watched undisturbed. Alarmed and with a conscience and sensitivity against lynching, African American leadership responded quickly, as Duke's murder had come amid an otherwise calm year. There were three Southern teams in the Negro American League, and therefore, anything that occurred in the Southern states, especially racial activities, caught the ball player's attention.

President Franklin D. Roosevelt received a letter from Tuskegee Institute's President F. D. Patterson, spelling out the historical details of lynching in America. "I find according to the records compiled at Tuskegee Institute in the Department of Records and Research, that there was not one lynching in the first six months of 1938," Patterson noted, then he added, "This is the first time since a record of lynchings has been kept that the first six months of the year went by without a lynching."[319]

Six months without a lynching--a fact hardly worth celebrating--provided a glimpse of hope for a bigoted America grappling with restraining the oppression of its African American citizens. For fifty years, the number of national people lynched occurring every ten years was smaller than the number that occurred in the preceding ten years--but one lynching of an American citizen was still too many. Entangled in the web of violence, African American athletes were forced to play in an unforgiving foreground of racial hate as Americans unleashed a reign of paranoia in communities all over the nation. By contrast, the lynching of African Americans in most decades far outpaced the number of wins achieved by Negro baseball's most outstanding teams. The number of wins by these great teams symbolized the disparity of the problem.

During the Cuban Giants' ten-year reign, ending in 1896, there were roughly 1,035 African Americans lynched, a number that far exceeded Cuban Giant wins as one of America's greatest baseball attractions. Throughout the Philadelphia Giants championship run, 1897-1906, there were approximately 884 people lynched. From 1902 to 1906, Philadelphia Giant wins exceeded a phenomenal 500 games, 384 less than the number of people lynched in almost the same number of years. In the period which covered O'Neil's boyhood, public lynching declined to 608 in the ten years from 1907 to 1916 to 419 during the next ten years, 1917 to 1926, and finally to 136 in the ten years ending with 1936, when O'Neil joined the Acme Giants. In all, a total of 3,082 African Americans were recorded as lynch victims by the records kept to 1936. Most often, articles involving a lynching were not covered with any demand to arrest the lawbreakers who executed the capital punishment or with much human compassion in daily newspapers although, minority newspapers were making the stories prominent with front-page headlines. In addition, this does not cover the numbers of African Americans that were shot and killed in cities all over America for reasons related to race. Judson W. Lyons of Georgia, the first African American licensed to practice law in the state, was quoted as saying, "It is as much murder for a mob of 500 men to take a life as was the crime that provoked their action."[320]

The fall of 1938 was exceptionally bloody. In Ruston, Louisiana, W. C. Williams, a nineteen-year-old African American, was lynched by a mob of several hundred men. Williams, captured by a posse at the home of his mother, was reportedly tortured with a hot poker before he was strung up to a tree, and his body riddled with bullets. In Wiggins, Mississippi, Wilder McGowan, a 24-year-old African American, was also lynched. The angry mob, which grew from eight men in the early morning hours to about two hundred at daybreak, captured McGowan and hung him from a tree beside a highway. McGowan's lynching was the second recorded in Wiggins within four years and the sixth in the South during 1938. McGowan and Williams were accused of robbery; Dukes reportedly shot an officer of the law.[8] They never received a trial, and no one was prosecuted for their murders. Such inhumane treatment continued to be more fact than fiction, and a constant reminder of the terror one might experience as they traveled America's highways and rural roads. And, as veterans of the highways, Monarch players were well-aware of Missouri's infamous tradition of lynching. "Between 1900 and 1931, mobs in the state lynched twenty-two men, seventeen of whom were black."[321] Most assuredly, traveling athletes were conscious of their surroundings in both the North and in the South. O'Neil offered,

> We would have more problems North, I believe, than South. Because South was
>
> this, you knew what you had to do. They had good black hotels; they had good
>
> black restaurants in the South. But when you passed the Mason-Dixon Line, now

---

[8] A photograph of Williams' lynching can be seen on the website
http://www.withoutsanctuary.org/main.html Williams.

you're getting into places where you didn't have it. Now we wouldn't go in a white restaurant in Atlanta, but we might just go in a white restaurant when we got to Washington, and the guy wouldn't serve you.[322]

The Black Barons' two-game set at Ruppert Stadium, which began on July 10, were home games thirteen and fourteen on the Monarchs' 1938 schedule. Those players--Parnell Woods, David Whatley, Harry Barnes, Dewitt Owens, Jack Burton, and "Nish" Williams--who were with the Barons in 1937, hoped that Willard Brown would remain on the injured list. During a 1937 doubleheader at Ruppert Stadium, Brown slammed three home runs against Birmingham.[323] With Willard Brown's return to the lineup, Kansas City settled for a 9-1 and 5-2 split of the double-bill. A small crowd of two thousand fans howled as Brown continued to torment Birmingham's best pitchers.

In Kansas City's doubleheader opener, Birmingham was unable to get a hit off Mose until the sixth, when the southern batters connected for two safeties to log their only run. Mose started the seventh by walking two batters before being replaced by Markham, who retired the side on two strikeouts and a fly-out to the outfield. By contrast, the Monarchs chased Birmingham's pitcher in the first frame.

Osley, the Birmingham hurler, pitched to three batters in the first and surrendered a hit and two runs before being yanked by manager Dismukes. A new pitcher named Oatman, Osley's replacement, allowed ten hits and seven runs over the next eight innings. Willard Brown's home run, triple, and single in four trips to the plate highlighted his return to the Monarchs' lineup

During game two, Jack Burton, pitching in near perfection, held Monarchs batters to four hits; two of them--a single and a double--were registered by outfielder Henry Milton. For Kansas

City, Willie Jackson and Dick Bradley worked the nightcap, with Jackson taking the loss. Kansas City scored their only runs in the seventh when O'Neil singled, stole second, and advanced home on two infield outs. Birmingham outscored the Monarchs 5-to-2 for the win.

Gaining a split of the doubleheader, Kansas City's record at Ruppert Stadium went to ten wins and four losses. At their home field, Monarchs' base runners outpaced their opposition seventy-seven to forty-seven, a thirty-run difference. After July 10, in light of the league's sagging attendance, the Black Barons failed to make a return trip to Kansas City. Attendance totals weren't much better in Alabama. As one of the Deep South's last strongholds on Jim Crow, city officials in Birmingham shamelessly banned African Americans from playing baseball and football with or against whites. The city also enacted similar laws against the mixed competition in softball, basketball, and such parlor games as cards, dice, dominoes, and checkers.[324]

As the teams collected their gear and dressed for the road, Wilkinson had the public address operator announce Frank Duncan's trade to the American Giants for a player, or players to be named later. Duncan joined the American Giants on July 12 in St. Paul, Minnesota, where the Monarchs and Giants were scheduled to start a fourteen-day caravan of the upper Midwest and Canada. Gone for the moment was the face of the familiar grinning Monarchs catcher.

While waiting for Johnny Dawson, a new catcher, to arrive, Wilkinson worked an agreement with H. G. Hall to borrow American Giants' receiver Ernie Smith. Harry Else was retained as the Monarchs' reserve catcher. Else, after starting 1938 with the Chicago Palmer House Hotel semi-professional team, he was re-signed in Milwaukee on June 28. The newly acquired catcher was born in 1904 in Terrell, Texas. His parents Elmo and Elby Else lived on West End Street, where Harry had grown up around many relatives. The last name Else was fairly common in his community. Harry broke into big-time baseball in 1930 with the Dallas Black Giants of the Texas Oklahoma

Louisiana League. He was behind the plate in 1930 when the Kansas City Monarchs defeated his team in the first-ever night baseball games in Dallas, a game that drew 7,000 fans.[325] He moved to the Monroe Louisiana Monarchs of the Negro Southern League for the 1932 through 1935 seasons and came to the Kansas City Monarchs with former teammates Willard Brown, Eldridge Mayweather, Floyd Kranson, and Bob Madison. Else was behind the plate when the Monarchs played the Sioux City Cowboys of the Nebraska State League on July 11, in Sioux City, Iowa. The game was attended by what the *Sioux City Journal* called "Probably the largest [crowd] of the season."[326] Among the interest parties in attendance were Heinie Groh, a scout and former member of the New York Giants, and Bill Essick, a scout for the New York Yankees. Managed by Pete Monahan, the Cowboys were on their way to capturing the league pennant.

Kansas City arrived in Sioux City with one handicap. Mayweather was not active. In his absence, a recruit named Betts was picked up to cover the right field. There was a big build-up before the Monarchs' arrival where a league game against Sioux Falls had been postponed and moved to a later day to squeeze Kansas City into the schedule. The newspaper advised,

> Tonight's assignment is particularly difficult since there really is a great difference
>
> between the caliber of the ball in the Negro National Leagues, a major circuit,
>
> and in the class D Nebraska league. A defeat for the Cowboys then would not be
>
> any disgrace, while a victory--no remote possibility--would be quite an
>
> achievement.[327]

On this night, they faced a troublesome foe in the Kansas City Monarchs and were bumped in a tight 3-1 pitchers' battle. Sioux City showed great effort and took an early lead. In the fourth, John Schinski and Pete Monahan had back-to-back singles. Doug White struck out. Barnes became rattled and balked, which allowed Schinski and Monahan to advance a base. Jay Russell walked to load the bases with one out. Ken Meyer laced a clutch single to center, scoring Schinski to give the Cowboys a one-run lead. In the sixth, Milton doubled and was eventually brought home on a sacrifice bunt and a sacrifice fly to tie the game at 1-1. The Monarchs were not to be denied. They took the lead and never looked back.

Milton led off with a single to center and promptly stole second base. Cox followed with a sacrifice bunt, but the infielder covering first on the play missed Larson's toss allowing the ball to roll to the dugout as Milton scurried across the plate with the tie-breaking run. Allen followed with a single, and Cox advanced to third. Allen stole second. Larson was caught daydreaming when Allen and Cox staged a double steal with Cox sliding across home plate on a play that wasn't even close. The two runs that won the ball game were unearned.

Cowboy batters outhit the Monarchs, six to four, but they couldn't stop the Kansas City base runners on the path. Milton, Cox, Brown, Else, and Allen, with two, stole a total of six bases while Sioux City logged none. If the Monarchs had less than six or seven hits, you could be reasonably assured that one or two of those hits belonged to Henry Milton, who had a pair of hits in this game. O'Neil went 0-for-3 against a trio of Sioux City pitchers: Rueben Fischer, a 21-game winner in 1938 who would appear in two games for the National League Giants in 1945; Bud Lawson, a University of Illinois pitcher who went 8-4 in 1938, and Brosamle, first name unknown. When Merrill Burnette penned his article about the game's best plays, O'Neil's name was mentioned twice,

> Two Cowboys came up with brilliant fielding plays, White going far to his right
> to spear O'Neil's smash in the fourth and Meyer making a fine leaping catch of
> O'Neil's liner in the sixth.[328]

The trade that sent Frank Duncan back to Chicago was another illustrious stop for the well-traveled Monarch receiver. When Duncan joined the Monarchs in 1921, there was much rejoicing as the Kansas City *Sun* announced a major trade with Joe Green's Chicago Giants. The two-for-one trade sent Monarchs' first baseman Lemuel Hawkins and catcher Otto "Jay Bird" Ray to Green's Giants in the exchange.[329] Duncan needed little introduction to local fans because Kansas City was his hometown. His father, also named Frank Duncan, was a well-known salesman of coal and block ice in the central city.[330] Duncan, the son, was born in Kansas City, Missouri, on February 14, 1901. He attended Attucks Elementary and Lincoln High School. At age eighteen, Duncan married Julia M. Lee, the younger sister of George Lee, leader of Kansas City's famous George E. Lee Jazz Orchestra. Julia, age seventeen at the time of her marriage to Frank, was well on her way to becoming a Capitol Record recording artist.[331] Duncan was among baseball's best catchers. And, while not known as an exceptional hitter, he was an excellent receiver with an accurate and powerful arm. O'Neil insisted,

> Frank could really catch and throw--a shotgun arm, and a great memory. Before
>
> Frank died, he would talk about a ballgame; he would tell you the inning, the
>
> pitch the guy hit, and how the score ended. He had a wonderful memory.[332]

Julian Bell, who played with the Memphis Red Sox, Birmingham Black Barons, and Detroit Stars in the 1920s, liked to compare Duncan to Larry Brown. "Duncan and Brown were about equal in catching ability, but Frank was more popular," he admitted before adding, "Brown was a better catcher."[333] According to the Altoona, Pennsylvania *Mirror* newspaper, "Duncan, a world traveler, "[had] played baseball in 15 countries in addition to the United States."[334] Canada, one of the countries he visited, had several stops on the upcoming fourteen-day caravan. This time, however, the legendary Monarch would be wearing an American Giants' uniform.

John "Buck" O'Neil. *"When I got to the Monarchs," stated O'Neil, "That was just like going to the Yankees for a White boy." (Wilborn & Associates collection)*

"There is little that can be added to the record of the Monarchs for this is their eighteenth tour of the West, and without exception, they have always turned up with a fine club featuring such star players as Newt Allen, Johnny O'Neil, and others."

The Estevan Saskatchewan Mercury, July 21, 1938

Buck O'Neil *says...*

"In those days, the women made their own hats. The reason for this is at the department stores, at Woolf Brothers if you were black, you could look at a hat, but if you tried it on, you had to buy it. Well, women started making their own hats, and they would wear them to the ballpark. They were the prettiest things you ever saw."

Into Minnesota And Beyond

July 12-St. Paul, July 13-Fargo, July 14-Crookston, July 15-Winnipeg, July 16-Winnipeg (DH), July 18-Winnipeg, July 19-Portege La Prairie, July 20-Brandon (DH), July 21-Regina, July 22-Regina, July 23-Estevan, July 24-Bismarck (DH), July 25-Fargo, July-28 Des Moines, July 29-Kansas City, July 31-Chicago (DH)

(NAL) O'Neil's Batting: G-11 AB-43 R-1 H-13 2B-1 3B-0 HR-2 SB-0 RBI-1 BA-3.02

O'Neil's Fielding: PO-110 A-4 E-2 DP-2 TC-116

In preparation for the Monarchs 300-mile jaunt from Sioux City to St. Paul, the team settled in for what was now a fairly routine overnight ride without hotel lodging. The American Giants had also consented to embark on the Northern excursion with them. In so doing, the teams commemorated, for the first time, regional play in the upper-mid-west between rival Negro American League opponents as a truly ritual barnstorming experience. Kansas City had played in the Northern region many times before 1938; although Chicago had not, both teams were well primed for such an activity. As road warriors of the unordinary kind, few teams had as many good pitchers as the Monarchs or American Giants. They were well-stocked for rigorous barnstorming. Not including himself, Cooper brought seven pitchers on tour. The American Giants, with six pitchers, weren't pitching-rich like the Monarchs, but they certainly had the hitters, all of whom would be on tour, except for Norman "Turkey" Stearnes Mayweather, one of the Monarchs' best hitters, was unable to take the tour because of his injuries.

Hilton Smith and Family. *In 1937 Smith earned the name "No-Hit" Smith, by tossing a 4-0 no-hitter over the Chicago American Giants in Kansas City. (Authors collection)*

Manager Taylor, a most powerful leader in a gentle way, was eager to capture the barnstorming series. It resulted in him choosing to use Cooper's strategy of shuffling and rotating pitchers to beat the Monarchs' manager with his own unique strategy. Taylor made his feelings known in a statement to the media,

> Other managers have told us we were foolish to make a trip of this kind, but these
>
> two teams seem to be the real contenders, and we thought we might as well bunch
>
> the rest of our games together into one tour and get it over with.[335]

Taylor's strategy was to throw "Sug" Cornelius, Ted Trent, Bill Johnson, Johnny Reid, or Jess Houston on one or two-days rest throughout the series. Buck watched and took mental notes as the two crafty managers strategized on how to beat the other. He was learning valuable lessons for the future when he would become a manager himself.

The Minnesota and North Dakota portion of the traveling series opened July 12, on a Tuesday evening at St. Paul, Minnesota, where numerous runs were scored, a total of 21 combined. Kansas City went to work on three American Giants pitchers: Houston, Reid, and Johnson. Johnson, a new addition, had come to the Giants from St. Louis. Kansas City eventually trounced the American Giants in an 18-3 final.

Monarch batters took delight in visiting Lexington Park, the home field of the American Association St. Paul Saints. They certainly enjoyed themselves and rewarded fans with a tremendous offensive attack. Roosevelt Cox laced a pair of homers, a triple, and drove in six runs to lead his team to victory. All totaled, three Monarchs: Cox, Newt Allen, and Willard Brown collected four hits each. O'Neil finished with three hits. Catcher Ernie Smith, a new addition to the Monarchs, inaugurated the occasion by obtaining five hits which included two triples. The former Bastrop, a

Louisiana native, was on loan to the Monarchs from the American Giants. Kansas City was seeking a catcher and another left-handed hitter when they signed Smith, a catcher who threw from the right but batted on the left.[336] It was all Monarchs from the opening pitch because of Hilton Smith's complete game hurling.

Smith held American Giant batters to seven hits and struck out five. Alex Radcliffe, with three hits, was his most troublesome foe. Alex, the younger brother of Memphis' manager Ted Radcliffe, was a perennial All-Star pick and a marvelous hitter. He participated in eleven East-West games and appeared for a final time in 1946. Apparently, very little of the Monarchs' momentum was saved for the next game in Fargo.

On July 13, Kansas City was edged in a close 4-3 game at Fargo, North Dakota. It was an exciting exhibition of America's national pastime as 3,000 people paid their way into Barnett Field to watch a true night game that started at the late hour of 9:00 p.m.[337] Cornelius, the American Giants' ace, provided all the excitement on this night when he struck out thirteen Kansas City batters. He started horribly, yielding multiple runs in the first and second innings before settling down to pitch-winning baseball. He allowed three scattered hits for the remainder of the game while his teammates staged a comeback from their 3-0 deficit. John "Buster" Markham, who was credited with the loss, entered the contest as a reliever for Dick Bradley after the sixth inning.[338] The American Giants had tied the series at one-all as the teams headed to Crookston, Minnesota, for game three. The build-up for the Monarchs and American Giants in the Minnesota town of 7,000 residents was occurring daily.

Publication of headlines like: *"Giants, One of Oldest Negro Team, Playing"*[339] and *"Colored Clubs Here Thursday for Loop Game"*[340] kept the town buzzing with baseball excitement before the Monarchs and American Giants' arrival. "The teams rested here today, noted the *Crookston Daily*

Times, "after a short jaunt from Fargo and were in the best of condition."[341] A capacity crowd of 2,000 people was present at game time.

(L to R) William "Sug" Cornelius and William "Nat" Rogers. *Cornelius, ace of the 1938 American Giants hurlers is shown here with Rogers who played for the Memphis Red Sox in 1938. (Authors collection)*

Spectators were in every available grandstand and bleacher seat by game time. They lined the foul lines down to the outfield and were rewarded with what the local newspaper called "a great array of stunts on the field."[342] Willie Jackson and "Lefty" Mose pitched in tough luck for Kansas City, with Mose taking credit for the 4-1 loss. Chicago touched them for eight hits. Johnson tossed a four-hit complete game for the American Giants. He walked two hitters and struck out six. At-bat, Johnson added a pair of hits. Because of the game's late start, 9:00 p.m., the teams boarded the bus around midnight for further overnight travel and more sleeping on the bus. The distance measured as miles in America became kilometers as both teams crossed the international border into Canada for four games in the Canadian Province of Manitoba at Winnipeg's Osborn Stadium.

Up to this point in the tour, all the scheduled games were well attended, and the strategies used by both managers were many. Three games had been played, and three pitchers had thrown complete games: Smith for Kansas City, Cornelius, and Johnson for Chicago. O'Neil was sporting a modest three-game hitting streak. That's where the gut-wrenching truth about Negro League play, and oppression ended the observation. The Monarchs' history of drawing large crowds in Winnipeg, coupled with the fact that they had not visited Winnipeg in 1937, should have increased anticipation of their arrival and enhanced their overall coverage, but many aspects of the games were not written, and fans found it difficult to follow the results. No box scores would be printed for the four games at Winnipeg, and only one of O'Neil's hits was recorded in print.

Since their initial stop in 1932, Monarchs' teams had played more than nineteen games in Winnipeg. Available records indicated they won sixteen while losing three. Facing an array of illustrious foes, Kansas City had defeated the St. Paul All-Stars, Grover Cleveland Alexander's House of David, and Bismarck's National Baseball Congress champions of 1935, which featured Satchel Paige in prior exhibitions. As one of the best sporting attractions on the barnstorming trail, the Monarchs drew twenty thousand Winnipeg fans to a four-game series in 1933.[9] In reaching

---

[9] The Monarchs played a four-game series in Winnipeg against Grover Cleveland Alexander's House of David on August 10 – 12, 1933, in front of a combined 20,000 people.

Winnipeg in 1938, local fans received their earliest glimpse at rival Negro American League opponents in actual games. O'Neil's return to Osborn Stadium conjured up memories of a game he had played there two years before.

In 1936, while performing for Welch's Acme Giants, O'Neil recalled how a pitcher named Michael Schroeder, on the mound for the Winnipeg Pucksters, whiffed seventeen of his teammates in a single game. Held to four hits, the tourniquet was applied in the form of a "lights out" rule at Osborne Stadium, a rule used to stop sports attractions from being played on Sundays. The game was halted at midnight after eleven innings had been played, with the score tied at 8-8 when local regulation seeped in the results.

Naturally, O'Neil wanted vengeance for that disappointing showing; however, Kansas City opened with a loss as a crowd of 2,000 watched. Leading by a 5-1 score headed into the seventh, Cooper made the grave mistake of having Barnes enter the fray to pitch to Alex Radcliffe with American Giants standing on all three bases. Monarchs in the field and on the bench watched as helplessly as any fan in the bleachers as Barnes' first pitch was hit to the base of the scoreboard in deep center field. The lead vanished as Radcliffe circled the bases. It was a grand slam that started a Chicago rally. The next two Giants also singled off Barnes. Bradley was rushed to his rescue, his teammate but had little success. Four pitchers were used, Cooper, Barnes, Bradley, and Mose, to halt the Chicago onslaught. The American Giants countered with three of their own: Trent, Reid, and Johnson in gaining an 8-6 win in the Friday, July 15 opener.[343] It was a strategically played game. Seven pitchers, three pinch-hitters, and a pinch-runner saw action on that night. Young, Radcliffe, and Bibbs each had a pair of hits for Chicago. Six of the Monarchs' 14 total hits were doubles, and one was a triple. The *Winnipeg Tribune* gave a glowing report the following day that noted,

[The] reaction of the big crowd to last night's exciting inaugural was so gratifying that the park management placed reserved tickets for today's two matches on sale immediately afterward.[344]

Kansas City landed two victories in the Saturday, July 16 day and night doubleheader, winning by a 13-10 score in the opener and 10-4 score later that evening. Markham, Bradley, and Smith pitched for Kansas City in Saturday's opener, while Thornton, Reid, and Johnson pitched for Chicago. Kansas City got the better of the hitting when they rattled Osborne stadium for fifteen hits. Newt Allen's home runs into the center field bleachers with a mate aboard iced a five-run ninth and the win. Willie Simms raked Kansas City pitchers for three doubles while Young laced a pair of doubles and a triple for the American Giants.

In Saturday's nightcap, Chicago's Trent and Houston were pitted against a trio of Monarchs' pitchers in Bradley, Mose, and Smith. Kansas City took an early lead with runs in innings one and three. In the fifth, Chicago moved ahead by a single run. After scoring two in the bottom of the fifth, Kansas City kept going until they regained the lead in inning number six with four safe blows that included O'Neil's screaming triple that highlighted a four-run outburst and a Monarch victory. In their only mention of the Winnipeg game, the *Chicago Defender* noted, "Only 800 paid admissions came out for the afternoon game. The second game which was played at night drew 1,500 fans."[345]

Canadian Blue Laws--Sabbath day restrictions that prohibited professional baseball from being played on Sunday kept the teams idle.[10] The rest that came from a day off was much

_____

[10] Two games were scheduled at Brandon on July 20, 1938. No Brandon newspapers are available for July 21. Scores for these games have not been located.

appreciated. When rain washed out Monday's game, both teams jumped over to Portage la Prairie for their next encounter, fully rejuvenated after two days of rest.

Newton Henry Allen *The veteran infielder was in and out of the line-up often in 1938. A report in the Kansas City Call explained his absence by stating, "Allen, second baseman of the Kansas City Monarchs is in the hospital suffering from ulcers of the stomach." (Authors collection)*

Taylor's American Giants were winners at Portage la Prairie on July 19. Cornelius, in gaining yet another complete game, his second of the tour, never faltered in beating Floyd Kranson, who was making his first tour appearance for Kansas City. He was replaced by Mose, who dished up some lefty pitching to stop the opposition's scoring, but the damage was already done. The final score was 4 to 2 in Chicago's favor.[346] The next day the teams were scheduled for a day and night doubleheader in Brandon. There were lots of media leading up to the day of the big affair. On the day of the game, July 20, the *Brandon Daily Sun* reported,

> The sun came out today after overnight rains and promised ideal weather for this
>
> afternoon and evening's doubleheader between the Kansas City Monarchs and
>
> the Chicago American Giants.[347]

That's where the trail runs cold. No newspaper article has been found for the day after on July 21, which would have carried scores of the games. A later note reported in an Estevan newspaper said that the game played there was the second tie ending of the series. This implies that one of the games in Brandon may have ended in a tie. Not including the Brandon games, the series stood at three wins for each team. Overnight both teams traveled in the Province of Saskatchewan for a pair of games at Regina. The battles were inside Regina's Park de Young ball field, where games on July 21 and 22 were won 3-2 in ten innings and 4-3 in nine innings by the American Giants.

On their first day in Regina, Chicago scored on an error by shortstop Byron "Mex" Johnson that allowed Simms to scamper across for the American Giants' first run. Retaliating an inning later, a Monarch scored on Ted Trent's wild heave to first base. In the sixth, Chicago jumped in front when Duncan walked and romped home on a hit by Bibbs. Kansas City tied the score in the eighth when Milton drove Johnson across the plate with a long double into right field. That same inning, manager Cooper pulled Barnes, who was rolling along with a five-hitter and eleven strikeouts, for a pinch hitter. After that inning, Mose, who entered as Barnes' relief, stumbled upon the difficulty, and eventually handed the ball to Markham, who lost in extra innings.

The game was already into extra innings when Mose walked two runners to start the tenth. Markham, with little time to collect his thoughts, descended from the bench to the mound to rescue Mose. Edward "Pep" Young, up next, sacrificed to advance the base runners to second and third. Alex Radcliffe was purposely walked, loading the bases. Duncan came to bat, and Cooper instructed Markham to retire the former Monarchs' backstop regardless of the cost. Duncan upset Cooper's strategy by dumping the pellet over the left fielder's head to give Chicago a one-run edge and a 3-2 victory.[348] Mose was credited with the loss. Trent tossed all ten innings for the complete-game victory. The *Regina Leader-Post* offered, "Although Trent hurled a sparking game, it was Barnes who caught the [public's] eye. He had plenty on the ball and had a fast one that really was fast."[349]

On the final day of their Regina visit, the Monarchs took an early two-run lead in the bottom half of the third and added another in inning five. In the meantime, Kranson was breezing along through six innings until Young tripled. This, combined with a balk, an error, and two outs sandwiched between hits, led to Kranson's early exit. Bradley played the rescue role after Kranson's departure. In the ninth inning, Radcliffe singled and was sacrificed to second by Duncan. Bibbs singled, and Radcliffe was held on third. Cornelius followed with a double to the fence sending Radcliffe and Bibbs home for the 4-3 win. Chicago used two pitchers, Johnson, and Cornelius, to defeat the Monarchs, who used Kranson and Bradley on the mound. As a unit, Kansas City was slumping badly and losing the series.

In the two games at Regina, only Milton and Brown collected more than one hit. Kansas City's two catchers, Smith and Else, failed to make a creditable showing on offensive or defensive. They indexed a combined 1-for-11 showing at-bat, while American Giants base runners stole six bases. Dave Dryburgh's column in the *Regina Leader-Post* was quick to explain away Kansas City's misfortunes,

Pitcher Markham was told off about slipping one down the alley to a hitter like

Frank.... [the] Monarchs claim they're off-form because they lack a catcher (the

new receiver hasn't joined them yet), and Mayweather is still on the injured list....

Brown played, but this lad ranked as the greatest hitter in Negro baseball, wasn't

getting a hold of them... he was injured too and was on the sidelines for a while

after colliding with Mayweather in the field during a series with Memphis.[350]

Continuing the tour, an overnight drive from Regina to Estevan, Saskatchewan, consisted of

a 226-mile jaunt. In Estevan, the teams battled to a 3-3 tie game, the tour's second tie. Played at the

local fairgrounds, the arrival of two Negro American League clubs sparked front-page recognition.

The *Estevan Mercury* newspaper offered,

> [The] Monarchs turned up with a club capable of giving the same lively caliber
>
> of baseball that has characterized this outfit in their Western tours during the past
>
> several years. Chicago[s] Giants were right up to advance notices, for they were
>
> worthy opposition for the Monarchs, there being little to choose between the
>
> clubs on the field or at the bat.[11]

Leaving Estevan, Canada, both teams headed towards the border for a return to the United

States. They hurried past Minot to reach Bismarck for a July 24 twin-bill. Bismarck's festivities were

promoted by local sportsman Neil Churchill, proprietor of Corwin-Churchill Motors. Churchill had

sponsored Bismarck's 1935 team, winners of the National Baseball Congress tournament in

---

[11] No box score was located at Estevan. An article about the game started on page 1 and concluded on pages 6 and 7. Unfortunately pages 6 and 7 are missing from that date's bound editions of the publication.

Wichita, Kansas. For Hilton Smith, a member of the 1935 champions, it was a homecoming of sorts. The 1938 game was billed as "The first return of big-time baseball since Bismarck's famous semi-pro champions of 1935 disbanded."[351] In the widely publicized doubleheader, Monarch and American Giants batters did not disappoint the paying public. Both teams combined for ten home runs.

Taking the opener, Chicago outscored Kansas City 10-to-6. The Monarchs returned later that afternoon to win 10-to-8. Game one was won by Jess Houston with Monarchs' Hilton Smith losing. Game two's pitching victory was captured by I. V. Barnes with Ted Trent taking Chicago's loss. O'Neil, as the Monarchs' first baseman, finished the doubleheader with a 5-for-9 performance and two home runs—one circuit blast in each game. Ten home runs, three by Hilton Smith, two each by Wilson Redus and O'Neil, and one each by Ernie Smith, Frank Duncan, and Richard "Subby" Byas accounted for forty-four hits and thirty-four runs in the Bismarck doubleheader.

Kansas City shot to an early lead in game one, adding to their total in the third, when Ernie Smith and Hilton Smith both homered. Smith pitched well enough for three innings before suffering a reversal of form in the fourth when three runs scored. In the fifth, Smith fared no better, finally going to the outfield when successive batters touched him for doubles. Giants' batters, having already pushed across three in the fourth to tie, added one in the fifth to gain a 5-4 lead and clinched the victory with three in the sixth and one each in innings seven and eight.

Duplicating Kansas City's early jump, in game two, the American Giants moved into an early lead. The Giants' initial tally was a gift when three errors allowed Simms to gingerly around the bases. The Monarchs grabbed another lead in the third and added two additional runs in inning four when Hilton Smith pounded his third homer of the day. A Giants' run in inning six, and two in the seventh, tied the game at five-all. In inning eight, Kansas City scored five runs on four singles, a double, and a walk for the victory. Seemingly, Richard "Subby" Byas who accounted for one of Chicago's home runs, remained an unsung factor in his team's success.

Richard "Subby" Byas. *At Chicago's Wendell Phillips High School Byas, an academic all-American in the classroom was also a superb two-sport athlete. (Authors collection)*

Byas, the American Giants' catcher, was among the league's most intellectual thinkers. Born in Beaumont, Texas, his family later moved to Chicago, where he attended Wendell Phillips High School and achieved a very high score on an IQ. Examination.[352] Byas always loved baseball more than school. Listed among his many high school classmates was Earl Foster, son of the legendary Andrew "Rube" Foster. At Phillips, Byas, an academic all-American in the classroom, was a superb two sports athlete. He became the first African American to achieve all-city in both baseball and basketball. When his school played the 1927 city baseball championship at Chicago's Wrigley's Field, Byas may have been the first African American to ever grace the North Chicago big-league diamond. As one of the league's many switch hitters, Byas remained steady as a defensive and offensive standout, having joined the American Giants in 1931. He had also performed in the Negro National League with the Newark Dodgers.

With the Chicago American Giants leading the exhibition series in wins, the tour returned to Fargo, North Dakota. Prior to the game's start, Kansas City announced the signing of infielder Julius "Rainey" Bibbs as completion of the deal that sent catcher Frank Duncan to Chicago. Bibbs became the left-handed batter they were seeking. Bibbs joined the Monarchs, and Ernie Smith was returned to Chicago. The trade began to make sense when it was announced that Newt Allen was ill. When the team returned to Kansas City, Allen was admitted to the hospital due to "ulcers of the stomach" and would be out for an undetermined period.[353] Hilton Smith went the distance in that final game, yielding eight hits with eight batters struck out. Bill Johnson was Chicago's starter and the losing pitcher, despite Trent's one strong inning in relief.

Picking up two runs in the first and another in the second gave Kansas City an early lead. Chicago hobbled into the scoring column, making it 3-1 in inning four. Successive doubles by Bibbs and Milton netted Kansas City's fourth tally in the seventh. Chicago added another run in the ninth but fell short, losing 4-2. O'Neil continued his hot hand, getting two hits in four at-bats. Bibbs, playing in his inaugural Monarchs game, also hit safely.[354]

Though not as efficient as Allen in the infield, and few players were, Bibbs was more than adequate at-bat and a perfect leadoff man as well. A better hitter than Allen, it was Bibbs's fielding that made him a liability. In an August 22 game at Junction City, Kansas, a contest marred by thirteen combined errors, Bibbs chimed in with three of his team's eight miscues.

Switch-hitting Bibbs, a native of Henderson, Kentucky, the son of a waiter and the grandson of slaves, was a one-time member of the Cincinnati Tigers and a 1927 graduate of Terra Haute Indiana's Wiley High School. He had broken into professional ball with the Detroit Stars in 1933. He was also one of a select few in the Negro league who attended a predominantly white college. As a fullback on the varsity football team, and a varsity baseball infielder at Indiana State, it was noted in an edition of the 1935 yearbook that "State's versatile colored athlete plays all positions in the infield with ease, bats left-handed for a high percentage, and plays an all-around good brand of baseball."[355]

As one of the few African Americans on the school's athletics squads and one of the few members of his race in the conference, Bibbs' memories on Indiana State's gridiron were defined by several unpleasant events. "Many times, my own teammates would not block for me and got a kick from seeing me get hit." Bibbs continued,

> Once Evansville, the opposing team, did everything imaginable to me, and by the
> half, I was bleeding from both ears, beaten and bruised all over. Wally Marks,
> our coach, asked me if I wanted to play the second half. I told him the biggest lie
> ever--I said, 'Yes.[356]

While attending Indiana State, Roy Herndon, one of Bibb's white teammates on the college baseball team, was scouted and signed to a minor league contract. Herndon hit .266 in 100 games in 1935 for New Iberia in the class-D Evangeline League and never reached the American or National Leagues after eight seasons in the minors. By contrast, Bibbs, originally a first baseman, was switched to shortstop after Herndon's sudden departure. Bibbs made the transition and later jumped from collegiate play to the Negro American League and played brilliantly all along the way. His posthumous honors put him into the Indiana Baseball Hall of Fame and the Indiana State University Hall of Fame.

On July 28, both teams pulled into Des Moines, Iowa, where the American Giants gave a sparking exhibition of major league play when they captured an 11-4 victory over the Monarchs. That game's big hitter was Alex Radcliffe, who blasted a pair of triples and a double in four at-bats and scored two runs. All totaled, Chicago collected fourteen hits off Barnes, Jackson, Mose and, Markham Monarchs' pitchers. Barnes the starter, was declared the loser by allowing eight hits and eight runs in four and two-thirds innings. Kansas City picked up eight hits off Houston, who lasted just one and one-third innings, and Johnson, who finished, with Bibbs, Cox, and Else collecting a pair of hits each. O'Neil went 1-for-3 and scored one of Kansas City's four runs. The written account of the game in the *Des Moines Register* was informative as it listed Jess Houston, "Train" Jackson, and Mose with names attached. While the game was listed as an official Negro League contest, it was anything but official because Ernie Smith started in right field for the Monarchs, picking up one of the Monarchs' hits in four at-bats, then jumped over to the American Giants roster to finish the game as their right-fielder.[357]

The crowds who witnessed the Monarchs versus American Giants games during the Northern United States and Canadian tour were not encouraging. Painstakingly checking the tour's skewed ledger, the attendance results were not as disappointing for promoters. In Fargo, where the park was at capacity for two games, the teams drew 5,600 in paid attendance. A trio of games in

Winnipeg, Canada, drew 4,300. At Crookston, the teams played to a crowd of 2,000, which was that park's capacity. The same thing occurred in Regina when the teams played to an opening night crowd of 2,000. In Bismarck, 1,200 fans attended the scheduled doubleheader. A reported 1,500 fans saw the Des Moines game. All totaled, about 20,000 had paid to see the two prodigious Negro American major league major teams in action.

There were conflicting results in the reporting of the games played. Where results are located, the series ended with seven wins for the American Giants, six wins for the Monarchs, with one, possibly two, games ending in a tie. This does not include the missing results of the doubleheader at Brandon on July 20. In summarizing the thirteen-day barnstorming tour, the *Chicago Defender* announced,

> The Giants have been away from town for two weeks on a trip thru the northwest
>
> and Canada. There they have been successful, winning nine and losing five to the
>
> Monarchs, but these games were not league games.[358]

The teams resumed their Negro American League schedule with a single game in Kansas City on July 29 before heading on yet another meteoric drive to Chicago for a doubleheader there on July 31. At Kansas City's Ruppert Stadium, the American Giants defeated Cooper's Monarchs by a 2-1 score. The contest, one that was played in an hour and thirty-eight minutes, was a pitchers' battle between Chicago's Ted Trent and Monarchs' Hilton Smith. During pre-game warm-ups, Frank Duncan appeared on the field, sporting his unblemished American Giants' uniform, and received boos and jeers from a crowd that was estimated at just 2,500 fans.

Trent allowed five hits and fanned seven for the win. Smith struck out eleven and yielded seven safeties in his team's losing effort. It was, however, yet another of his ten-plus strikeout performances in 1938. Bibbs, now hitting in the leadoff spot, collected two of the Monarchs' hits. Else scored the Monarchs' only run in the losing effort. On Sunday, July 31, both teams jumped 500 miles overnight to Chicago, where they were scheduled to participate in what was probably the fourth double bill since they left for Canada.

Chicago opened the doubleheader with a 7-2 win. Cornelius held the Monarchs to two hits--a double in the sixth by Bibbs and a ninth-inning double by Willard Brown. Kranson, Kansas City's selection for mound honors, allowed Chicago to score first when Ernie Smith's single drove home Simms who had reached on Bibbs' error. Mayweather, back in the line-up after a long absence, tied the score at one-all when he walked, stole second base, and counted when O'Neil hit into a double play. Chicago scored two additional runs in the second frame when, with the bases full, Horn skied to Mayweather in right field, Radcliffe scoring after the catch. Duncan scored when Simms followed with a hit off Cox's glove. Another run tallied as Sparks scored on Ernie Smith's sacrifice fly to Milton. In the sixth, Sparks and Horn tallied on Simms' single to center field. Smith, the catcher, singled to the right, scoring Simms. Kranson was lifted in the sixth six and replaced by Bradley, who fanned Young to retire the side. Bradley returned in the ninth, holding Giants batters to one hit, a double by Horn, and no runs. Henry Milton walked to start the ninth. Johnny Dawson, playing in his first game as a Monarch, was safe on Young's error. Mayweather forced Dawson at second base. Willard Brown stepped in, and with one stroke of his mighty bat, spoiled Cornelius' one-hit game with a double to the left, scoring Milton.

In the nightcap, Andy Cooper scattered six Chicago hits as Kansas City won 3-1. All of Kansas City's runs were scored in inning one. Amazingly, Bibbs, who tallied first, did so without hitting safely. Bibbs dumped the ball softly in front of home plate. Duncan lunged forward from behind the plate and threw to the initial sack for the force, but Young failed to cover the base allowing the ball to roll towards Smith in right field; the relay to third was wide and wild. As the ball rolled toward the dugout, Bibbs intuitively scored on his own batted ball, a tap that traveled no more than five yards and was followed by two errors. First baseman Edward Young was also a factor in the Monarchs' other scores. After Milton singled and stole second base, Young, taking Else's bounder, charged the middle diamond trapping Milton off third. With the runner dead in his sight, Young threw wildly over the third baseman's head. As the ball rolled to the grandstand, Milton scored. The game's final run came as Else hurried home, scoring, while Chicago's Joe Sparks was robbing Brown of a hit with a bit of acrobatic fielding in the outer garden. Alex Radcliffe, who reached safely after being hit by an Andy Cooper wild pitch, was a prelude to Duncan's hit-and-run, which pushed across Chicago's only tally in the home second. The victory was Cooper's only complete game in 1938.

American Giants pitchers held O'Neil and his hard-hitting teammates to eight hits during the doubleheader and limited the Monarchs to thirteen hits in their last three games, two of which were won by Chicago. Because of inequity in the Negro American League schedule, the American Giants appeared in just three games at Ruppert Stadium in 1938. The July 29 game was their last. In July, however, the Monarchs played the American Giants more than any other opponent, yet most of the games were played outside of Kansas City and Chicago.

By the end of July, Kansas City had played at least nineteen games against the American Giants, only two of which reportedly counted in the certified Negro American League standings. What remained were contests classified as exhibition games--pure money-making opportunities to keep Negro league teams struggling along until others saw fit to integrate their "lily-white" leagues.

The bigotry supported the discrimination and prejudice thinking that encouraged baseball fans to believe that African American athletes were of inferior ability, playing in a substandard league with a second-rate schedule and no ballfields of their own. They valued Negro American League

211

events but seldom saw the players as equal to National and American League stars, especially so in 1938. Things, however, were starting to change.

Abe Saperstein. *O'Neil joined the Chicago-based Zulu Cannibal Giants in 1937, a team that was promoted nationally by Saperstein. O'Neil's Zulu name was Limpope. (Authors collection)*

Promoter Abe Saperstein who just completed his fifth season of booking the American Giants, Monarchs, Cuban Stars, and the annual East-West game at Comiskey Park, advised,

With the worldwide notice attracted by such performers as Joe Louis, Jesse Owens, Henry Armstrong, etc., the public has become colored athlete-minded and [will] pay real money to view the top performances in the various sports.[359]

212

Jake Powell. On July 29, 1938, Powell made insensitive remarks about African Americans over WGN radio during an interview with announcer Bob Elson. Powell's team, the New York Yankees were in Chicago to start a three-day series against the White Sox. The Monarchs arrived in Chicago two days later. (Authors collection)

Judge Kenesaw Mountain Landis. *As National and American League Commissioner, Landis punished Yankee Jake Powell with a ten-day suspension for an uncensored racial slur made over the radio. (Authors collection)*

"Of the many great ballplayers who have worn the uniform of the Detroit club, Stearnes has served the longest. The Turkey came to Detroit back in 1922 and was here continuously until 1933 when he went east. He returned to the fold last year."

Detroit Tribune, January 22, 1938

Buck O'Neil *says...*

"We could be in Hattiesburg, Mississippi, and when we'd drive the bus up, people would say, 'Where did you come from?' And we'd say, 'Well, we're coming in from Memphis.' They'd say, 'I got a sister' or 'My grandmother lives in Memphis.' People wanted to know what was happening on Beale Street. And we were actually carrying the news of what's happening because we didn't have this media that we have now. So, this was the way of knowing what was happening in the next city or the next part of the world."

Baseball, Bigotry, And Turkey Stearnes

<u>August 1-Davenport</u>, August 2-<u>Kansas City, Ks. (DH)</u>, <u>August 3-Wichita</u>, August 4-Oklahoma City, August 5-Little Rock, <u>August 7-Birmingham</u>, August 8-Memphis

(NAL) O'Neil's Batting: G-3 AB-11 R-1 H-5 2B-1 3B-1 HR-1 SB-0 BA-4.55

O'Neil's Fielding: PO-33 A-0 E-1 DP-1 TC-34

(E) O'Neil's Batting: G-1 AB-5 R-1 H-2 2B-0 3B-0 HR-0 SAC-0 SB-0 RBI-2 BA-4.00

O'Neil's Fielding: PO-13 A-0 E-0 DP-2 TC-13

Henry Milton. *O'Neil recalled, "Most of your [bus] conversation would be with the person that sat beside you. I did a lot of talking with Frank Duncan. I set right up in front of the bus and Frank would drive a lot. With [Henry] Milton I talked [about] college life and different things like that." (Authors collection)*

The Monarchs were making octave leaps all over the Midwest while trying their best to turn a profit. Included among these many stops were exhibitions games in Kansas, Missouri, Arkansas, Alabama, and Illinois. In addition to a copious number of exhibitions, the Monarchs tangled with three Negro American League opponents in over a dozen games outside of league cities in early August. They seldom played the ABCs in Indianapolis, the Red Sox in Memphis, or the Black Crackers in Atlanta. The team's roster was also changing. In early August, Manager Cooper, seeking to add yet another left-handed batter to the line-up, cut a deal with the American Giants to bring

216

outfielder Norman "Turkey" Stearnes to Kansas City. Stearnes, an eccentric veteran with a long history of Negro League play, began the season as the American Giants' centerfielder. He was released at the start of the second half.[360] He turned in his American Giants' uniform for one with the red-lettered MONARCHS embossed across the chest and worked his way into the starting line-up. O'Neil, as were all the league rookies, was working to familiarize themselves with Stearns and the other talented men that comprised the Negro American League. Newspapers were one of the best sources for this information. In addition to learning what was happening in their league by reading the Kansas City Call, they took notice of arrogant remarks made by New York Yankee reservist Jake Powell over a Chicago radio station that was covered in-depth in national daily newspapers. It was important news in the world of baseball and race relations. O'Neil, along with the men on other leagues teams, held firm to their mission of providing high-quality baseball despite the racial agitation stirred up by Powell or any other player. Taking all these events under consideration, August of 1938 would become a month worth remembering for many years to come.

In 1938, American and National League representatives made at least two significant moves that openly revealed its agenda towards race--key moments that served as "wake-up calls" concerning the fate of African Americans in baseball and how deeply racism had affected the national pastime. The first occurred when Alvin "Jake" Powell made a slip of the lip over a national radio program. The second was the hiring of a Cuban, Mike Gonzalez as an interim National League manager for the St. Louis Cardinals. Whirled into the belly of the media controversy, the Monarchs were headed to Chicago for a series with Horace G. Hall's American Giants when Powell made his ill feelings known.

Powell, a part-time outfielder of the New York Yankees, was spending too much time bad-mouthing the Negro race. His left-field comments sparked ten days of suspension from

Commissioner Judge Kenesaw Mountain Landis, provoking the first punishment of its kind given to a player for making Tongue-in-Cheek slurs of a racial nature. Elected as baseball's Commissioner in 1921, Landis was hired to rekindle baseball's integrity after the 1919 Black Sox scandal. It is debatable whether he achieved that goal on matters of racism. In 1938 Landis reluctantly suspended Powell for making a maniacal remark about his "cracking niggers over the head" while employed in an off-season job as a police officer during a live radio interview. His uncensored remark about the police brutality he revealed was an outgrowth of a July 29 pre-game interview at Chicago's Comiskey Park, where Powell bragged on how he enjoyed the off seasons in Dayton, Ohio. A deluge of protest from insulted African American radio listeners resulted in Commissioner Landis suspending Powell for ten days. Landis, in an obvious defensive stance, told the press the "remark was due more to carelessness than intent."[361] For many, Powell's sheepish comment typified the National and the American League's official "solemn study of the problem" to bar African American players from their circuits.

Community leaders, who badgered white leagues and sportswriters to admit African Americans into their circuits, viewed Landis' comments with raised eyebrows. An article in the Kansas City *Call* newspaper suggested,

> If this expression by any means typifies the type of baseball players that are now
> present in the big leagues, it will be some time before Negroes will have the doors
> of major league baseball opened to them.[362]

Powell's negative spirit bedeviled him until the day he committed suicide in 1948. His was a message of racial hate that should have never existed. League executives showed little urgency to assimilate American-born players of African American ancestry into their circuits while being more gracious to Anglo-looking Cubans and other foreign-born players. In 1938, Miguel Angel Gonzalez was hired as interim manager by the St. Louis Cardinals, making him the National League's first Cuban manager. The continued polarization of the major leagues' "discrimination by color" code of ethics went forward without interruption and often without discussion. Thus, Gonzalez's hiring gave little reason for hope. It would be another twenty-four years before O'Neil's achieved his milestone as interim coach for the National League's Chicago Cubs in 1962 and another thirty-six years before Frank Robinson was hired as a full-fledged American League manager in 1974. Until those changes occurred, African American players, fans, and their supporters continued to challenge any oppression intended to block their path. In the meantime, interracial play continued. The Monarchs started August with a barnstorming trip to Davenport, Iowa.

At Davenport, Kansas City faced a formidable squad in the Illinois-Iowa League All-Stars. As the August sun grew fiercer, night games were pushed back to start times of 8:00 p.m. and later. Playing in an 8:15 p.m. start in Davenport, the boys from Kansas City convincingly defeated a team led by Johnny Valsoana, a veteran Western League hurler and pilot who formerly pitched in the Mississippi Valley League for nearby Rock Island, Illinois. Valsoana managed the Relleville, Iowa Legion club for several years and helped develop Phil Cavarretta, right fielder for the Chicago Cubs, who batted .462 in the 1938 World Series against the American League Yankees. Buck and his teammates ran into former minor league players often as they traversed the Midwest.

Tickets for the Quad City appearance were priced at 40 cents for grandstand, 25 cents for bleachers, and 15 cents for children's seats--fees that over 800 people were willing to plunk down to see an interracial baseball game. With bleachers at capacity Kansas City slew the All-Stars in a 6-to-1 final at Davenport's Municipal Stadium, a scenic park that bordered on the Mississippi River.

Three Monarchs' hurlers, southpaw Willie Jackson, right-handers Buster Markham, and Dick Bradley limited All-Stars batters to a lone third session tally while holding them to six safe blows. A combined eight batters whiffed over nine innings. Nipping at Davenport's Al Barnes for a quartet of singles, Kansas City erupted for four first-inning tallies and then ended with fourteen total hits. O'Neil's 2-for-5 effort, with two runs driven in, highlighted the Monarchs' scoring.

Willard Brown was missing from the Kansas City line-up. His place in the outfield was filled by newly acquired "Turkey" Stearnes, who immediately plucked out two of the Monarchs' hits. Stearnes, since gaining his freedom from the American Giants, had sought employment with several Negro league teams before signing with Kansas City. By returning to the Monarchs, a team he performed with briefly in 1931, and again in 1934, Stearnes found a much desirable refuge. Born May 8, 1901, in Nashville, Tennessee, Stearnes, even at the advanced age of 37, was considered one of the league's best hitters. He lived the good life as his advice to younger players was, "You've got to take care of yourself good. Be careful what you eat, what you drink, where you go, and what you do when you go to those places."[363] His specialty was lifting home runs out of Detroit's old Mack Park,

> I hit so many [home run], I never counted them," Stearnes suggested with easy confidence, "And I'll tell you why: If they didn't win a ball game, they didn't amount to anything. It didn't make any difference if I hit four or five over the grandstand; it didn't make any difference to me, as long as I hit them to try to win the game. That's what I wanted; to win the game.[364]

Not counting his home runs unless they won games was quite contrary to how statistics were kept in all other leagues where insignificant home runs were used to inflate a player's lifetime achievements. After the game, O'Neil and his teammates were off to the races with another long drive back to Kansas City.

A return trip from Davenport to Kansas City, covering roughly three hundred and sixty miles, was made on August 2. The direct return allowed the Monarchs to cross the Missouri River into Kansas--to Rogan's hometown, Kansas City, Kansas--where fans eagerly awaited their arrival. Instead of playing at Kansas City's Ruppert Stadium, the Monarchs battled the Memphis Red Sox on unfamiliar turf at Ward Field in Kansas City, Kansas. It was supposed to be an 8:30 p.m. league event.[365] They were often compiled to play in nearby cities when the Blues, the primary tenant at Ruppert Stadium, were at home. Ward Field, owned by a local Catholic high school, was routinely used during the late 1930s. In 1937, Willard Brown hammered four home runs in a single game while playing at Ward Field.[12] The Red Sox were absent at the game time.

Memphis had participated in a doubleheader in New York City, which drew a reported 18,546 fans to see them lose a 9-1 game to Pittsburgh's Homestead Grays in a four-team doubleheader that also included the Newark Eagles and Birmingham Black Barons on Sunday, July 31. In pure agony, members of the Red Sox went from the "House that Ruth Built" to a field that the Pope ordained at a local Catholic high school around the corner from Tom Baird's bowling alley. Still, Buck and the other Monarchs were holding the Red Sox in high esteem for their Yankee Stadium appearance. The Monarchs had never played in Yankee Stadium, but Memphis and Birmingham had. It wouldn't happen in O'Neil's rookie season, but their Yankee Stadium debut wasn't far off. Memphis, in moving across the country, hadn't arrived at game time. They were late. To reach Kansas City, Kansas, the bus ride was more than 1,200 miles, a ridiculous jump even by Negro Leagues standards. An aggregation of Wyandotte County All-Stars was quickly summoned to

---

[12] Brown hit four home runs at Ward Field in an 8-1 Monarchs win over the Kansas City, Kansas Semi-Professionals, October 3, 1937.

fulfill a portion of that night's scheduled events. Memphis arrived at Ward Field with enough evening remaining to play an abbreviated game against the Monarchs that started at 10:00 p.m. Sam Brown, the Red Sox's traveling secretary, had lots to report regarding the exploits of the Red Sox who had left New York at 3:00 a.m. early Sunday morning.[366] The Red Sox had just finished a nine-game series in the east with the Homestead Grays. They suffered dearly behind the hitting presence of Josh Gibson, who hit nine home runs in nine games, which included four in a single game in Zanesville, Ohio. In losing the game to Kansas City, the Red Sox's number of losses had reached sixteen consecutive.

The Monarchs captured a 5-3 seven-inning curtain-raiser over the All-Stars in the haphazardly scheduled doubleheader. Mose and Barnes shared mound chores while Harry Else did the receiving. Later that night in the regularly scheduled league game, the Monarchs defeated a road-weary Red Sox team. The players were exhausted, the fans were tired, and it was nearing midnight when the game was called after Memphis batted in the sixth inning. The final score favored the Monarchs 14-to-1.

Buster Markham, the winning Monarchs' pitcher, whiffed a season's best nine men and limited Memphis to seven hits to gain the win. "The game was played before a capacity crowd," avowed the *Kansas City Kansan*," although no attendance totals were ever presented.[13] O'Neil's hitting featured. He went 2-for-3 with a triple and a clutch home run and scored twice. His bomb, which left the park in a hurry, was hit off the Memphis ace, 28-year-old Porter "Ankle Ball" Moss. The pitcher's scouting report reads like a fairytale,

---

[13] No box score was printed for the Monarchs' game against the Wyandotte County All-Stars.

[Porter] Moss was playing softball in Cincinnati [when I found him]," Ted Radcliffe recalled. "He had a good sinking curveball and pinpoint control."[367] In another interview, Radcliffe recalled, "Going to the ballpark one day. Some kids were playing softball on the playground, and Moss was pitching. He was throwing that softball underhanded by all the batters. I went up to him and signed him to a contract, and he became one of the best submarine pitchers in our league.[368]

Speaking matter-of-factly about his former teammate, Marlin Carter offered, "Moss couldn't throw overhand. He had developed his unique style while skipping rocks across the Ohio River."[369] Carter added, "When he fielded a ground ball, he returned the ball underhanded. Many times, his hand would hit the ground when he threw the ball. When he was tired, he would tell his infielders, 'You better get me some runs because I'm going to coast a little bit.'" Moss, nicknamed "Ankle ball," never lived to see his 35th birthday. He died from a gunshot when a card game went bad in Jackson, Texas. His assailant shot back into the train and made his exit.

After an overnight stay at Streets Hotel, located down on the Vine where all ladies, bars, and nightlife action was happing in Kansas City, early the next morning, both teams stumbled out of their hotel rooms and to the bus for a game later that day in Wichita, Kansas, a distance of nearly two hundred miles. They would travel from there for games in Oklahoma City on August 4 and into Little Rock on August 5.

Playing before a crowd that numbered 3,500, the Monarchs staged a 9-3 come-from-behind victory at Wichita's Lawrence Stadium. Injuries forced Memphis to use pitchers Allen and Radcliffe in the outfield. The substitutions cost the Southerners dearly. Memphis took an early lead due to some clever base running and timely hits, but with the score tied 3-3 in the seventh, two outfield mistakes sparked a five-run Kansas City rally. Seven egregious errors, one each by Bubba Hyde,

Ducky Davenport, Neil Robinson, Willie Jefferson, and Clifford Allen, and two by catcher Larry Brown, dashed any hope Memphis had for an affirmative outcome. "Memphis looked like a ball club for six innings and then put on a grand balloon ascension act," noted Wichita's *Eagle* newspaper, "allowing Kansas City to capture the victory." Willie Jefferson pitched an eight-hitter, but errors behind him accounted for the loss. He was yet another Southern pitcher with a colorful past. When commenting on Jefferson, Manager Ted Radcliffe offered no apologies,

> I got him out of prison in Mississippi around Greenville. A white Coca-Cola salesman told me about Jefferson. Claybrook [owner of the Claybrook Tigers] gave the warden $300 to let him go. He [Jefferson] was in prison for stealing in Cleveland, Mississippi, with six months to serve.[370]

Jefferson was not a Southerner by birth, according to at least one record. He allegedly was born in Kansas City, Kansas, which was noted in a printed 1937 Cincinnati Tigers' roster. If he was born in Kansas City, Kansas, he would have grown up in the shadows of Riverside Park, home to the old Kansas City Kansas Giants, down in the segregated region of town where Rogan, Eddie Dwight, and Alfred "Army" Cooper had grown up. Jefferson and his Memphis crew couldn't solve the slants of the Monarchs' Hilton Smith.

Smith tossed a ten-hitter and struck out six batters in the Wichita win. Smith spoke with coolness as he recalled, "I had a fastball estimated at ninety-five miles per hour and one of the best curveballs that have ever been in baseball."[371] Smith, one of the best pitchers in the Negro American

League, lacked what Leroy "Satchel" Paige and others had plenty of--colorfulness. It may have been bad for publicity, but it never stopped him from being a league leader in wins.[14]

Born in Sour Lake, Texas, the eldest of six children born to John H. and Mattie Smith, he was the son of a Prairie View College educator.[15] His environment was well structured. He was prepped to be an educator. Hilton never entered the field of education; he loved baseball too much for that. "Even as a child," according to one of Smith's sisters, "Hilton loved to take rocks and hit them with broomsticks." He was gifted with great hand and eye coordination. After graduating from a Giddings, Texas, High School, which was followed by a short stay at Prairie View College, Smith joined the Senators, a regional team based in Austin, Texas. In 1932 he reportedly won thirty-three consecutive games, a total that included two wins over the champion Monroe Monarchs of Louisiana in the Dixie Series.[372]

The following year he joined the rival Monarchs in Monroe. The team, which was managed by Frank Johnson, toured the Midwest in 1934. Willard Brown, Floyd Kranson, Harry Else, and Eldridge Mayweather, all members of the Monarchs in 1938, were on that team. It was during this season that Smith first visited Kansas City. Upon his return home, Hilton married Louise Humphrey in Monroe, Louisiana. The next year the Monroe Monarchs returned to the Midwest and barnstormed into Canada. When unexpected finances derailed their efforts, Smith jumped to the Bismarck, North Dakota team, and ultimately a deal was struck with Kansas City in 1936 to have Smith, a two-time Monarch but with different clubs to come to Kansas City. In 1937 he earned the

---

[14] Hilton Smith was elected to the Hall of Fame in Cooperstown, New York, in 2001.

[15] Hilton Smith said that he was born in Giddings, Texas. An older sister, Norva Burdine, informed me that Hilton was born in Sour Lake, Texas

name "No-Hit" Smith by tossing a 4-0 no-hitter over the Chicago American Giants in Kansas City.[373]

He was just as dominant in 1938.

(L to R) (Unknown), Floyd Kranson, Hilton Smith, and an unknown player. Kranson, from Louisiana, was the product of a bi-racial union--his father was white, his mother African American. After graduating from Natchitoches High school in the city of his birth, he attended Piney Woods College. (Authors collection)

While Smith held Memphis scoreless, Monarchs' batters selectively chopped at the opposition for six singles and a pair of doubles. Infielders O'Neil, Bibbs, and Byron Johnson collected two hits each. O'Neil and Turkey Stearnes picked up the doubles. The Monarchs' supporting cast, except for O'Neil's error, played flawlessly in the field for a 9-3 win. Bibbs' performance so impressed Manager Cooper that he shifted the infielder into the team's leadoff position, a spot generally held by speedy Henry Milton. Bibbs, since joining the Monarchs, had collected ten hits in twenty-seven at-bats, a respectable .270 batting percentage. Olan "Jelly" Taylor the Red Sox's fancy-dan first baseman, was batting for a higher average off Monarchs' pitchers.

In four games, played as back-to-back doubleheaders against Kansas City in early July, Taylor went 8-for-17 with a trio of runs scored and a pair of stolen bases, thereby helping his team clinch the first-half pennant. Much could be written about Taylor. The *Negro Star* newspaper declared, "Taylor [is] rated as the most sensational fielder in the game, and Taylor is a one-man circus around first base." [374] He caught and threw left-handed and had sacrificed nearly everything to play professional baseball. Marlin Carter evoked,

> His [Taylor's] wife told him if he played ball, he wouldn't have a wife. And sure, to
> her word, she left. [Taylor] was a flashy first baseman. He always caught with one
> hand and was pretty fast for a big man. [375]

O'Neil, giving some thought to Taylor's one-handed catching, realized that he also adopted the practice. "Showboating" is what they were calling it. "The showboat term," O'Neil suggested, "came from the mediocre ballplayer who called the other guy a show-boater and tried to bring the other guy down to a level. Baseball, when you bring it right down, is entertainment. [376]

When it came to snagging balls one-handed for the fans, few mastered the technique better than Taylor, born July 7, 1910, in London, Ohio. He was the son of Burl and Gertrude Parsons-Taylor. When his parents relocated to Pittsburgh, he attended the Watts Streets School and finished at Schenley High, a mixed-race school. [377] He was the oldest of five brothers in a family without sisters. They lived on Watts Street across from the school before leaving the Hill District for Pittsburgh's North Side. He was a good size kid, and always, a prodigious eater. Baseball was always his thing. Taylor was discovered playing ball in the East Liberty neighborhood around Pittsburgh. He left

Pennsylvania headed for Ohio with DeHart Hubbard, owner of the Cincinnati Tigers. After professional baseball, he joined two of his brothers who were living in Cleveland, Ohio, where he coached local ball teams and eventually died.

Holland Field was playing host to the Monarchs for the third time in 1938. The *Oklahoman* newspaper said these games were scheduled "because of schedule conflicts with Kansas City's American Association Blues."[378] Kansas City's misfortune was Oklahoma City's good fortune as both teams made a Thursday 8:15 p.m. appearance. Dick Bradley got the call to pitch the Oklahoma City game.

Bradley blanked Memphis for five scoreless innings before Neil Robinson banged one of his offerings off the wall. Larry Brown singled, and Robinson scurried home to give Memphis a one-run lead. That one run was enough because Radcliffe was pitching a three-hitter and whiffing the Monarchs' best hitters. His strikeouts were coming all too regularly and so frequently that the game was stopped several times to search for doctored balls. They found no foreign substance, no cuts, or scratches but immediately after the game wired a protest to league officials. Radcliffe fanned ten batters in capturing the 1-0 win to end the Red Sox losing streak at eighteen consecutive games.

After another night of travel, on August 5, the Monarchs were victorious in an 11-1 romp over the Red Sox in Little Rock, Arkansas' Traveler's Field. Kansas City scored in nearly every inning. Who did the scoring and who got the hits will remain a mystery? Box scores and attendance totals for Negro American League teams weren't something that concerned many of the local newspapers. Turkey Stearnes' home run blast in the fourth with a man on base wasn't something the newspapers missed. Moss and Allen pitched in tough luck for Memphis. Moss was especially rapped hard by Stearnes' big lefty bat.

For Kansas City, I. V. Barnes hurled a solid three-hitter. The lone scoring blot against him occurred in inning one when Neil Robinson singled to center, scoring Bubba Hyde, who had singled and stole a base. Cowan Franklin "Bubba" Hyde had become one of the Negro American League's best players. Hyde, the second batter in the Memphis line-up, was a native of Mississippi. Born in Tippa County, on the outskirts of town, he had turned 29-years-old in the start of the 1938 season. As one of many college-educated Negro American League players, Hyde attended Rust College in Holly Springs, Mississippi, and transferred to Atlanta's Morris Brown College after his freshman year. At Morris Brown, he received baseball instruction from Joe Robinson, a former professional with the Philadelphia Hilldale team.

This was a homecoming for Little Rock natives Wayman "Red" Longley and Byron "Mex" Johnson, a game that revived some old-time Southern sentiment. Longley, a second baseman, formerly of the Negro Southern Leagues' Little Rock Black Travelers, and Johnson, a graduate of Little Rock's Dunbar High School, grew up in the city. Johnson was discovered while playing semi-professional ball with the local DuBisson Tigers before graduating to the Little Rock Stars. In between time, Johnson earned a teaching degree from Wiley College, where he excelled in football and baseball under legendary coach and former Negro National League player Fred Long. Johnson arrived in Kansas City about midseason of 1937 as a replacement for shortstop Willard Brown. Johnson thought it important for us to know why the change was made,

> Brown couldn't make the double play well. [Manager] Andy Cooper, after
> watching me field ground balls, looked at Brown and said 'Sonny'--they used to
> call Brown Sonny--you better get your glove and go to center field, I have found
> a shortstop.[379]

Arkansas was also the birthplace of Monarchs' promoter and co-owner Tom Baird. Baird's mother, Japha Duncan, was the daughter of Sarah Ann "Sally" Younger Duncan, a sister of Cole Younger, the famous Missouri outlaw that rode with Jessie James.[380] Baird's family named him Thomas Younger to keep the family's legacy going, but to hide that identity, he always used the initials "T. Y." Baird's early life was spent in Pinnacle, Arkansas.[16] In 1902 the family moved to Kansas, as his father, a plumber by trade, was seeking better employment opportunities. Baird's family lived in Kansas City's Armourdale district until a flood destroyed their home in 1903, after which time they moved to Kansas City, Kansas. As an athlete, Baird, a second baseman, formerly played with Procter & Gamble and later his own team, the T. Y. Baird's in Kansas City. He eventually went to work with Rock Island Railroad as a brakeman, and in 1918, an accident while sitting train brakes in White City, Kansas, broke his leg just below the hip. The injury ended Baird's career as a player and left him with a permanent limp. Unable to play ball, he began managing the Peet Brothers baseball team and operated a ball diamond with one of the most colorful names ever. Billion Bubble Park at Mill and Osage Streets in Kansas City, Kansas, was their home field. He also operated a billiards hall at Twelfth Street and Kansas Avenue. On most afternoons, you could catch Tom in his place of business shooting pool. He was said to be an outstanding pool player. While guiding Peet Brothers, Baird developed Charles Roy "Lefty" Meeker, who went to Connie Mack's Philadelphia Athletics after an outstanding career with Columbus in the American Association. As a promoter, Baird made a small fortune off Negro League baseball. His baseball career, which spanned from 1920 to 1955, rarely affected his racial views. He remained a staunch segregationist who, as late as 1956, refused service to African Americans in his place of business. Tom operated a bowling alley

---

[16] Sally Duncan (born 1846, died 1925) was Tom Baird's grandmother.

on Minnesota Avenue in Kansas City, Kansas. Bob Milan, an African American, took Baird and his associates to task the year after Baird sold George Altman, J.C. Hartman, and Lou Johnson to the Chicago Cubs for something like $11,000. According to Milan,

> Before the Public Accommodation laws were passed, Mr. Baird wouldn't let Black people come into his bowling Alley, and if we did, we were promptly shown the door. When the laws changed, Don Sewing, a local businessman, and I tried to bowl at Baird's business. Although no one was there at the time, we were not allowed to bowl. The manager said a bowling league was about to start. When we asked if we could bowl until people in the leagues arrived, we were told no. We filed suit in the Wyandotte County district court. Baird was found guilty of breaking the law and fined $50.[381]

Regardless of how well Baird promoted or how well Bryon Johnson performed on the field--no one was able to stem the tide of oppression facing the Monarchs at the turnstiles. Kansas City's American Association team was playing to a sizable human mass of 8,000 with St. Paul as their opponent. The midseason crowd was larger than any crowd that attended a Monarchs game in all of 1938. Another crowd of 8,000 packed into Ruppert Stadium for a twin-bill two days later when the Blues battled Minneapolis. The day-to-day disparity in attendance totals was troubling. Despite driving day and night, barnstorming across the country, the Monarchs were not drawing crowds over 4,000, especially in the Southern states where local promoters, growing tired of the low turnouts, were starting to get creative with their promotions.

The Monarchs versus Red Sox barnstorming series resumed in Birmingham, where a game was played on Sunday, August 7. It was part of something new, a four-team Southern twin bill. Because of the escalating cost associated with renting Birmingham's Rickwood Field, Barons' management became creative in scheduling events. The cost of doing business had increased. According to manager William Dismukes, "It cost the Black Barons $100 more for the use of Birmingham's ballpark at night than it did in the daytime." The park's management, men who were always seeking ways to bleed out Negro League teams, said the extra cost was charged because, "It took, [Negro American League clubs] on an average of 17 minutes [more] to play a game than it does white ball clubs."[382] Wilkinson faced similar increases at Kansas City's Ruppert Stadium, where night rentals had increased by $20 over the previous year's rate. If the average cost for entering the park was 40 cents, and many nights it was, fifty extra people would need to enter the park to cover the additional expense--250 more at Birmingham.

The Birmingham festivities included four teams in a Sunday afternoon doubleheader. The teams scheduled to participate were the Baltimore Elites, the Memphis Red Sox, Birmingham Black Barons, and Monarchs. Kansas City shut out the Red Sox 7-0 in the Birmingham opener. Smith hurled the Monarchs' victory with a four-hitter. Bibbs, batting leadoff and playing third base, had a superb game. He went 4-for-4 and drove in two key Monarchs runs. Kansas City's other runs were driven across by Milton, Stearnes, and Allen. Game two was captured by the Baltimore Elite Giants, who knocked off Birmingham in a 6-to-2 final.[383] The following night, three of the teams jumped over to Memphis, Tennessee, where another four-team doubleheader occurred on August 8 at Martin's Park. The winner of game one was guaranteed two games and a larger cut of the gate. Kansas City was matched against Memphis in the opener but lost in a 6-5 final.[384] Later that night, the Red Sox lost to Baltimore by a 3-1 score.

After the loss, Kansas City headed due north at a speed that would carry them to Springfield, Missouri, by daybreak, where the ABCs of Indianapolis were scheduled to meet them. August and some intense league plays were about to heat up!

"Big names of the ABC's include Joe Green, comedian coach, George Mitchell, 43-year-old managing relief pitcher, and Ted Strong, leading hitter in the Negro American League. Strong is also among the leaders in home runs and is a classy first sacker."

Fort Madison Evening Democrat, September 12, 1938

Buck O'Neil says...

"A slump is totally different. The line drives get a big hump in them. You pop up pitches you should rip for base hits, you strike out often, start guessing with the pitcher, change stances and worry yourself to death. That's the time the wife hides the cat when you come home, fixes your favorite dinner, which incidentally tastes like sawdust, and then speaks out of sight. Believe me, a slump is unpleasant for everybody."

Baseball, Bios, And Ted Strong

August 9-Springfield, <u>August 11-Kansas City</u>, <u>August 12-Topeka</u>, <u>August 14-Kansas City (DH)</u>, August 15-St. Joseph, August 16-LeLoupe, <u>August 16-Chanute</u>, <u>August 17-Independence</u>, <u>August 18-St. Louis</u>, <u>August 19-St. Louis</u>

(NAL) O'Neil's Batting: G-5 AB-15 R-4 H-5 2B-1 3B-0 HR-0 SAC-1 SB-4 BA-.333

O'Neil's Fielding: PO-58 A-1 E-1 DP-1 TC-60

(E) O'Neil's Batting: G-3 AB-12 R-3 H-3 2B-1 3B-0 HR-0 SAC-0 SB-1 RBI-2 BA-.250

O'Neil's Fielding: PO-16 A-1 E-0 DP-2 TC-17

Catching up with the ABCs in Springfield, Missouri, three hours from Kansas City, O'Neil and his Monarch teammates opened a series of Negro American League games against Indianapolis at that city's appropriately named White City Park. Having already visited six states in the past nine days, they were now to start a seven-game series with the ABCs in two states. Four games were to be played in Missouri and three in Kansas. Following the series against the ABCs, the Monarchs left immediately to join the Atlanta Black Crackers in another round of barnstorming contests.

The Monarchs won a slugging bee at Springfield on August 9 against the ABCs with a dramatic bottom of the ninth 13-12 come-from-behind triumph. Tallying two in the first, five in the fifth, and finally four big runs in the ninth, when they drove out four doubles, and a single gave Kansas City an important win to start the series. Dick Bradley, I.V. Barnes Buster Markham, and Hilton Smith pitched, but the win was credited to Smith. It was Smith's third victory in five days. James Armstead of Indianapolis was bumped for the loss. After this game, the teams reversed directions and headed back to Kansas City.

On August 11, the Monarchs were back at Ruppert Stadium, where game two of the five-game set was slated. It was the Monarchs' sixteenth home appearance of 1938. The festive affair was played as a benefit for Wayne Miner's Post Number 149. Numerous pre-game attractions were planned for this day. A local drum and bugle corps from Wayne Miner Post 149, Sons of the Legion of Argentine Post in Kansas, and two troops of Negro Boy Scouts ceremoniously paraded around the outfield and drilled before the game. As a special box office attraction, women entered for a mere 10 cents service charge. Allowing ladies into the park for a dime was a way of attacking more men to a ball game on a Thursday night in Kansas City. It was yet another evening game with an 8:00 p.m. start time that resulted in an Indianapolis win.

Theodore "Ted" Strong. *Before joining the Kansas City Monarchs in the fall of 1938 Ted was one of the ABCs' biggest attractions. He specialized in two sports, baseball and basketball, having signed with Abe Saperstein's Harlem Globe Trotters basketball team in 1936. (Authors collection)*

Indianapolis defeated the Monarchs by a 7-to-5 score in a free-swinging slugfest. Floyd Kranson, Kansas City's starting pitcher, was jerked after three innings when he allowed four runs on three hits. The offense continued to falter as Kranson was crowned loser despite Hilton Smith's stellar relief effort. Smith, pitching in relief, allowed six hits, and fanned twelve ABCs batters to no great benefit. It was the third time that Smith surpassed ten or more strikeouts in a 1938 game. Both teams missed numerous scoring opportunities.

The ABCs scored in the first inning, then added to the total in the third, fourth, and fifth frames. As a unit, they laced hits into every nook and cranny of Ruppert Stadium. Robert Dean pitched a splendid game, and in so doing, limited Monarch batters to seven well-spaced hits. He was following a family legacy. Dean's father, Nelson Dean, was a former Monarchs pitcher from Muskogee, Oklahoma, who burst into the Negro National League with great promise in the early 1920s.

O'Neil picked up a pair of hits three times up, stole a base, and scored two runs. Henry Milton and Ted Strong excelled for their respective teams. Milton had three hits, which included a triple, a pair of runs scored, and three stolen bases. Ted Strong Junior, also the son of a former Negro Leaguer, raked Monarch pitching for three hits, one of them a prolific home run. He scored twice and stole two bases. Ted's father, Theodore Sr., had been a professional boxer before coming to the Negro major leagues. Strong Junior at 6-foot-3 inches tall was difficult to overlook, on and off the field. Young Ted's athletic lineage was well defined in the minority press.

Theodore "Ted" Strong Jr., born January 2, 1917, in South Bend, Indiana, was tagged as a coming star in baseball. He was a 1935 graduate of Chicago's Wendell Phillips High School.[385] Formerly a standout at Baltimore's Morgan State College, he was a right-handed throwing switch-hitter infielder who came into professional baseball briefly as the tallest shortstop in baseball with the 1936 Chicago American Giants.[386] In 1937, he performed for a brief period with the Monarchs during the fall exhibition season after spending most of the season with the Mounds Blues, a team co-owned by his father, Ted Strong Sr.[387] From that moment forward, Wilkinson and Cooper had to have that powerful bat in their line-up permanently. That winter, Strong signed with Abe Saperstein's Harlem Globe Trotters basketball team. By the summer of 1938, young Ted had become one of ABC's biggest attractions. In a baseball uniform, he was a force to be reckoned with. Summarizing his skills, one writer ascertained,

> In baseball, he can field his position like Turkey Stearnes, or the late [Herbert]
> 'Rap' Dixon; can hit on par with Buck Leonard; would rival Josh Gibson in home
> run hitting if he were in the Negro National League, and plays basketball in the
> style that makes managers and owners like Bob Douglas of the Renaissance Big
> Five perk up the eye and nod the head.[388]

Strong stood an inch taller than Kansas City's tallest player, Buck O'Neil. Yet Strong's hands were extremely large and much larger than Buck's. Abe Saperstein's public relations advertised Strong's hands as "The largest pair of human hands in basketball."[389]

Reflecting on a time when his teammate was young, alive with possibilities unlimited, and in the prime of life, O'Neil shifted expertly to a scouting evaluation. "When Ted came here [Kansas City], we played him at shortstop. Ted was a pretty good shortstop. What Ted was, was a good outfielder. Ted had a good arm – he was a good right fielder! He was one of the best right fielders I've ever seen, other than maybe a [Roberto] Clemente."[390] Basketball Hall of Fame inductee Marcus Haynes was Strong's 1946 roommate on the Harlem Globe Trotters. He discussed openly with the author of this book some of the inner demons that plagued Strong. Haynes ultimately acknowledged, "Ted had a drinking problem."[391] There were others, like Strong, who struggled with the everyday socializing that came with being a professional athlete. Because of the way ballplayers traveled, they were frequently up at night when the bars and nightspots were open. O'Neil readily admitted,

The ballplayers, they were drinkers. We would go to the bars after the ball games because that is where everything was happening. They were more or fewer drinkers. We never had the dope problem. During that time, we didn't even think about that. In Cuba, you could get Scotch whisky; over here [in America], you were getting bootleg whiskey. You got the best, and it was cheap. So the guys would drink, [and] a lot of guys just drank too much. The difference between the drink and the dope was a guy could get drunk tonight, but he could take a good shower in the morning, and he's all right. You had to play ball again.[392]

Unknown to O'Neil and many others was the increasing presence of marijuana and a drug case that involved John Leonard Jones, a former member of the 1931 Homestead Grays. These were stories occurring and circulating outside of baseball's inner circle that was printed prominently in small-town newspapers. One incident of note occurred in Chester, Pennsylvania, a town of nearly 60,000. According to a 1938 edition of the *Chester Times* newspaper,

Jones, who appeared briefly on the rosters of the Bacharach Giants, Baltimore Black Sox, Homestead Grays, and other teams, "was arrested in a house on [Chester's] East Street with [another suspect] Goldie M. Green, at which place several cigarettes made of marijuana were found. Previously, an informer working undercover for a federal narcotic [agency] purchased several cigarettes from Jones.[393]

Getting back to baseball, at home as well as on the road, Kansas City continued to dominate in runs scored. After sixteen home games, Kansas City had outscored their opponents eighty-three to fifty-six. Having achieved a respectable home record of ten wins and six losses and with little time to celebrate, both teams jumped 70 miles to Topeka, Kansas, for a game on August 12.

Topeka's Monarchs versus Indianapolis ABCs event was a Friday 8:30 p.m. affair that was advertised as a "regularly scheduled Negro American League fray." Expecting one of the largest crowds of the season, park officials installed temporary bleachers to accommodate six hundred extra people, increasing park seating to twenty-six hundred. It was the Monarchs' first Capitol City appearance in six seasons.[394]

A published paid attendance of 1,682 entered Topeka's Ripley Park, a total well short of the park's capacity. And while there was a dash for seats inside the park, others, the less fortunate unable to pay admission, peeped in from beyond the covered wire fence. Two home runs, one a seventh-inning grand slam, and a solo shot by infielder Ted Strong gave Indianapolis a 6-5 victory. Numerous strategies abounded as five pitchers, two pinch hitters, and seven errors impacted the game's outcome.

Barnes, the Monarchs' starting hurler, worked seven innings, giving up nine hits and six runs. Indianapolis' initial run resulted from Bibbs' error, a sacrifice by Raymond Taylor, and an RBI single by Walter Calhoun, the starting ABCs pitcher. Ted Strong poled what locals believed to be the longest home run in the brief history of the park. It was a third-inning solo shot. The mammoth blast cleared the north end of the scoreboard in the right-center field and provided a rare souvenir for fans assembled outside the park. In the seventh, a single by Lyles and an error by Stearnes put two men on base for Indianapolis. Manager Cooper came storming out of the dugout. Strong was next up. Always a prolific hitter, Strong was intentionally passed on many occasions. Cooper ordered

Barnes to walk Strong, and he did. They wanted to take their chances on Bradford. The strategy was futile. The intentional pass to Strong set the stage for Bradford's inside-the-park circuit smash.

Kansas City skirmished throughout, but Mitchell, the Indianapolis manager, took few chances with Calhoun, a left-hander, and removed him in the sixth after Kansas City scored on successive singles by Brown and Stearnes. Arkansas born Frank "Chip" McAllister, a lanky right-hander from Forrest City, said to be a real strikeout king of the Satchel Paige variety, retired the side but was the victim of a rousing four-run Monarchs' rally in the last half of the seventh when Mayweather, batting for Barnes, got life on a fielder's choice and scored on back-to-back singles by Bibbs and Milton.[395] Allen followed with a double that drove in two additional runs. Allen later tallied on an infield out. McAllister tightened and faced only seven batters in the final two innings.

Dick Bradley showed Indianapolis his fastball in the eighth, striking out the side in a game that was already lost. Markham entered and hurled the ninth without a blemish. Indianapolis' victory, their second consecutive over the Monarchs, set the stage for the August 14 doubleheader in Kansas City.

Games seventeen and eighteen of the Monarchs' Ruppert Stadium schedule were part of a Sunday afternoon two-game sweep. Kansas City captured both ends of the doubleheader beating Indianapolis by 4-1 and 5-3 scores before an enthusiastic crowd that numbered 3,000.

In the opener, Smith, a good hitting pitcher, drove in two early Monarchs' runs when he caromed a fourth-inning double off Ruppert's left-field wall, scoring O'Neil and Johnson. A double by Allen and Stearnes' triple accounted for another Monarchs' run in the fifth. Singles by Brown, Else, and Johnson accounted for Kansas City's final tally in the eighth. Indianapolis' only run was a long home run by another good right-handed-hitting pitcher "Chip" McAllister, who drove the ball the length of the left-field wall and about sixty feet beyond on the fly and into the parking lot where cars were parked.[396]

For game two, Manager Cooper assigned himself with the task of starting on the mound. He held the ABCs to five hits, two coming in the sixth when Indianapolis scored the first of their runs and three in the seventh when they scored two more times. Cooper was aided by Henry Milton, who had another outstanding game.

Milton finished with five hits, two in game one and three in the nightcap. Milton also stole three bases, although Raymond Taylor and Quincy Trouppe--two superb throwers--were catching. In game two, with Trouppe behind the plate for Indianapolis, Milton and his teammates stole seven total bases, giving them a total of eleven pilfered on the afternoon.

Kansas City's sweep of Indianapolis placed the Monarchs' home record at twelve wins and six losses inside Ruppert Stadium. In the process, they had outscored their opponents ninety to sixty-two, a margin of thirty-two runs more than the opposition.

The Monarchs made a quick jog over to St. Joseph to face that city's White Eagles in an 8:30 p.m. August 15 game at Goetz Field. The visit received lots of pre-publicity in the *St. Joseph Gazette,* and their coming was highly anticipated. "Manager Andy (Lefty) Cooper has assembled one of the strongest teams in the history of the Monarchs," was expressed with caution.[397] The articled mentioned every member of the Monarchs with some detailed descriptions. When speaking of O'Neil, the newspaper stated, "John O'Neal, six feet two inches tall, plays first base."[398] Al Stahlin, the White Eagles' manager, readied Bill McCoy, and Bob Eisiminger to pitch.

Kansas City was scheduled to take the field at 7:30 p.m. to perform one of their peppers shows and infield drills, but rain prevented the game from being played. Eagles' management promised another date with the Monarchs before the seasons' end, which never occurred.

The canceled St. Joseph game was followed by a two-city barnstorming doubleheader against Indianapolis. Kansas City played the ABCs in Le Loup, Kansas, on the afternoon of August 16, and later that night, the same teams battled in Chanute, Kansas, where rain continued to affect playing conditions.

Standing on a field that was clay on top but moist beneath on the morning of August 16, Kansas City and Indianapolis locked horns in the small community of Le Loup. A small town located 11 miles from Ottawa, Kansas, and 7 miles from Wellsville, towns which the Monarchs had played before, increased attendance substantially. The Monarchs' arrival marked the first "big-time" baseball game to be played in Franklin County since 1929, when the Monarchs last visited Le Loup.[399] The teams were the big attraction at the Modern Woodmen of the World annual picnic. Kansas City captured an 8-7 victory. Indianapolis, in losing, made eight hits and three errors. The Monarchs gathered nine hits in harnessing the win. Having played to a $375 crowd at the annual lodge picnic, local officials called the event a success. Both squads boarded buses directly after the game's conclusion for an eighty-mile sojourn to Chanute, Kansas, for that day's second clash.

In Chanute, the Monarchs and ABCs played for the benefit of that city's charity fund. All of the local proceeds went directly into the coffers, which provided food baskets and other assistance to needy families during the Christmas holidays. Three local umpires, George Cox, Bill Shaw, and Bill Brennan, donated their services in an attempt to defray costs.[400] Opening the August 16, 8:00 p.m. encounter for Indianapolis was pitcher Robert Dean.

Dean hurled Indianapolis to a 4-to-2 victory over Kansas City with a five-hitter, despite Floyd Kranson's eleven strikeouts. His double-digit strikeout effort was his only ten-plus performance of 1938. It was one of the few highlights of the most unproductive seasons in his career.

Chanute's charity fund, some $100 richer, received a big boost from the Monarchs' visit. In playing the final event of the seven series block of games, Indianapolis finished with four wins and three losses to preserve their league supremacy over Kansas City. Without much hesitation, the Monarchs motored to Independence, Kansas, a distance of forty miles to face yet another regional opponent. This time it was a team of talented semi-professionals on another historic day for baseball in Montgomery County.

Facing Independence's local Ban Johnson team at Shulthis Field on August 17, the Kansas City's Monarchs captured a 15-1 victory. Herb Romig, a resident of Independence and a semi-professional hurler of much renown, was the losing pitcher. Triples replaced home runs as Brown, with two, along with Cox and Stearnes, ripped three-base clouts. Included in the Monarchs, fourteen hits were three each by Else and Brown. Barnes, having pitched a four-hitter with a phenomenal seventeen batters struck out, was Kansas City's winning hurler. The astronomical number of strikeouts highlighted Barnes' third game of ten or more men whiffed and was tops for all Monarchs' pitchers for a single-game performance in 1938. Pulling some of their old tricks as a pre-game delight, Kansas City revived their pepper game and their long-distance throwing antics. Else, showing his remarkable arm strength, stood atop home plate and threw the ball over the right-field fence, a distance of nearly 300 feet. That day's other historical feature was given by boxer Henry Armstrong in far-away New York, but thanks to radios, people all over the Midwest were listening.

O'Neil and his teammates sought to find a radio--any A.M. transmission--to catch the results of Armstrong's championship bout, which was going on while they engaged the Independence

Ban Johnson club. Armstrong, fighting at New York's Madison Square Garden, whipped reigning champion, Lou Ambers, to capture the world lightweight championship. It was Armstrong's third title in less than a year. With this win, Armstrong became the first fighter in the ring's long history to hold three crowns simultaneously. He knocked out Pete Sarron in December 1937 to win the featherweight championship and beat Barney Ross in May for the welterweight title, and finally Ambers. The match was a box-office smash as 18,240 paid their way to see the 25-year-old African American in action. Gross receipts amounted to $102,280 and netted $86,841.[401] That sum of money rarely circulated in Negro baseball league circles, especially in 1938. As a consequence, they decided to revisit St. Louis, Missouri, a stop they avoided for many years.

St. Louis was then and still is an epic city for African American baseball history. Until recently, the Cuban Giants of Babylon, New York, were assumed to be America's first African American professional team. An April 28 edition of the 1883 *National Police Gazette* of New York reverses that trend. "The Colored Champions of St. Louis are called the Black Stockings, and they claim to be the only ebony professional team in the country," noted the Police Gazette. An earlier reference on April 12 in this same publication ascertained, "The champion smoke club of St. Louis, the Black Stockings, contemplate a trip to Ohio, and are anxious to know if there are any coon clubs in that state who have sufficient nerve to tackle them." During the season of 1883, numerous references support St. Louis' claim of having America's first African American professional baseball team. Fully two full years ahead of the Cuban Giants, St. Louis, not Babylon, New York, holds the destination as being the birthplace of African American professional play. At least two of the Black Stockings' players, William Whyte, and Richmond Robinson, would graduate to well-documented careers with the famous Cuban Giants.

Before the Monarchs' 1938 St. Louis visit, it had been seven years since they last appeared in the city. They scheduled two games on a Thursday and a Friday night against the South Ends and St. Louis Giants, with both games scheduled for South End Park. Kansas City played great baseball in a Thursday night slaughter of the South Ends.

The Monarchs marked their return to St. Louis in celebratory fashion by logging nineteen hits in a 14-1 win.[402] The only Kansas City player to make the press was Willard Brown, who smashed a 385-foot home run, but there were lots of highlights to acknowledge, like five stolen bases and nine extra-base hits. In addition to Brown, who went 3-for-5 with a home run, a stolen base, and three runs scored, Buck O'Neil and Henry Milton both had a superb game.

O'Neil went 3-for-5 with a double, stolen base and a run scored. Milton was also a 3-for-5 batter and finished with two doubles, a triple, a stolen base, and a trio of runs scored. On defense O'Neil at first, and Else the catcher, recorded twenty of the Monarchs' twenty-seven putouts while Buster Markham pitched six and two-thirds innings for the win. The following night Kansas City returned to South End Park to battle the St. Louis Giants.

The city of St. Louis, although no longer a member of any official Negro League, had assembled a most interesting array of talent and renamed them the St. Louis Giants. Sponsored jointly by the St. Louis Titanium Pigment Company and the National Lead Company, the new Giants became a potent factor in upsetting worthy opponents who cared to come to St. Louis.

Managed by Monroe "Shane" Vincent, the St. Louis non-Negro League Giants were one the best African American teams in the Midwest, not a member of the Negro American League. Pitcher Herbert "Doc" Bracken, boasting a record of "117 strikeouts in about nine games pitched," was St. Louis' choice to face Kansas City. Infielder Jesse Askew, a standout at Jefferson City's Lincoln

University, John Huntley, Johnny Lyles, and Dan Wilson were also with the Giants. Eli Chism, Carl Whitney, and Luscious "Luke" Easter rounded out the squad that faced Kansas City at the Kingshighway and Arsenal Street ballpark. Huntley and Askew were former members of the Arkansas-based Claybrook Tigers, a well-known traveling aggregation of players once managed by Ted Double Duty Radcliffe. Easter, St. Louis' unsung first baseman, was already slugging a wicked willow.

Easter, a Jonestown, Mississippi native that stood six feet four inches, was among Negro baseball's tallest first basemen, amateur or professional. Batting left-handed and throwing with his right helped Easter to graduate to an American League career with the Cleveland Indians. The man that the Monarchs' missed in 1938 would go on to bang ninety-three home runs in 491 big league games. In eleven years of triple-A minor league play, Easter stroked an additional 269 career home runs. That's nearly 400 home runs, and it doesn't include the ones he hit in Negro League play or as an "amateur" in St. Louis.

About 2,600 local fans cheered and wondered why they had no entry in the Negro American League as the Friday crowd watched their St. Louis Giants hammer four Monarchs' pitchers in a blissful 9-5 triumph at St. Louis' South End Park. Bracken, backed up by spectacular fielding, retired the first eleven Monarchs in order. A report in the *Globe-Democrat* reported the score as being 10-5 and that Bracken whiffed seventeen Monarchs."[403] His dazzling speed, sharp breaking curves, and almost perfect control handcuffed numerous Kansas City batters. Bracken struggled in only two innings.

In the sixth, John Huntley's finger was busted, and play halted while they looked at the severity of the injury. Bracken appeared bothered by the game's delay. When the action resumed, Bracken appeared to be sluggish as Milton and Else were walking. Stearnes, next up, caught an outside pitch and lined it against the outfield screen for a double, scoring Milton. Bracken pitched very carefully to Willard Brown, who finally walked after a full count. After Brown's at-bat, Bracken recovered his bearings and whiffed Mayweather and O'Neil to end the threat. Bracken was also rattled in the eighth when Monarch batters bunched three hits and a base on balls to score three runs. After that brief rally, Bracken tightened and struck out three of the final five batters he faced. There were other attractions to go along with Bracken's remarkable performance.

Herbert "Doc" Bracken. *The St. Louis Giants' pitching ace defeated the Monarchs during an exhibition game in St. Louis when they weren't even a member of the Negro American League. (Authors collection)*

Before the game, Kranson informed members of the Giants that he "didn't pitch against rookie teams and all of his pitching was done in the league." When Kranson became the fourth Monarchs pitcher, he didn't last an inning. The Giants greeted him with an impromptu song, "I pitch in the league," bunching three solid hits, much to the local fan's enjoyment. The Monarchs offered numerous alibis for the loss, as was noted in *St. Louis Argus.* "We were tired," and "They're just lucky, wait till we meet them again," went the dogged reframe. In losing, Manager Andy Cooper who was always on the lookout for young talent, fielded fifteen players, including a recruit pitcher whose last name was Joseph. Appearing in his only game as a Monarchs' pitcher, Joseph struck out three batters then disappeared like the last light from the sun into segregated America. Cooper also missed an opportunity to recruit Easter, who finished with one hit. Teammate Jesse Askew instructed, "Easter hadn't played well against the Monarchs. It's just one of those things. He was a player you had to see every day to appreciate."[404]

"Among the players that the Monarchs are now featuring is John O'Neil, a six-foot, two-inch first sacker whose uncanny ability to stab wild heaves have made him outstanding in the Negro National League at his position."

Belleville News-Democrat, August 26, 1938

Buck O'Neil says...

"I think we are the cause of the change... We did our duty. We did the groundwork for the Jackie Robinsons, the Willie Mayses, and the guys that are playing now. We did our part in our generation, and we turned it over to another generation, and it's still changing--which is the way it should be."

A Wake-up Call

August 20-Topeka, August 21-Kansas City (DH), August 21-East-West Game, August 22-Junction City, August 24-Chanute, August 25-Elmer (Day), August 25-Keokuk (Night), August 27-Belleville, August 28-Chicago (DH), August 31-Atlanta

(NAL) O'Neil's Batting: G-5 AB-14 R-4 H-4 2B-2 3B-0 HR-0 RBI-2 SAC-1 SB-1 BA-2.86

O'Neil's Fielding: PO-48 A-2 E-2 DP-0 TC-52

(E) O'Neil's Batting: G-3 AB-13 R-0 H-0 2B-0 3B-0 HR-0 SAC-0 SB-0 RBI-0 BA-0.00

O'Neil's Fielding: PO-33 A-0 E-0 DP-2 TC-33

The Monarchs returned to Topeka, Kansas, on the evening of August 20, for a 9:00 p.m. start against the Atlanta Black Crackers. Unfortunately, Kansas City showed up minus six important players: Hilton Smith, Floyd Kranson, Newt Allen, Byron Johnson, Henry Milton, and Manager Andy Cooper. They had traveled to Chicago to perform in the annual East versus West All-Star game on August 21. Willard Brown and Turkey Stearnes were omitted from the big game's roster, but Floyd Kranson, who was having an offseason, was included. Unwilling to revise the league's schedule, the series with Atlanta was played as originally advertised. The entire Black Crackers series of five games would count in the league standings. The games went forward, although Kansas City was operating with a skeleton crew. Atlanta would not return to Kansas City, which made it important to put this series in the official standings. There was no break in the activities, no budget for idleness, teams had to play somewhere almost every day. They were still spreading the love, and it cost the Monarchs a second-half pennant.

Kansas City won a wind-swept, rain-threatened Negro American League game at Topeka's Ripley Park, spanking the Atlanta Black Crackers 13-2 on August 20. Four-hit pitching from Willie "Train" Jackson, aided by the pelting of three Crackers twirlers for fourteen total hits, helped the Monarchs to an easy win. Atlanta scored first on Jim Cooper's single and Joe Greene's solitaire single to the left. A walk, Rogan's single, Harry Else's triple, and a balk produced two Monarchs runs in the bottom half of the inning. A single by Stearnes, a passed ball, and a hit by Brown netted another run in the third. Kansas City did some lusty clouting in inning six and sent a half dozen runs into the scorer's ledger. Successive singles by Brown, Stearnes, and Mayweather bumped Duncan, Atlanta's lefty pitcher, in the sixth. Intermittent rain showers persisted throughout the early innings of the game. Throughout the sixth inning, rain threatened to halt the game and chased nearly 500 customers from the park. After that, the teams played to mostly empty bleachers. Reese, another left-handed hurler, entered in the seventh, and O'Neil stepped to the plate and greeted him with a two-run double. A walk, an error, and singles by Else and Bibbs brought in additional runs. Brooks, Atlanta's third hurler, allowed the last four. "Train" Jackson pitched like a seasoned veteran for Kansas City and was never in any real danger. He sat down eight Atlanta hitters on strikeouts, thereby capturing a win.

Claude Willoughby. On August 24, 1938, Willoughby, a former big leaguer, was lambasted by the numerous Monarch hitters in what was possibly the most embarrassing loss of his entire career, amateur or professional. (Authors collection)

Those who chose to stay, fans and players alike, were drenched. The rain had a toxic influence on the day's attendance which continued to sag throughout the league. Topeka's two Monarchs' appearances, one on August 12 and the weather-related game on August 20, attracted approximately 2,182 fans. Black touring teams were professional and loaded with star players, but their performance was rarely dictated by crowd size. This could be seen in the performance of catcher James "Joe" Greene. Having produced one of his team's runs at Topeka, he was in the midst of a career that would last from 1938 to 1951 and eventually land him a job with the Kansas City Monarchs.

Greene was born on October 17, 1911, in Stone Mountain, Georgia. While in his youth, his parents nicknamed him "Pig." He originally joined the Atlanta Black Crackers in 1933. In 1936 he came north briefly performing with the American Giants and the Homestead Grays as a backup catcher. He returned to Atlanta the following season. When speaking of Greene, teammate Thomas Butts raved about the catcher's quick release. "He had a good arm, could throw, could get the ball to you on time so the runner wouldn't have a chance to go through his act and spike you or something like that."[405] As a hitter, he demanded a heavy bat and eventually settled on a 37-inch bat but would choke up.[406] Another reference stated,

> James (Pig) Greene is about the peer of any catcher around. One thing is certain,
> Josh Gibson may be greater, as all agree, but he's not as consistent. Greene is the
> same decisive performer daily. Gibson seems to play his best only by inspiration
> from big crowds and great excitement.[407]

Upon their return to Kansas City, the Monarchs had a reversal of their prior good fortune. Atlanta woke from their slumber and won the next four games. Greene added mightily to the Monarchs' downfall.

A day after the capital city affair, both teams returned to Kansas City for an August 21 two-game set.[408] Kansas City's weakened line-up became more obvious. Willard Brown was shifted to third base, Roosevelt Cox to shortstop, and Rogan went to left field. The shift in the defense proved futile as Kansas City lost both ends of the double bill by 6-5 and 9-2 scores, thereby virtually handing the league's second-half race to Atlanta. Greene continued his onslaught and finished with four hits in the doubleheader.[409]

Atlanta won the opener behind the superb pitching of Felix "Chin" Evans and Eddie "Bullet" Dixon and some timely hitting by Thomas Butts. Evans pitched a masterful game, hurling eight innings, striking out seven Monarchs. "Lefty" Mose and John Markham worked in succession for Kansas City, but they weakened in the eighth and ninth when Atlanta scored five important runs. Up until that time, Kansas City was out in front by a 3-to-1 score. Atlanta came roaring back with a three-run rally in inning eight, then added two more runs an inning later to take a permanent lead. Kansas City rallied for a run in the eighth and another in the ninth. Then with the bases loaded, Dixon came on as a relief pitcher and forced Mayweather to pop out, ending the game. Mayweather's out resulted in Markham taking the Monarchs' loss. Butts, who delivered a key triple to ignite Atlanta's scoring, collected hits in both games. He, too, was a factor in his team's sudden late-season surge.[410]

Thomas Butts, nicknamed "Pea Eye," had all the appearances of a big-league veteran while still a senior in high school.[411] As a teenager, he moved with his family to Atlanta, Georgia, where he eventually attended Atlanta's Washington High School. Butts' baseball career continued well into the 1950s. He died in Atlanta in the early 1970s. It was strange to see Butts in the South because most African Americans were migrating North, and when they reached the North, many chose to stay--and never returned--but some, like Butts, did,

I started playing baseball with the Atlanta Black Crackers in 1936 when I was seventeen.[412] I stayed with the Black Crackers for three years, and then the Baltimore team came down and played us, and they gave me a tryout.[413]

The nightcap, a lop-sided seven-inning contest, was captured by Atlanta in a 9-2 finish. Both Monarchs' tallies came in the last inning on a Turkey Stearnes' triple that drove in a pair of runs. As an aging runner on the sacks, the 37-year-old outfielder was forced to hold at third. A few years earlier, it would have been an automatic inside the park home run. Up to that point, Monarchs' hitters were limited to just three hits by pitcher Dixon, who was making his second appearance as a pitcher in the doubleheader. On the other side of the ledger, Atlanta batters were keyed up. Three doubles, two triples, and a home run ringing up a total of fifteen hits told the whole story. Pelham, with a home run, a double, and a single, led Atlanta's onslaught. Donald Reeves, an alumnus of Atlanta's Clark University and right fielder, also picked up three hits, one being a triple. In a vain attempt to stop the carnage, four Monarch pitchers were ushered into the contest, but Barnes received the loss.

When Rogan hustled to the outfield for both games, few knew it would become his final professional appearance at Kansas City's Ruppert Stadium. That afternoon Rogan, stationed in his familiar position in left field, went 0-for-4 and 0-for-3 at-bat. That halfhearted performance was not up to Rogan's standards. As much as he hated to admit it, it was time to take his legendary 36 inches, 40 once bats, and retire from active play.[414] His was a lengthy professional career that lasted from 1920 to 1938.

While their teammates were being thumped at Ruppert Stadium in Kansas City, big doings were occurring in Chicago, where Hilton Smith pitched the Western All-Stars to a 5-4 win at Comiskey Park in front of a crowd estimated to be 30,000 fans. The Western All-Stars represented the Negro American League, the Eastern Stars the Negro National League. Manager Andy Cooper was credited as the winning manager. Oscar Charleston was the Eastern All-Stars manager. Smith was the game's winning pitcher with four shut-down innings on the mound. The game was close until the third inning when Neil Robinson of Memphis hit an inside-the-park home run off lefty Edsall Walker with two men on. Robinson and Chicago's Alex Radcliffe drove in all of the West's runs, while Willie Wells, the Newark Eagles' shortstop, featured at-bat for the East with several sensational plays in the field. Wells' triple and single were also responsible for three of the East's four runs. By contrast, Monarchs Smith, Milton, and Johnson went 1-for-3. Newt Allen went hitless, and Kranson never got into the game. 1938's East-West game was the sixth game played since 1933, with victories split three wins for each region.

Playing the East-West game in the afternoon allowed the West All-Stars to assemble for another game later that same night in Milwaukee, Wisconsin. The event was titled the "North-South All-Stars Game." R.R. Jackson, the league president, helped promote the event to Milwaukee fans. He selected the top players from the West, along with four African American umpires.[415] Andy Cooper managed the North squad; Larry Brown of Memphis handled the Southern team. Attendance totals for the 8-8 tie game were not published, but a box score of the event showed that Milton, Allen, Johnson, and Smith were in the North's line-up. Kemp, manager of the Atlanta Black Crackers, was there at second base for the South squad.[416] The Monarchs' Johnson at shortstop and Smith in right field had two hits each. Milton, hitless in the affair, stole a base and scored a pair of runs. Allen also contributed a hit. Sug Cornelius of Chicago and Chip McAllister of Indianapolis both pitched for the North. By contrast, the National and American League white All-Star game also drew well. They had a capacity crowd at Cincinnati's Crosley Field.

Performing to a capacity crowd of 27,067, the National League thumped the Americans by a 4-to-1 score. New York Yankees' manager Joe McCarthy and New York Giants' manager Bill Terry drew All-Star managerial assignments. While financial data was not given for the Negro League East-West game, the National League versus American League game, which was played on July 6, took in $38,469.00.[417]

Major league teams were renting their stadiums to Negro League teams and showing big profits. Some were getting into the action late. Negotiations were occurring in cities like Boston and St. Louis, where teams were yet to enter big-league parks. One such meeting took place with Boston Braves President, James Aloysius Robert Quinn Sr. when Mabe "Doc" Kountze, a young black reporter asked, and was invited to his office high atop Braves Field to discuss the opportunity of Negro league play at the National League stadium. He reminded the writer that he had come to Boston from Brooklyn and that he knew Abe and Effa Manley of the Newark Eagles. Kountze noted,

> Quinn, at that time, seemed very tired and had been through many baseball wars. Squinting through his glasses reflectively, he surprised [me] by agreeing on areas I expected to argue. He was honest and blunt, and he told me quietly he knew more about Colored Big-League player abilities than I did. He said he had played on teams with, and against, sepia stars in his younger days. He favored Colored teams playing in Braves Field and wished he could have sepia stars like [Will] Jackman, [Burlin] White, [Satchel] Paige, and others on his club.[418]

Quinn went on to prophesize that the National League would have Colored players before the rival [American] League, and the Braves would have Colored players before the Red Sox. Bob was a true prophet."[419] On April 18, 1950, Sam Jethroe made his major league debut for the Boston

Braves. Elijah "Pumpsie" Green, born in the predominately Black town of Boley, Oklahoma, did not make his major league debut with the Boston Red Sox until July 21, 1959.

Robert Bob Quinn Sr. In 1938, Quinn prophesized that the National League would have "Colored" players before the rival American League and added the Braves would integrate their team before the Red Sox. (Associated Press, Authors Collection)

With the American Association Blues scheduled to return to Ruppert Stadium, the Monarchs resumed action against Atlanta on the barnstorming circuit in Western Kansas. In an August 22, 8:15 p.m. invasion of Rathert Field at Junction City, Kansas, the Monarchs and Crackers battled for a third consecutive day. It wasn't a game for the faint of heart. This was a slugfest that featured twenty-eight hits and thirteen egregious errors. At the finish, the 12-to-11 score favored Atlanta. A five-run uprising in the ninth allowed Atlanta to squeeze by Kansas City in a game that was classed as yet another "officially sanctioned Negro American League road game." The Crackers entered the ninth inning trailing by four runs before blasting Barnes. They capitalized on two passed balls and a pair of walks in the inning. Monarch batters finished with fourteen hits, although their performance was marred by eight fielding errors. The Crackers also committed five fielding bobbles.

Three Kansas City batters blasted home runs at Junction City. "Turkey" Stearnes pasted a solo shot over the distant right-field wall. Barnes' home run flew over the left-field wall some four-hundred feet from home plate. Willard Brown's home run over the same right-field wall was hit with Else on base. Though his speed limited him to a triple, Mayweather's clout, which fell in front of the center-field scoreboard, was credited as being "the longest ball ever hit inside the park."[420]

Four Monarchs' pitchers tried, and all failed in their quest for victory. Barnes, the most effective of them, took credit for the loss. Felix "Chin" Evans, one of two Crackers' hurlers, got the win. Evans was not new to big-time baseball. He had played for both the Memphis Red Sox in 1936 and 1937 and the Atlanta Athletics before joining the Black Crackers in 1938. Born October 3, 1911, in Atlanta, Georgia, he grew up to be a scholar-athlete. He graduated with honors from Morehouse College, where he also excelled at basketball and football under former Negro Leaguer, Frank Forbes.[421] The win gave Evans victories over Kansas City in consecutive days.

Newly acquired Johnny Dawson had become a liability behind the plate. Atlanta stole six bases and took advantage of three passed balls before Dawson was replaced by Else in the ninth. Dawson from Shreveport, Louisiana, was replaced by Else, another Louisiana product. Having the stronger arm, Else was working his way back into Kansas City's starting line-up. On numerous occasions, he demonstrated his arm strength in pre-game workouts by "standing on home plate and throwing the ball over the right-field fence." In the four-game series, on bases, the Crackers' swiped ten and scored twenty-nine runs. The Monarchs headed to Chanute, Kansas, for the next day's encounter. Their defeat to the ABCs in Chanute provided a glimmer of hope that the local team might do the same.[422] Local promoters re-signed Claude Willoughby, the former Phillies' pitcher, to do just that--beat the Monarchs. He packed his grip for Chanute traveling from his home in Buffalo, Kansas bringing with him six seasons of National League pitching experience. Willoughby, who last pitched in the majors in 1931 and the minors in 1937, was easy prey for the mix of young and seasoned Monarchs.

On this night, Chanute took its worst beating of the entire summer.[423] When the Monarchs scored three runs in the first inning, defeat was almost certain. When four more runs were added in the third, Chanute's defeat was a sure thing. The only question remaining was the margin of victory. Dick Bradley was humming them past the locals with relative ease. He whiffed seven before handing mound duties to Hilton Smith, who proceeded to fan six more batters. The pitchers combined to toss a three-hitter. Willoughby, on the other hand, was ineffective.

Willoughby lasted the entire route but was handed one of the most embarrassing losses of his entire career, amateur or professional. He surrendered nineteen hits, struck out four, and hit a batter, but that was only half of what occurred in this game. Willard Brown went 3-for-3 and, after hitting his second triple, was pulled and Rogan inserted as his pinch-runner. On the next pitch,

Rogan stole home. The Monarchs weren't finished. They scored their final four runs in the top of the ninth after loading the bases. Everyone scored on Henry Milton's grand slam. The entire team took their pokes at the former big-league pitcher. Every hitter in the Monarchs' line-up, except for O'Neil, who went 0-for-5, had hits on this day. Bibbs went 3-for-6, Cox 2-for-5, Else 3-for-5 with a double. Mayweather was 2-for-5 with a home run over the right-field fence. There was a standing offer of "five gallons of gasoline to the player clouting a ball over the fence."[424] The final score was 15-0. Oh yes, Mayweather's gasoline contribution saved his team's owners a few bucks on fossil fuel and helped get the bus to Elmer, Missouri, for the next day's 1:00 p.m. game.

Back in Kansas City, there was anger and rage among Monarchs' fans and Booster club members incensed by Atlanta's wins. Boosters took their complaints public in a letter signed by twelve club members. The lengthy letter to the editor of the Chicago *Defender* contested,

> Since the Monarchs were in the Negro American League race, we didn't feel so bad when they lost the first half, but the second half seems to be a carefully planned scheme on the part of the league administrators to 'gyp' Kansas City out of the second half and if that is so (and it appears to be on the face of things) we, the Boosters are demanding some action either against the president of the league or against the local club owner. We are not sore because Atlanta beat Kansas City because we Missourians are better sports, but we don't intend to allow the league president who is secretary and stockholder in the Chicago American Giants who are out in front by a narrow margin in the second half to manipulate things to the benefit of his club. He will blame it on the scheduling committee, of course, but it's too plain. [Ted] "Double Duty" Radcliffe, [Neil] Robinson, and [Larry] Brown were taken from the Memphis Club, and the Chicago team was deprived

of [Alex] Radcliffe, Frank Duncan, and [Sug] Cornelius. Atlanta sent one man, [Gabby] Kemp. Why was Kansas City penalized by five players?[425]

An edition of the *Lincoln State Journal Times* hinted that "there is a chance that two protested games which Atlanta claimed from Kansas City will be thrown out by league officials," and that such an action by league officials "would give the Monarchs the second-half crown."[426] As the debate raged on, the Monarchs crossed the border into Missouri and headed for the little village of Elmer for a 1:00 p.m. game.

The Elmer, Missouri Reunion, where they whipped the local Panthers All-Stars 4-0 in an afternoon game on August 25, an event which drew "One of the largest crowds to ever see a baseball game there," was another exhibition win.[427] The Elmer team was being touted as one of the best hardball teams in Missouri. Fans saw Kansas City at their very best, facing Steve Buban, who held them scoreless for five innings. Buban, a part-time pitcher, was earning $30 to $150 a game to toss them up for the Panthers.[428] Against Kansas City, early on, he was nearly invincible. Kansas City finally broke through to score once in the sixth inning, twice in the seventh, and once more in the eighth for the win. Later that night, the Monarchs jumped over to Keokuk, Iowa, a distance of over one hundred miles for their second game of the day. Locally, promoter, W.R. Dickson manager of the Keokuk Indians, was doing everything possible to win the game. He stocked his line-up with players of local renown.

Rhea Flambeau returned to Keokuk in time to play with his hometown team. As a player with a contract owned by the St. Louis Browns, he was finishing off a season in the Kentucky-Illinois-Tennessee League. He was there to play center field. Junie Brust, a catcher, Harley Miller at shortstop, and Drake, a third baseman from the Mississippi Valley League, were all recruited. Bob Stoneking and Whitey Wilson were there to do the pitching for the Joyce Park encounter.[429]

The extra talent failed to produce the desired results. Kansas City scored a pair of runs in the second and added another in the eighth to beat the local Indians by a 3-1 score. "Dissension" by the Keokuk team gave the Monarchs the advantage they needed, as the local's "slowness in taking the field and don't care attitude on the diamond" wreaked havoc, wrote the *Keokuk Daily Gate City* newspaper.[430] The Monarchs, on the other hand, "Played with a snap in the field with ample life and pep at all times to delight the fans." They won the hearts of local fans. "Not once did they debate a decision but took the whole affair good-naturedly, seemingly getting a 'big jolt' and receiving as much entertainment and fun as the assembled multitude," wrote a local sports reporter.[431] There were no home runs hit in the game; however, Allen and Brown both collected a pair of hits each in the Monarchs' total of eight. Brown stole a pair of bases, and Stearnes doubled. A recruit named Vaughan was there to earn a spot on the Monarchs roster. He pitched a three-hitter and struck out nine. Flambeau, the highly recruited minor leaguer, went 0-for-4, as did O'Neil for the Monarchs.

While Monarchs' attendance totals remained essentially unchanged in both league and barnstorming games, the Kansas City *Star* was gloating on the growth and prosperity occurring in the American Association. "St. Paul's Saints, with 202,000 in paid attendance, were running, neck and neck," stated the article, "with [the] Kansas [City's Blues] vying for a close second with 195,000 in paid admissions."[432] Having averaged about 2,000 people a game, an insignificant total, by comparison, Monarch management sought fresh ways to attract larger crowds despite the systemic racism they faced. Association teams could boast of large attendance numbers, but they were rarely seen outside of Ohio, Indiana, Missouri, Kentucky, Wisconsin, and Minnesota. They could not match the territory covered by the Monarchs or the diversity of places where people would see them play. You never knew where the Monarchs might show up.

The Monarchs were back on the bus later that night. They motored towards Illinois for their next game at Belleville, where they were scheduled for a nighttime scuffle with the Belleville Stags on the evening of August 27. Belleville remained a frequent stop among Negro League teams, and, as always, they gave the Monarchs a good challenge. The missing East-West game participants: Johnson, Kranson, Smith, Allen, Milton, and Cooper rejoined the Monarchs at St. Louis. Newly acquired Eugene Bremer, a 21-year-old son of a New Orleans washerwoman, a late-season pitching addition from the Memphis Red Sox, was with them.

Single runs in the first, second, third, fourth, sixth, and seventh innings gave Kansas City a 6-5 win over Belleville's Stags. Milton's first-inning triple started Kansas City's scoring. In the second, Brown's single, a stolen base and a single by Cooper, the Monarchs' manager, produced another Kansas City marker. Bibbs' single--his steal of both second and third bases--and Stearnes' single pushed across a third Monarchs' run. A fourth-inning single by Else, a stolen base, an infield out, Milton's walk, and a double steal gave Kansas City the fourth run.   Mayweather's hefty clout over the right-field wall gave the Monarchs their fifth run in the sixth. Bibbs crossed with the winning run on his single that was followed by Brown's triple to the right. Monarchs' base runners essentially stole the victory by swiping six stolen bases. Bremer held Belleville to two hits in five innings, thereby getting credit for Kansas City's win. Heading into the final weeks of August, the Monarchs would face the American Giants and Black Crackers in exhibition games.

Reaching Chicago on August 28, the Monarchs and American Giants met in a doubleheader at Giants' Park. That final August doubleheader was the last of Kansas City's 1938 visits to Chicago. In the succinct two-game Sunday afternoon set, they divided the results. Chicago captured game one 11-9 and Kansas City game two 12-2. It was stated publicly that these games were "exhibition contest only" and would not count in the league standings.[433] This news must have surprised fans as there were no reasons or legitimate excuses for these games to be labeled as exhibitions.

The Monarchs banged on two Giants' hurlers for twelve hits in game one's losing effort. Henry Milton was a virtual one-man offense, scoring four runs in five times at-bat, getting three hits. Horn and Edward got three hits each to bring the Giants' total to nine. Hilton Smith, unable to arrest Chicago's wicked onslaught, was given poor support by his fielders. Barnes relieved Smith in the fourth, with two runs already across and one out. Before the side was retired, Candy Jim's Giants pushed the total runs to five and ultimately captured the opener for Sug Cornelius.

Cornelius pitched into the eighth but had a rocky finish. He allowed a third-inning homer to Stearnes, with two men on base, when the Monarchs seized an early lead. The Giants later tied the game at four-all. When the Monarchs run total reached nine, Taylor, the Chicago manager, waved Cornelius to the showers and replaced him with Ted Trent. Trent forced one batter to fly out, simultaneously ending the threat and the game.

Trent returned to start game two but was relieved by Percy Forrest. Kansas City banged both pitchers for eleven hits, three being hits for home runs. Willard Brown pasted a ball over the barrier in the right, with Stearnes on the path in the sixth. Harry Else caught one, pounding it against the scoreboard for a home run with a man on. Mayweather's slap for another home run with two on in inning-nine, facilitating three more runs.

Chicago scored twice off Buster Markham in nine full innings. Both runs were scored in the fourth when Edward Young walked and scored on Duncan's single. Houston scored while Duncan and Sparks were victims of a double play. Wilson Redus was making a mighty contribution. His double to start the sixth led to additional offense.

(L to R) Olan "Jelly" Taylor, Mrs. Robinson with husband Cornelius Randall "Neil" Robinson. From 1938 to 1945, Robinson started in five of eight East-West games, including four straights from 1938-41. He dominated in those games, hitting .476, second only to Josh Gibson's .483. (Authors collection)

Fans gazed at Redus in wonderment. Diminutive in stature, he stood five feet, five inches, weighing a brawny 155 pounds. Surprisingly, Redus was not the shortest Negro American League player. That honor belonged to Birmingham's "Goldie" Cephas, a five-foot, two-inch shortstop. Redus started professional play in 1920 with the Muskogee Oklahoma Wonders. In 1922 and again in 1923, he remained with the Tulsa Oklahoma Black Oilers, arriving there a year after the Tulsa race massacre. The bloody massacre occurred when a white mob descended on a Black neighborhood intent on murder, mayhem, and property destruction. They destroyed homes and businesses in Tulsa's Greenwood District. Countless numbers of unarmed African American citizens were killed, and more than 40 square blocks of the community were torched and burned to the ground. This act of violence is considered "The single worst incidents of racial violence in American history."[434] Redus eventually entered the Negro National League as a member of Kansas City's Monarchs in 1924. He also played for the Baltimore Black Sox and New York Lincoln Giants. Born in Tallahassee, a small Oklahoma town in Wagoner County, he batted and threw right-handed. Away from the game for two seasons due to illness, Redus returned to professional play in 1935.

All totaled, in 1938, Wilkinson and Baird scheduled nearly twenty games in Chicago. Thirteen of the games were against the American Giants; seven were exhibitions against Tri-State League opponents such as Chicago Mills and Spencer's Coal. Eleven games were won, and four were losses by the Monarchs. At least two events were rained out. Next to the twenty-three games played in Kansas City, Chicago, Illinois was the Monarchs most frequently visited city in 1938. As it had been for many years, the American Giants remained their most rivaled Negro League opponent.

Byron "Mex" Johnson. *"He was a competitor," recalled O'Neil, "He was going to outhit you, outfield you, anything he had to do to be the best." Johnson was the starting shortstop for Kansas City's 1938 Monarchs. (Authors collection)*

The Monarchs closed the month of August against the Black Crackers of Atlanta in Atlanta. Getting there wasn't easy. Most of these overnight drives were laborious and humdrum. They were, however, a necessity in the era of segregated baseball. The trip to Atlanta took two days to cover 700 miles across a sometimes subtle but always present landscape of oppression and segregation. They were headed to Ponce de Leon Park, where a two-game series was to be played on Wednesday, August 31, and Thursday, September 1, with both teams needing a sweep of the series. Kansas City arrived in Atlanta without the service of Byron Johnson and Roosevelt Cox, who both returned to college.

Atlanta had the distinction of beating the Monarchs four times in a five-game series, which included wins in the last four games of the series.[17] The Monarchs team they faced didn't have all the regular players. Those players were back, but others were missing, yet it heightened the enthusiasm within Atlanta's African American community, who were celebrating their team with fervor. If the Black Crackers won both games, they would achieve something that few teams had; win five consecutive games from the Monarchs.[435] To add to the excitement, Atlanta was rolling along with a nine-game winning streak and looking for wins number ten and eleven.[436] Lucius L. Jones, in his *Sports Bug* column for the *Atlanta Daily World*, wrote of Wilkinson's history in night baseball then added,

> No doubt, he'll pardon this department's prediction that his boys will be glad to
>
> get out of Atlanta after the Black Crax have 'done their number.'[437]

Evidently, Jones was more than a sportswriter; he was also a prophet. Kansas City came to Atlanta and lost both games. In the opener, Chin Evans faced two Monarchs' pitchers in lefty Willie Jackson and Eugene Bremer. Manager Cooper chose Jackson instead of the righty Barnes, and it cost the Monarchs dearly. Atlanta scored a pair of runs in the first when catcher William Cooper singled, and Jackson threw over O'Neil's head at first on a Spencer Davis bunted ball. Cooper came around to score, and Davis jogged home on Thomas Butts' sacrifice fly to right field. Atlanta added two more runs in the second inning after Evans helped his own effort with a single to centerfield. Cooper followed with a double; the second big error followed. Willard Brown was playing third base, and he threw the ball over O'Neil's head in an attempt to retire Davis at first, and two runs

---

[17] The Monarchs played a five-game series against the Black Crackers in the West, but only four of the games have been located. The missing game was played on August 23 a day after the two teams met in Junction City, Kansas. The game was continuously reported in the Atlanta Daily World and was included in Atlanta's nine game winning streak.

scored. Atlanta was leading 4-0 when Bremer replaced Jackson. The best Atlanta could do after that was to scratch two hits over the next six innings. Kansas City didn't score until late in the game.

In the eighth, Else singled and scored on Brown's second double and third hit of the day. Two more runs tallied in the ninth when O'Neil doubled and scored on Henry Milton's inside-the-park home run to the scoreboard. That was the end of the scoring for Kansas City. Atlanta had stopped the Monarchs in a 4-3 final. Evans finished with a four-hitter and matched Bremer's seven strikeouts. Late in the game, with the Monarchs mounting a scoring threat Hilton Smith was sent in to pinch-hit for Junius Bibbs. Evans, Kemp, and Cooper gathered around the mound for a conference, and it was decided that they would pitch to Smith. Evans made Smith hit back to him for an easy play at first and an Atlanta win. Rick Roberts' report in the *Atlanta Daily World* celebrated the day's action,

> The play of Bibbs and Butts featured. Cooper led the Crackers offense, scoring once on 2 hits but was fanned twice by Bremer's curves. The Crax played errorless ball. They close out the home season tonight, when ladies will be admitted free.[438]

The next night's game wasn't even close. It started as a "Telosh" Howard versus Buster Markham outing with a crowd of 3,000 people, mostly ladies, looking on. In the third, a fantastic play, "brought down the house."[439] In that frame, a Monarchs' scoring bid was repelled. Milton had slapped a double to the left and was flying around second when Babe Davis let the ball scoot past him. Davis retrieved the ball, relayed it to Butts, who rifled it to Joe Greene at the plate in time to retire Milton in a cloud of dust. Atlanta's big inning occurred in the fourth.

Atlanta chased Markham from the mound in the fourth after a Spencer Davis walk was followed by a Don Pelham single to the right. Joe Greene was purposely walked to load the bases. Donald Reeves followed with a sacrifice fly to Milton to score Davis. Newt Allen's error on Butts' liner loaded the bases a second time. "Gabby" Kemp followed with a single to score both Pelham and Greene for a three-run Atlanta lead. Hilton Smith was summoned to stop the onslaught; Markham retired to the bench with just 3 and 1-3 innings pitched. After a few warm-up tosses, Smith's first pitch to Howard resulted in a hot single up the middle to score Butts. The scoring ceased, but the damage had been done. Atlanta was leading 4-0. Smith pitched a one-hitter after that and struck out six batters, but Howard was matching his performance. After five innings of play, he too was tossing a one-hitter, and at one point, had retired sixteen hitters in succession. Howard ended the game with seven strikeouts through nine innings for the win. The game was full of great defense by infielders Butts and "Red" Moore. Kansas City was held to four hits and Atlanta to five, but the Black Crackers hits led to Howard's shutout victory. "One of the most dramatic games I ever saw at Ponce de Leon Park," was the description Ric Roberts gave at the finish."[440] The win was Atlanta's eleventh straight without a loss.

With that loss, the Monarchs left Georgia headed towards Alabama. Now that Atlanta was vanishing in the rearview mirror, they hurried over to Leeds, Alabama, and eventually to Birmingham's Rickwood Field for games against the Barons on consecutive days.

Buck O'Neil says...

"What would hurt you was the fact that you would have to go in a back door to get a meal. We played a lot of teams, White teams--we would play this ball club, and they could go in and eat. And somebody would have to bring us something, which was a horrible thing--a horrible thing."

Simple Mathematics

September 1-Atlanta, September 3-Leeds, September 4-Birmingham (DH), September 5-Birmingham (DH), September 8-Kansas City, September 10-Louisville, September 11-Kansas City (DH), September 14-Lincoln, September 18-Moberly

(NAL) O'Neil's Batting: G-5 AB-19 R-5 H-1 2B-2 3B-1 HR-0 RBI-0 SB-0 BA-2.63

O'Neil's Fielding: PO-38 A-4 E-1 DP-2 TC-43

The season was down to its final home series in a summer where it was well demonstrated that this Monarch team towered over nearly every Negro American League opponent in games won, except for Atlanta, and even those results were being disputed. As a unit, they demolished the Memphis Red Sox, first-half league champions, and other league members, but they had their problems with the Black Crackers, winners of the second-half pennant. Atlanta took six of the seven second-half games played between the two teams. Ultimately the Monarchs hadn't been declared champions of anything. O'Neil explained the contradiction in the league statistics versus the actual on the field results. "The way we played, now we probably [would have] won the thing [Negro American League [pennant] as far as games were considered."[441] He was probably right! Many of the games played by the Monarchs against other league teams were classified as exhibitions. Claiming the pennant or World's Championship was cumbersome and confusing. With the league pennant and league play behind them, Wilkinson and Baird were ready to barnstorm through the final weeks of the 1938 season. On tap was another long bus ride home from Atlanta, lots of visits to numerous Midwestern cities, and games with the Israelite House of David team. In preparation for an active September, extra players soon fortified Kansas City's already potent line-up. The late-season acquisitions included Barons' Clifford Blackman, a pitcher who was signed immediately after the final series in Birmingham, and infielder Ted Strong and catcher Raymond Taylor who joined from the Indianapolis ABCs. Having already acquired "Turkey" Stearnes and Eugene Bremer in late August, their presence added much more depth to the Monarchs' big-league line-up. Stearnes, born in Nashville, Tennessee, in the historic 14 Ward, was the son of Will and Mary-Everett, who resided on Fairfield Avenue during his youth.[442] He had worked as a Porter in a publishing house before signing his first professional contract with the Montgomery Grey Sox. Bremer, a native of New Orleans, Louisiana, where his parents Joseph and Amanda raised their family in the historic district of Ward 7, later lived on North Roman Street with his wife Elizabeth before moving north to Cleveland, Ohio.

(L to R) Ted "Double Duty" Radcliffe, an unknown woman, and James "Candy Jim" Taylor. In 1938 Radcliffe, born July 7, 1902, in Mobile, Alabama, managed the Memphis Red. (Authors collection)

The Monarchs league schedule was completed with visits to Birmingham and Atlanta. Kansas City bagged a 12-9 Saturday win over the Birmingham Black Barons in Leeds, Alabama, on September 3, then returned to whip the Barons in the next day's doubleheader at Birmingham by 7-2 and 8-6 scores on Sunday, September 4. Credit for the wins went to Willie "Train" Jackson, I.V. Barnes, and Hilton Smith--in that order. According to newspaper reports, a second doubleheader was played on Labor Day, September 5. This holiday double-bill was probably classified as an exhibition contest. Unfortunately, the results of that afternoon's scores have not been located.[18] Shortly thereafter, the Monarchs relaxed into an overnight excursion of long-distance driving for a seven-hundred mile, eleven-hour marathon turn-around back to Kansas City. Blackman, one of Birmingham's best hurlers, headed to Kansas City with the Monarchs.

On September 8, in a scheduled 8:30 p.m. start versus the Indianapolis ABCs a game preceded by a zany circus-styled promotion called Joe Engel's Wild Elephant Hunt, local fans were treated to some rare entertainment. Engel's show featured elephants, ostriches, giraffes, and one Donald Duck nine feet high. There was also an egg-laying contest between one of the ostriches and the big duck. The promoter, Engel, a former pitcher for the Washington Senators, was the current President of the Chattanooga Lookouts baseball team. His major league career started in 1911 when he joined the Washington Senators. His brief stay in the majors also included stops at Cincinnati and Cleveland, where he ended with a major league record of 17 wins 22 losses. He was better known as the P.T. Barnum of baseball, a title given him after he left the ball field for the box office. One of his most remembered promotions was the "Wild Elephant Hunt." On Opening Day 1938, Engel introduced the popular "Wild Elephant Hunt" before the game [at Chattanooga]. It was so successful he took it to ballparks throughout the South.[443] Fans waiting outside the stadium could hear wild elephant noises blaring inside. They were expecting to see real elephants. Once inside, they witnessed men in bamboo hats chasing after men running around in elephant suits."[444] In some cities, there were actual live animals in the park. "This is the widely known 'Wild Elephant Hunt,' with live elephants," wrote one newspaper. "This feature has been shown in many southern ballparks

---

[18] An article in Birmingham's *Age-Herald* advertised the Labor Day doubleheader but no scores were found.

and only recently in Oriole Park in Baltimore City."[445] How this promotion ended up in Kansas City is anyone's guess. After the pre-game activities, the Monarchs were victorious by a 5-to-1 score behind Blackman, Bremer, and Smith's seven-hit, eleven strikeout pitching. Blackman, who was pitching his first game for Kansas City, finished with four strikeouts.

Scoring three in the first, one in the third, and another in the fourth cemented the victory for Kansas City. Not including Milton's double, the game's other extra-base hits were launched by Quincy Trouppe who had two doubles, and Alfred "Buddy" Armour, who chipped in with a double and a triple. Indianapolis' lone score was on a fourth-inning home run by Trouppe. A Georgian by birth, a child of the great migration, Trouppe graduated from Vashon High School in St. Louis. He played amateur baseball for the local Post 77's American Legion when professional scouts started calling. In 1930, at age 18, he turned professional with the St. Louis Stars. In 1932 he played for Cumberland Posey's Homestead Grays and for a brief period J. L. Wilkinson's Monarchs––two of the most prominent teams in baseball. Trouppe recalled in his book, *Twenty Years Too Soon*, how he signed with Indianapolis in 1938,

> I got in touch with "Mountain Drop" Mitchell, manager of the Mound Blues
> team of Illinois, which was also known as the Indianapolis ABCs and we got
> together on a contract."[446] Speaking pompously, Trouppe added, "The fans
> voiced their sentiments, through the *Chicago Defender*, by voting Ted [Strong]
> and me into the East-West All-Star game, in Chicago, where I played left field for
> the West.[447]

Years later, in 1952, after signing a Cleveland American League Indians contract, Trouppe made baseball history by becoming the American Leagues' first African American catcher. He was the only player from the Negro American League season of 1938 to reach the majors--a feat he achieved at the advanced age of 39-years-old.

It wasn't surprising that Henry Milton chipped in with his team's only extra-base hit. As Willard Brown said, "Milton was the fastest man on the Monarchs for years."[448] Milton was adept at turning infield hits into singles and singles into doubles. The boy was a flat-out speedster and an all-around athlete in several sports. He was born in Montgomery County, Mississippi, formerly the homeland of the Choctaw nation, but later an area where the decedents of African American slaves who once labored in the district's many cotton plantations were routinely lynched. His home was the town of Winona, the county seat. It wasn't a safe place for a growing young Black boy. His widowed mother, Roxie Milton left in the Great Migration and moved the family to East Chicago, Indiana. The family lived in Ward Six, where Henry attended Washington High school, which was an integrated public institution. According to yearbook information, he excelled in baseball beginning in spring of 1927, track and field in 1928, and football.[449] Beneath Milton's 1929 senior picture was a quote, he enjoyed, "Diligent work makes a skillful workman." By 1930 Milton was living on Catalpa Street, biding his time as a laborer at a local chemical plant while being heavily recruited by Wiley College, an African American institution of higher learning in Texas. He left Indiana for Texas, where he was made a second baseman on Wiley's baseball team, a halfback on the football team, and a forward on Wiley's basketball squad. It was as an amateur track and field athlete that gave Milton his first national recognition.[450] In 1931 Milton, representing Wiley College at the Tuskegee Relays, ran the 100-yard dash in 9.9 seconds.[451] His time was only slightly behind that of Edward Tolan, an Olympian and holder of the World's Record at 9.5/10 seconds in the great dash. One newspaper declared, "They have the fastest man in the nation in Milton, the speed king who matched [Mozelle] Ellerbe [of Tuskegee Institute] stride for stride as a Wiley College star.[452]

Milton had "Cool Papa" Bell and Eddie Dwight's accelerated speed, but his on-base feats are seldom celebrated. His hitting is also overlooked. Milton was Kansas City's most persistent hitter in 1938, with many impressive days on the paths and at-bat throughout the season. The Monarchs won lots of games because of Willard Brown and Hilton Smith, but they won even more because of Milton. Some of his 1938 performances are worthy of extra recognition. In Davenport, Iowa, against the Illinois-Iowa League All-Stars, Milton went 3-for-5, scoring two runs and pilfering a base. On August 28, in a doubleheader against the American Giants he scored four runs in five at-bats and got three hits, including a triple. Milton returned in the nightcap to pick up three additional hits–a total of six hits for the doubleheader. He also gathered four hits in a July 25 game at Fargo's Barnett Stadium against the American Giants and picked up four hits on September 12 against Memphis. Equally effective on base, he stole four bases on May 22 against Indianapolis. Milton would wave his cap to fans, then take it and contort the bill in such a style that allowed it to fit into his back pocket. He was a class act on a baseball diamond.

In gaining the victory over the Indianapolis ABCs Kansas City surpassed 104 runs scored compared to 76 by their opponents in games played at Ruppert Stadium.

After the final Indianapolis game, infielder Ted Strong and catcher Raymond Taylor joined the Monarchs for the late season barnstorming tour. Fully revamped, Kansas City headed off to Kentucky for eight arduous hours of travel and another exhibition appearance in Louisville. It was a scheduled three-team doubleheader.

September 11 found the Monarchs at Louisville's St. Xavier Park. Leonard Mitchell, the local promoter, announced in the *Louisville Leader* that the Memphis Red Sox would meet Chicago's American Giants in game one, with the winner battling Kansas City in game two.[453] With that event concluded and the gate receipts settled, Wilkinson and his Monarchs boarded their bus for an anticipated overnight return of five hundred miles and eight more hours on the bus to Kansas City. These long road trips seldom bothered the Monarchs. They took the traveling in stride. Jim LaMarque and Allan Bryant, left-handed pitchers who came to the Monarchs during the 1940s, made their feelings known. We sometimes traveled five hundred miles a day to play baseball," recalled Jim LaMarque, a member of the 1940's Monarchs, "and actually, I never got tired." Allan "Lefty" Bryant, another member of the 1940's Monarchs, added, "It was a beautiful thing to see the world.[19]

On September 12, a doubleheader crowd of 3,000 watched as Kansas City thumped rival Memphis in 6-5 and 18-1 finals at Kansas City's Ruppert Stadium. The opener was a tug-of-war mêlée with Memphis getting an early two-run lead, a lead that held until the last half of the fifth. Kansas City recaptured the lead with a two-run outburst on the first of two Willard Brown home runs. Brown's second home run came in the sixth. Home runs were important to Brown's success, but his four-ply blast wasn't hit in abundance in 1938. He was having an off-season in the power department. One writer stated it best when he said,

> "Brown is up there swinging, and when he connects, there isn't a great deal of
> doubt where the ball is headed for usually it goes over the wall. Brown bats in a
> crouched position and the stance at the platter is unusual for his type of long-
> distance hitter, but the results speak for themselves"[454]

---

[19] Pre-game notices of the Louisville game appeared in both the *Chicago Defender* and *Louisville's Leader* newspapers, but scores were never located. Another reference in the *Pittsburgh Courier* said the games were played at Parkway Field and that Toad Franklin promoted the games.

Entering their half of the ninth, with the score 5-4 against them, newly acquired Ted Strong tied the score with a solo shot over the right-field barrier. Mayweather, pinch-hitting for O'Neil, tripled to the left-field wall, giving Kansas City a dramatic 6-5 ninth-inning win. Smith was the game's winning pitcher. Ted "Double Duty," who allowed two hits and a pair of runs in two and two-thirds innings, was the loser.

Memphis jumped out front in game two, scoring a single run early. Kansas City came storming back with a three-run third. All hell broke loose in that same frame when the game was marred by an argument. In 1938 there were no African American umpires at Ruppert Stadium, much to the annoyance of African American fans. Roy McDonald and Al Wallin were the two white men who umpired Monarchs' home contests. The Memphis third baseman and second baseman were ejected after squaring off in the face of umpire McDonald and disrupting the game with their indignant opposition to the umpire's call. The disputed play occurred at first base on Willard Brown's grounder. So disruptive was the ruckus it prompted the *call* to respond,

> When a player loses his head and resorts to physical objection to a decision, he
>
> has completely overstepped his bounds not only of good sportsmanship but of
>
> the rules of the game. This type of action on the part of our ballplayers is certainly
>
> not a step toward the major leagues.[455]

Some years later, Jackie Robinson would exemplify such a case. Should anyone man speak for an entire race of people? The obvious answer is no, but people are still debating the topic. Being a Black athlete meant you were naturally going to work harder, both on and off the baseball field. The travel was rigorous, the pay hideous, and recognition of your accomplishments were mostly undocumented. Ballplayers were not to be too threatening--although some, like Andrew Payne, Oscar Charleston, and Jud Wilson, were indeed just that. Above all, each team was to be a positive representation for the entire race, which was hardly individualistic. At the center of the Kansas City disagreement were third baseman Marlin Theodore Carter and second baseman Fred Bankhead.

The third inning dispute ultimately broke the Red Sox spirit, and it was all downhill from that point. Kansas City scored twice in the fifth. In the sixth, they sent a season's record of fifteen batters to the plate. Even more amazing, eleven of the sixth inning batters hit safely, and twelve scored as the Monarchs walloped Memphis 18-1. First baseman O'Neil pounded his old teammates' pitching for three hits, chipping in with two doubles, a triple, and two runs scored. Mayweather, the Monarchs' right fielder, went 3-for-4 with a double, a triple, and two runs scored. Blackman, the new Monarchs' pitcher, recorded a complete game. It is important to know more about Carter and Bankhead to understand how such an argument might occur.

Carter was born on December 27, 1912, in Shelby County, Texas, in the sawmill town of Haslam. Southern segregation was in order, and separate communities were laid out for the families of white and black workers.[456] His family moved to Louisiana, whereupon graduation from Shreveport's LCI High School, he began to play professionally for the Shreveport Louisiana Sports in 1931. Carter plowed his way through an assortment of teams before reaching Memphis in 1938. In 1932 he joined the Monroe, Louisiana Monarchs and eventually worked his way to Memphis but failed to stay the entire season. He later went to Cincinnati, Ohio, where he remained until some heavy influence from Olan "Jelly" Taylor assisted in his return to Memphis for another shot at the Red Sox. The other arguer was Fred Bankhead, a younger brother of Pittsburgh Crawfords' Sam Bankhead.

Fred was a new addition to the 1938 Memphis Red Sox after starting the season with the Birmingham Black Barons. He was no stranger to southern oppression, having been born in Lamar County in the town of Sulligent, Alabama, on November 22, 1912, in a historic cotton-producing region. The family migrated to Walker County, where his Father, Garnett, and Sam, an older brother, worked in a local Coal mine.[457] Fred, like many of the Negro major leaguers, was college-educated after escaping the harsh conditions of his childhood. He attended the all-black public school in Empire, Alabama. His alma mater was Daniel Payne College. To break into baseball, Fred hoboed to Chicago after college but ended up back in Birmingham, where he was signed by the Black Barons in 1937.[458] Why he ended up on the roster of the Memphis Red Sox is unknown when it was announced on September 18, 1938.[459]

Carter and Bankhead were not known to be temperamental. Neither was ever classified as disruptive brutes. They had grown tired of racial oppression and the perceived unfairness they felt on the field in Kansas City.

The two-game sweep concluded the Monarchs' 1938 home schedule at Ruppert Stadium. In winning fifteen games to their opponents' eight, they had played .652 percentage baseball on their home field. While winning these games, O'Neil and his teammates outscored their discontented foes by a whopping 128 to 82 differentials for an advantage of 46 points and an average of two more runs per contest over their opponents on their home ballfield.

The Monarchs concluded the home portion of their 1938 season with twenty-three games played at Kansas City's Ruppert Stadium. Eleven of the dates were parts of scheduled doubleheaders. Included in that total were five doubleheader sweeps captured by the Monarchs. All of the games, except for six, were played on Sunday. O'Neil performed well in all twenty-three of the contests, and so had Mayweather, who missed six of the home games because of injuries.

Appearing in every home contest, twenty-three in all, and in games for which every box score was publicly printed, O'Neil recorded a robust .289 batting percentage. He totaled fifteen runs scored, five doubles, one triple, eleven stolen bases, and two sacrifice hits to highlight the home portion of his Monarchs' rookie season. Some of these games were classed as exhibitions, even though they were all played against Negro American League teams. Modern-day historians have distorted the results even further by not presenting all of these totals, choosing instead to ignore some games.

For the Monarchs' thirteen home dates, attendance figures are sketchy. Attendance totals were not published for seven of the home games. The remaining six events drew 18,100 paid customers, an average of 3,016 paid for each game. The American Association Blues drew 257,913 fans to the stadium, an average of 3,416 per game for the total games played--but they played many more games at the Kansas City ball diamond. Once asked, "What will create a better interest in [Negro] baseball in the west," Wilkinson response was classic,

> Get some better ballplayers. There is a crying need for good talent in this league.
> And every club owner should go out and try to get the best material possible. If
> other owners in the league will go out and get some strong young prospects for
> next year, we will have crowds similar to those of the days of [the] the 1920s.[460]

The Blues returned to the Stadium on September 14 to face the league's Indianapolis Indians, thereby forcing Wilkinson's Monarchs back on the road. Road games were best for the Monarchs because of their unfavorable home attendance totals.

Hesitating long enough to avoid a small-town hotel stay, on September 14, two days after their final doubleheader in Kansas City, the series with Memphis resumed in Lincoln, Nebraska. Nebraska's long association with African American ballplayers is worthy of discussion.

The Lincoln Giants of 1890 were the first professional African American team in the Midwest. Sporting a roster of such well-known players like William Castone, Frank Maupin, John "Pat" Patterson, and George Taylor, their pioneering efforts were featured in *Sol White's History of Colored Base Ball* published in 1907. White noted,

> The Lincoln Giants made a great record during the season of 1890 playing
>
> Western League and State League teams: but their backing was not strong enough
>
> for continuance in the business, and 1890 saw the last of the Lincoln Giants.[461]

In 1892, when the Nebraska State League added Bud Fowler and William Castone to Lincoln; John Patterson, John Reeves and Frank Maupin to Plattsmouth; and George Taylor to Beatrice--six African American players on three teams--area correspondents to the *Sporting News* labeled the circuit as the "Coon League." In the summer of 1892, Nebraska's State League was America's only professional league with African Americans on its rosters. The unpleasing treatment that players received in Nebraska had not stopped Frank Maupin, Will Lincoln, and Jack Reeves from performing with David City, Nebraska, in 1894, although most African American athletes refused to perform in such a negative environment. These events appeared to carry little historical significance when the two Negro American League teams began to play in Nebraska's capital city.

Lincoln's Landis Field tussle between the Monarchs and Red Sox was a Wednesday 8:00 p.m. event. A crowd of six hundred, which included Coach Major Biff Jones and his entire Nebraska University grid football team, was on hand to observe the sedulous African Americans in an event sponsored by Pug Griffin.

Few things went awry in the Monarchs' 22-2 rout of Memphis. Monarch batters were having much more fun than the box score indicated. Committing only one error on defense, Monarchs' batters lashed a plethora of hits, twenty in all of four Memphis hurlers. Kansas City pounded six doubles, two triples, and twelve singles. Newt Allen led the way with a 3-for-5 evening at-bat that included a double, four runs scored, two runs were driven in, and a stolen base. O'Neil went 1-for-5 with a run scored. While his mates were gathering hit after hit, Barnes pitched six innings, scattering five hits. Eugene Bremer took over after Barnes's exit and tossed a five-hitter the remainder of the way. In Buck's recollection, this was the Monarchs' last Negro American League opponent, although there was nearly a month remaining in the 1938 season.

Now that the official Negro American League campaign was over, a September 17 edition of the *Pittsburgh Courier* announced the Atlanta Black Crackers as official winners of the league's second-half pennant.[462] Atlanta, with a 12-4 record and a .750 winning percentage, finished ahead of Chicago, the second-place contender, with a 17-7 record and a winning percentage of .682. Wilkinson, quarreling on behalf of the Monarchs, asked that the games played in the West between the two teams be tossed out. He was overruled by league officials. According to Robert R. Jackson, league president, "Kansas City's owner knew about them [the games] and ruled that the Atlanta victories stand."[463] Had Wilkinson been successful in eliminating Atlanta's victories over his Monarchs, they were still behind the American Giants in the official American League standings. W. B. Baker, Black Crackers business manager, proceeded to announce plans for a World Series with games planned for Memphis on September 18 and 19, a single game in Birmingham on September 20, and three games at Ponce de Leon Park in Atlanta on September 21, 22 and 23. The location of the series' final game was to be announced later.

As far as Kansas City was concerned, their publicized 13-10 second-half record was just part of the missing story. Publicized as a distant third-place finisher, behind the Black Crackers and American Giants, in reality, the Monarchs were probably the circuit's strongest team. The difficulty in proving their superiority could be credited to the puzzling way in which league games were scheduled and counted in the official standings.

Summarizing Kansas City's second-half setbacks, there was a 5-2 July 10 loss to Birmingham and a 2-1 loss to the American Giants on July 29, and a 7-2 loss to the same team on July 31. There were two losses to Indianapolis, 7-5, 6-5, and a third 4-2 loss in Chanute, Kansas, on August 16. The Atlanta Black Crackers accounted for six of the Monarchs' losses, by scores of 6-5 and 9-2 in Kansas City, a 12-11 loss in Junction City, another loss that hasn't been located, and two more setbacks in Atlanta on August 31, and September 1. Additionally, there was an 11-2 August 29 loss in Chicago that did not count in the official league standings--or did it? Despite the ten losses printed by league officials--of which there were thirteen second-half possibilities--Kansas City had a winning record, or at least a tie record, over every Negro American League opponent except the Atlanta Black Crackers during the 1938 season. O'Neil explained,

> The way we played, now we probably won the thing [Negro American League Championship] as far as games were considered, but Wilkinson didn't want to play nobody for the championship because that year we were going to barnstorm with a major league ball club where he was going to make more money than he would if we had played in the world series. We were going to pick up the House of David and take them all the way to Canada. We were going to be out of the league [for] maybe a month and a half.[464]

No further Monarchs' baseball games were played on the grounds of Ruppert Stadium after September 18. On that date, the American Association Blues were in Indianapolis playing the Indians. This same day, the Monarchs dashed over to Moberly, Missouri, and defeated Bill

Gatewood's Browns 6-to-0. The name Gatewood was one that O'Neil and his teammates treated with respect--and for a good reason.

William "Bill" Gatewood, an erstwhile Negro League pitcher, had performed in professional and semi-professional baseball circles since 1905. He was on the rosters of such illustrious teams as the Chicago Leland Giants, the Chicago American Giants, the St. Louis Giants, and Indianapolis ABCs. He was a pitcher of great ability. His specialty was throwing no-hitters. He tossed many, but most are yet to be found. On August 3, 1907, he no-hit the Kankakee Browns in Kankakee, Illinois. He returned on April 10, 1910, to no-hit the Louisville Stars, winning 11-0 in St. Louis, Missouri. He tossed other no-hitters, one of the last coming on June 6, 1921, when he no-hit the Negro National League's Cuban Stars. He had played for such men as Andrew "Rube" Foster in 1909 and J.L. Wilkinson in 1915, which explained to some degree why the Monarchs always came to Moberly.

Moberly's Gatewood Browns, both the team and their local park, owned and operated in tandem by Herbert Brown and Bill Gatewood, produced some well-known talent. Negro Leaguers Jimmy Crutchfield and Leroy Matlock of the Pittsburgh Crawfords were graduates of the Gatewood Browns. Moberly's 1938 team featured Raymond Bagby, Felix Fowler, Charlie Bundy, and Alfred "Army" Cooper. Kansas City collected eight hits off former Monarch Army Cooper to gain the victory. Cooper, a native of Kansas City, Kansas, had originally joined the Monarchs in 1927, playing his last Monarchs games in 1931. Members of the Gatewood Browns collected four hits in their team's loss. The playoff series between Atlanta and Memphis started that same afternoon.

In the Negro American League playoffs for the league pennant, Memphis defeated Atlanta 6-1 in the opener behind Ted Radcliffe's five-hit pitching and captured game two by an 11-to-6 score.[465] That's where the series ended as President Robert R. Jackson declared the playoff series a "no contest." Things had gotten complicated when Atlanta arrived late at Rickwood Field for a 7:00

p.m. game on September 20. Arriving at 8:30 p.m., Manager Radcliffe thought it was too late to start the game and asked the umpires, Moore of Birmingham, and Goodman of Memphis, to halt the night's activities. Dr. B. B. Martin, business manager of Memphis, conferred with Radcliffe and the two umpires, Black Barons' owner A. M. Walker, and with the owners of Rickwood Field. They all agreed with Radcliffe and stopped the game from starting.

The games scheduled for Wednesday, Thursday, and Friday in Atlanta were also called off. Atlanta's white Southern League team was using the park on Wednesday and Thursday. On Friday, a softball championship game had been billed, making the park unavailable. Atlanta's fans and owners thought the game should be postponed until Sunday. Dr. B. B. Martin refused to agree to this because of the heavy expenses of keeping his team in Atlanta. President Jackson was contacted, and a decision to halt the series was made. There would be no Negro American League World Series winner for 1938. The Monarchs, no longer a participant in the discussion, had already started a barnstorming tour.

"The Kansas City Monarchs' wrecking crew, who won a 22-2 encounter their last trip here this year, didn't have much respect for Count Clay, former Cub pitcher, Tuesday evening and closed the 1938 baseball season as far as Lincoln is concerned with a decisive 11-to-8 victory over House of David at Landis field before a 'cool' thousand fans."

Lincoln State Journal, September 28, 1938.

Buck O'Neil says...

"It's only human that people should have likes and dislikes, even have racial difference. But I think that if politicians--some of them, not all--let people decide for themselves, we'll stop tearing each other apart. It's a little more than just winning an election."

Barnstorming With The House Of David

September 20-Rock Island, September 22-Waterloo, September 23-Viroqua, September 26-Rock Valley, September 27-Lincoln, September 28-Concordia, September 30-Manhattan, October 2-Oklahoma City, October 6-Oklahoma City, October 9-Oklahoma City (DH)

(E) O'Neil's Batting: G-4 AB-9 R-0 H-1 2B-0 3B-0 HR-0 SAC-0 SB-0 RBI-0 BA-1.11

O'Neil's Fielding: PO-27 A-0 E-0 DP-0 TC-27

After several barnstorming events, just as O'Neil had forecasted, the Monarchs finished the 1938 season with a series of encounters against the Benton Harbor, Michigan-based Israelite House of David. All the games were played away from Kansas City, some in areas so remote scores have never been located. These two teams were as peripatetic as they came. Long forgotten and rarely discussed were the many quarts of oil, bus washes, tin cans of Gulflex grease, road tolls, and rubber tires that made barnstorming baseball profitable. Each had experienced the rigors of barnstorming as the best-known road warriors in baseball history.

As near as O'Neil could recall, the Monarchs began their season-ending series with the Israelite House of Davids on Tuesday, September 19, in Rock Island, Illinois. The series matched two of touring baseball's most popular attractions in games across the Midwest. The summer of 1938 had been a banner year for one of the Davids' former members. Grover Cleveland Alexander, a baseball great who managed the Israelite's from 1931 to 1935, although not a member of the House of David colony, saw his notoriety grow by leaps and bounds when he was elected to the Baseball Hall of Fame at Cooperstown, New York.

On January 18, 1938, Nebraska-born Alexander, known to many as just "Old Pete," was added to the list of baseball immortals at Cooperstown, New York. He surpassed the minimum of 197 votes or 75% of the total votes when 212 of the 262 members of the Baseball Writers of America voted for his entry.[466] When asked what he thought of the honor, Alexander, who had been flat broke, sick, and discouraged the year before, offered, "The Hall of Fame is fine, but it doesn't mean bread and butter. It's only your picture on a wall."[467]

House of David Ball Players

House of David.

The "Bearded Beauties" of 1938 had origins dating back to when the colony was started by

Benjamin Purnell, a former broom maker and twice-married circuit pastor from Kentucky. He

declared himself to be the seventh and final messenger of God, based on what he had read in the

book of Revelation, the last book of the New Testament. The founding year was 1903. He preached

with charisma from the Bible and found enough support to start a small colony on donated land in

Benton Harbor, Michigan. Colony converts weren't allowed to have sex. They were prohibited from

eating meat, drinking alcohol, tobacco smoking and surrendered all their personal property in

exchange for communal living.[468] Purnell's House of David religion was classified as a cult by

mainstream religions. He ignored their complaints and watched as the colony doubled, tripled, and quadrupled in size. He continued to preach the return of Jesus and the restoration of the Garden of Eden. His was an end-time ministry. The colony welcomed outsiders as tourists and supported itself locally by opening and managing businesses for tourism. A bowling alley, a local movie theater, jewelry shops, a greenhouse to sell produce, a large dance hall, a billiards parlor, and souvenir stands were built. They operated a vaudeville show and the world's largest miniature railroad. The attractions brought thousands to the little hamlet of Benton Harbor. Outside of Benton Harbor, they generated funding with their traveling jazz orchestra, a basketball team, and of course, a baseball team. Men did not cut their hair or beards, which was also based on scripture. The hairstyle of each baseball player was an individual decision. It could be braided, teased, curled, or brushed.

Like the Monarchs, the Israelite team had loaded up for the barnstorming series. Many former and future major and minor leaguers were added to their roster. Included among them were Ollie Marquard,**Error! Bookmark not defined.** Clifford "Count" Clay, George Zahn, Ardys B. Keller, Arnie Velcheck, Bill Pike, Hub Hansen, Eddie Lick, and Nick Gregory. Marquardt, real name Albert Ludwig at second base, had managed the Clinton, Iowa Owls to an Eighth place Three-I-League finish in 1938.[469] He was better known for having played with the Boston Red Sox in 1931 when he appeared in 17 games, getting 39 at-bats, 7 hits for a .179 batting percentage. Clay, formerly in the Chicago Cubs farm system, a player with Western Association and Western League experience, was the ace of David's pitching staff. Zahn, a one-time Western League pitcher, who had been on the Tulsa Texan League roster in 1938, was another starter. Keller, a former Nebraska native, was reputed to have hit .325 for the Davids in 1938.[470] Based on his 1938 performance, he was signed by the St. Louis Browns in 1939 and spent several years in their minor league farm system. When WWII broke out, Keller joined the 36th Texas Infantry. Shipped overseas, he died in action on September 29, 1944, near the French town of Biffontaine.[471]

Other members of the Davids also had careers in minor league baseball. Velcheck had played for the Alexandria Aces in the 1937 Evangeline League, where he batted .275 in 61 games. Pike had played in the Texas League. Hansen, the second baseman, was a former member of the Des Moines Western League team. Gordon O'Brien, formerly of Milton College in Wisconsin, was another pitcher. Eddie Lick, Jesse "Doc" Tally, George Anderson, and John Tucker had been with the team for several seasons and were classed as star athletes. The latter quartet was recognized as the original masters of the pepper game, a House of David specialty that entertained crowds all over America. The power-stroking Tally, in his younger days, was known as the "Bearded Babe Ruth." The team's record was undaunted regardless of the opposition dating back to 1934, with Alexander as manager.

Reportedly, in 1934 the House of David boys played 188 games and won 142 of them. The next year the schedule increased to 198 games, of which the Davids won 146. By 1936, when the House of David played a reported 211 games, they boasted a record of 147 wins.[472] Many of the Davids' losses over these years had come against the Monarchs. The Davids' record for 1938 included 162 games played and only 47 losses.[473] O'Neil remembered,

> They [the House of David] always had a good ball club, and it was a payday for our bosses because we were on salary. So many guys that were in the major leagues, or were on their way to the majors, played with the House of David. It was quite an experience, but a lot of travel because you played someplace [different] every day.[474]

The Monarchs and David's first stop was Rock Island, Illinois. In Rock Island, there were no hotels to accommodate African Americans, so O'Neil and his teammates split into groups and stayed with three different families. Some stayed at the home of Frank and Harriette Brown, while others stayed with Isaiah and Bertha Aldridge.[475] The remainder of the team lodged at the home of Reverend Albert and Hannah Collins.[476] Game one of the barnstorming series was already in jeopardy! The final game of the Illinois Iowa League, scheduled the day before at Rock Island, had been called off because of cold and wet grounds. Local fans were denied their chance to see the last game of the Double-I League schedule and the last chance to see Joe Engel Wild Elephant Hunt.

Bad weather kept the Monarchs and Davids from performing in Rock Island on the following evening, September 19. The field at Douglas Park was too wet. Combined with cold temperatures, it wasn't a good night to play an 8:00 p.m. game of baseball. The two teams were scheduled to play in Clinton, Iowa, on September 20, but a wire from that city read, "Ball Park in that city was underwater due to the flood condition of the Mississippi river."[477] Both teams agreed to remain in Rock Island for an attempted game on September 20.

On Wednesday, a night game was played. Hilton Smith's fastball and quick breaking curves whiffed twelve batters in seven innings, but the Monarchs lost 5-1. Zahn was pitching equally well, holding Monarch batters to seven hits and four batters struck out. Kansas City's only run was scored in the sixth. In that inning, Willard Brown laced a triple off the centerfield fence to drive in Bibbs. In the last frame, fog settled over the playing field and made continued play impossible for the players and the 500 people who were inside the park watching the action. Milton, Stearnes, and O'Neil all went hitless in that first loss, while Eddie Lick went 3-for-3 for the winners.[478] As the teams made their exit, commentary in the local *Argus* newspaper acknowledged, "The fielding, hitting and throwing was far superior to any around the Rock Island Park this season."[479] It was an audacious statement considering that the Rock Island team won both halves of the Double I schedule. Both teams boarded buses, exited Illinois, and eased into Iowa. The Davids traveled in a stuffy 15-

passenger Dodge bus. They cut a swatch across some very familiar territory as they headed towards Waterloo, Iowa.

Hilton Smith. *After graduating from a Giddings, Texas, High School, and following a short stay at Prairie View College, Smith joined the Senators, a team based in Austin, Texas. (Authors collection)*

In returning to Waterloo, one of the Monarchs' many scheduled Iowa stops, O'Neil's memory must have drifted to his first visit to the city in 1936. In that game, his former team, the Acme Giants, lost a close 4-3 game to the Waterloo Hawks.[480] Now that he was with the Monarchs, there was every reason to believe that his earlier setback would be his last in Waterloo. However, the scheduled Thursday night affair at Waterloo's Lions Field was canceled. Waterloo's *Daily*

Courier newspaper reported that the cancellation was due to "Weather conditions and the fact that the floodlight transformer which furnished lights for night games was transferred to the football field."[481] It was a lame excuse to scratch the game after tickets had already been sold. Both teams appeared in Viroqua, Wisconsin, a day later as afternoon entertainment for the Vernon County Fair. Waterloo and Viroqua were 150 miles apart.

Included among the Fair's tractor pulling contest, stock parades, and other attractions on Friday, September 23, was the Monarchs versus House of David game. A purse of $500 was at stake; the winner takes all.[482] As part of the pageantry, the 2:00 p.m. game drew thousands. The *Vernon County Censor* noted, "The grandstand was jammed, and the playing field fully surrounded. Five to six thousand people watching the game alone would be a conservative estimate."[483] Kansas City responded with a 12-to-7 win over the bearded beauties. On this same day, Harold Scherwitz, writing in the San Antonio Light, advised his readers that, "Most of the San Antonio Missions have agreed to play a post-season series against the touring Kansas City Monarchs, a strong negro team."[484] The Missions, a farm team for the St. Louis Browns operating in the Texas League, were on the Monarchs' schedule for a series of games starting Sunday, October 2.

On Monday, September 26 at Rock Valley, Iowa, Gordon struck out six over nine innings, allowed five hits to aid the House of David in a 1-0 win over the Monarchs. He allowed hits to Allen, Stearnes, Bibbs, and newly acquired Raymond Taylor. Blackman and Smith pitched in tandem for the Monarchs. Blackman, the Monarchs' starter, pitched a four-hitter and struck out six in seven innings before he was lifted for a pinch hitter but was credited with the loss. Still stewing over their defeat, the despondent Monarchs boarded the team bus for what was now a routine two-hundred-mile trip. They ended up in Lincoln, Nebraska, where another night game was scheduled for September 27.

(L to R) John "Buck" O'Neil, Ted Raspberry, and Wilber "Bullet" Rogan. Thomas "T. Y." Baird operated the Monarchs until 1955, then sold out to Ted Raspberry of Grand Rapids, Michigan, the only African American to ever own the Monarchs, but Baird's daughter told the author he never finished paying for the team. (Authors collection)

The Monarchs resumed their victorious romp with an 11-8 triumph over the Benton Harbor crew at Lincoln's Landis Field. Allen, Milton, Stearnes, and Strong, the Monarch's first four batters, collected a dozen hits between them as Kansas City slipped out front and kept piling up runs. In addition to sixteen total hits, Monarch batters accounted for three doubles and two triples. Hilton Smith was equally spectacular. He struck out eleven Israelite batters through eight innings before handing mound duties to reliever John "Buster" Markham. Smith's total strikeouts gave him at least five games of ten or more strikeouts during the summer of 1938. A fan that had come over from Plattsmouth, Nebraska, gave the game an adverse review. He wasn't amused by what the teams offered. In his estimation, "The game proved to be more of a circus than a contest for supremacy on the diamond."[485] The Monarchs' series of games scheduled to start on October 2 at San Antonio was reportedly canceled only days before they were to start when a local newspaper noted,

> Rumors that the San Antonio Missions baseball roster would be held together for some exhibitions games starting Sunday were dispelled today when Ralph Rhein, Art McDougal, Johnny Berardino, and Bus Payton left for the west coast.[486]

The cancellations forced Monarchs' owners to scramble for other exhibition dates. The infusion of better talent had sparked new life into the season-long banter of the now routine bus rides. Everyone was eager to keep the exhibition season going a bit longer. When traveling, athletes sought engaging conversation. No doubt they were also chatting with their comrades on the House of David team regarding the end of the 1938 season and how inclement weather had played a factor. The next stop for the teams was a jaunt to Concordia, Kansas.

The *Concordia Kansan* newspaper advertised the Wednesday evening Monarchs-House of David game for the local fairgrounds on September 28. Advertisements had been running for weeks.[487] The game, which was sponsored by the local Ban Johnson Baseball Club, was promoted as a fundraiser for the local baseball program. The follow-up to the game, however, wasn't much to write home about. The local promoter wasn't impressed after witnessing Kansas City squeak out a tight 9-8 final in what the *Kansan* described as a "very poor exhibition of what might be expected of these two teams."[488] Two days later, on Friday night, September 30, both teams landed in Manhattan, Kansas, where neither team needed an introduction. When Harold Larson, manager of the local

Ban Johnson team, booked the Griffith Field affair, they were hopeful for a large crowd. A newspaper report before the game announced the Monarchs' line-up as Milton, right field; Allen, second; Bibbs, third; Strong shortstop; Brown, left field; Stearnes, center field; O'Neal, first base; Else catching, and Taylor pitching.[489] Kansas City dominated the night in a 13-3 final as Monarch batters finished with sixteen hits off three House of David pitchers, Gordon, Tally, and O'Brian.[490] Only a small crowd assembled on this night to see Smith and Markham limit David's batters to seven hits. Details of that night's game were also limited.[491]

Back in Kansas City, the American Association Blues finished the 1938 regular season with an 84-67 league record, six games in arrears of league champion St. Paul. Joe Gallagher, a Blues outfielder, led American Association batters with 200 hits. The top four American Association teams went into a playoff, which Kansas City won. A win that put them into the Little World Series against the International League's Newark Bears of New Jersey. At the same time, an article in the Kansas *Plaindealer* newspaper provided details on the Monarchs' final games. The newspaper stated the Monarchs' next game would be "Sunday afternoon" October 2 in Oklahoma City.[492]

As September turned into October, men were exchanging their straw hats for jackets and overcoats. However, there were several exhibition games remaining on the 1938 schedule. Four of the Monarchs' final events were played in Oklahoma City starting on October 2. The Monarchs' first Oklahoma City opponent would be the House of David. Three other games, all against Jack Fitzpatrick's Oklahoma City All-Stars, were scheduled for Thursday, October 6, and as part of a Sunday doubleheader on October 9. Oklahoma City's Holland Field hosted all the games. The *Daily Oklahoman* wrote that the Monarchs versus David series stood at four wins in seven games played for the House of Davids.[493] The falsely advertised record was apparently used to increase fall attendance.

On October 2, the bewhiskered House of David team went down in a 14-3 defeat after the Monarchs scored three runs in the first on a Willard Brown circuit blow over the outfield wall in left field with two men on. Zahn and Gordon O'Brien pitched for the House of David, while Barnes went the distance and won for the Monarchs. Fitzpatrick, a local ballplayer of high regard, believed he could defeat the Monarchs and quickly organized some of the local professionals into an All-Star squad.

Fitzpatrick's All-Stars were composed of former Oklahoma City Indian players. Clay Touchstone, Jack "Lefty" Brill heart, Joe Bilgere, Lou Brower, Jim Keesey, Jack Calvery, Ray Flood, and Jim McLeod were the heart of Fitzpatrick's All-Stars. About 1,100 fans watched game one and enjoyed nine innings of spectacular pitching. Touchstone, a 16-game winner for the Texas League Oklahoma Indians in 1938, pitched a seven-hitter and struck out seven while holding the Monarchs scoreless for eight innings. On this day, catcher Jack Fitzpatrick's arm was tested. He failed horribly as Brown, Allen, Strong, Stearns, and Bibbs--five different players--all stole bases. Hilton Smith was the better pitcher on this day. He tossed a four-hitter and struck out six batters in a 1-0 win. The winning run was scored after Willard Brown singled to the right, stole second, and scored on Bibbs' single.[494] This set the stage for the much-anticipated Sunday doubleheader.

Before the game, the *Daily Oklahoman* reported the Monarchs' barnstorming record as 21 games played, with 16 wins and five losses since Labor Day.[495] The same newspaper gave the Monarch seasonal record as 131 games played. It reported further that this Monarch team had only been shut out twice in the entire 1938 season.

The weary Monarchs manhandled the All-Stars in both ends of the doubleheader, winning 6-4 in the opener and 5-0 in the abbreviated five-inning nightcap that was called because of darkness. A crowd of 1,300 looked on in wonderment at who these men were. Surely some might have wondered if they were better ballplayers than those in the Texas League. Kansas City strung together fifteen hits in the opener and seven hits in the nightcap to get wins for Markham and Barnes. Touchstone and Skedzel were the losing All-Star hurlers.[496] Brillheart, a former big-league pitcher with the Washington Senators and a winner of 19 games for the Oklahoma City Indians in 1938, tossed in the opener. The All-Stars were leading 4-2 until the third inning when Kansas City tied it at 4-all. When Brillheart made his exit in the sixth, the score was still even. Touchstone entered, and the Monarchs scored a pair of runs for the victory.[497] Kansas City obtained fifteen hits off the two Texas League pitchers and then added seven additional hits off Skedzel and Rogers in the nightcap for a total of 22 hits on the day compared to 16 for the All-Stars. Fitzpatrick's All-Stars, their season now over, didn't win a game.

With few fields left to conquer, the teams pushed back against the fidget winds of fall and yielded to football and other autumn activities. This closed O'Neil's rookie season, his first summer in a Monarchs' uniform, a neatly colored ball suit he would continue to wear for seventeen more seasons. It was the beginning of the young first baseman's legacy in Kansas City, a city where the rookie was soon to become a man with a legacy. Yet, and despite the details, both missing and discovered, this one season is only a snippet of all that John Buck O'Neil would experience in his baseball travels.

There was a price to be paid for choosing baseball, especially Negro baseball, as a professional occupation. While earning only a fraction of what players on National and American League rosters were being paid, they endured an endless travel schedule that started each season in April and ended in October. They covered thousands of miles over an American landscape that routinely denied them the simple pleasures of a meal in a restaurant or an overnight stay to wash up in a small-town hotel. For those who were fortunate, there were winter league opportunities in Cuba,

Puerto Rico, the Dominican Republic, Mexico, or California. Yet, for most, the Negro American League was the beginning and the end before eventually fading into history not yet told or fully appreciated for its contribution to the growth of America's great national pastime. Statistics alone will never explain the life they lived or how O'Neil and his teammates made this nation a better place for us all with a baseball, a baseball bat, and a dosage of good humanity. There is, however, a glorious ending to this story.

Lawrence "Biff" Jones (Center). As the head football coach of the Nebraska University Cornhuskers, Jones brought his entire football team to Lincoln's Landis Field to see the Monarchs manhandle the Memphis Red Sox on September 14, 1938. (Authors collection)

The Negro American League would continue to operate for many seasons. The league gave birth to such baseball royalty as Jackie Robinson, Sam Jethroe, Eugene Baker, Sam Jones, Hank Thompson, Ernie Banks, Willie Mays, Hank Aaron, and many others. John "Buck" O'Neil, as a first baseman, later a manager of the Kansas City Monarchs, and ultimately as a big-league coach and scout, played a pivotal role in this history. He could certainly make a claim, "I saw them all and helped many," without any fear of contradiction.

KANSAS CITY MONARCHS ROSTER, 1938

MANAGER

Andrew "Andy" Cooper

UTILITY

Wilber "Bullet" Rogan

PITCHERS

Alfred Marvin – (Not on roster after May)

Brantley – (July 1 only, first name unknown)

Charlie Beverly – Houston only, left April 10

Clifford Blackman– Joined September 8

Eugene Bremer – Joined August 26

Floyd Kranson

Hilton Lee Smith

I.V. Barnes

John "Buster" Markham

Joseph – (St. Louis only, first name unknown)

Gad McLemore – (Spring Training only)

Mosley Moses/Mosley Mose "Lefty"[20]

Richard "Dick" Bradley

---

[20] Who this player was is one of the great mysteries of the 1938 season? An April 30, 1939 article in the *Dallas Morning News* gave his name as Mosely Mose, and another article in a September 22, 1939 edition of the Wichita, Kansas *Negro Star* newspaper, also wrote about a Mosley Mose being a member of the Kansas City Monarchs. The Monarchs' second team scrap book in the author's collection has a photograph of a player which Newt Joseph, the team manager, wrote Mose on the image.

Ryan – July 17, Chicago, first name unknown)

Vaughan – (Keokuk only, first name unknown)

Willie "Train" Jackson – (Joined July 4)

INFIELDERS

Byron "Mex" Johnson

Eldridge Mayweather

Jack Marshall – Left May 15

John Jordan "Buck" O'Neil

Julius Alexander "Rainey" Bibbs – Joined July 25

Newton Henry Allen

Roosevelt Cox

Everett "Packinghouse" Adams, Joined – June 13

Luther Gillard – May 15 only

CATCHERS

Ernie Smith – Joined July 12, left July 28

Frank Duncan – Left July 12

Harry Else – Joined June 28

Johnny Dawson – Joined August 22

Raymond Taylor – Joined September 9

OUTFIELDERS

Betts (first name unknown)

Henry William Milton

Norman "Turkey" Stearnes – Joined August 1

Theodore "Ted" Strong – Joined September 9

Willard Jesse Brown

William "Bill" Simms – Left May 15

Endnotes

Somewhere Else, Someplace Better

1 "United States Census, 1920," database with images, Genealogy Bank (https://genealogybank.com/#), Warren O'Neal, Carrabelle, Franklin, Florida, United States. (Original index: United States Census 1920, FamilySearch, 2014)

2 "United States Census, 1920," database with images, Genealogy Bank (https://genealogybank.com/#), John J O'Neil, Sarasota, Sarasota, Florida, United States. (Original index: United States Census 1930, FamilySearch, 2014)

3 Wulf, Steve & Conrads, David. (1996). I Was Right on Time, Buck O'Neil, 20.

4 "Giants to Train In Everglades," Jersey Journal, 20 November 1923, 17.

5 "Communications," The New Smyrna Daily News, 24 April 1925.

6 "Salute Due Cub Scout Buck O'Neil," Sarasota Herald-Tribune, 17 February 1956, 11.

7 http://www.sarasotahistoryalive.com/history/articles/leagues-of-their-own/

8 "The Way We Were, with Phil S. Dixon," Kansas City Kansas Community College, 1986.

9 Ibid.

10 Cablevision Interview in Author's collection, January 21, 1984.

11 "Salute Due Cub Scout Buck O'Neil," Sarasota Herald-Tribune, 17 February 1956, 11.

12 "Buck O'Neil: Man With A Storied Past," Sarasota Herald-Tribune, 20 June 1971, 26.

13 "Baseball Great Coming to Town," Atchison Daily Globe, 16 February 2002, sports.

14 http://www.pbs.org/kenburns/baseball/shadowball/oneil.html

15 Ibid.

16 Cablevision Interview in Author's collection, January 21, 1984.

17 https://www.pbs.org/kenburns/baseball/shadowball/oneil.html

18 Cablevision Interview in Author's collection, January 21, 1984.

19 "Negro Teams Play Sunday," Sarasota Herald-Tribune, 1 December 1933, 6.

20 Dateline Sarasota, interview by Kerry Kirschner on YouTube, 1998.

21 Ibid.

A Whole New Ballgame

22 "White Fans May Finance Negro Team," Sarasota Herald-Tribune, 22 April 1930, 10.

23 "White Fans Go In For Fund To Equip Negroes," Sarasota Herald-Tribune, 25 April 1930, 12.

24 "Black Tigers Play Orlando," Sarasota Herald-Tribune, 27 April 1930, 12.

25 "Buck O'Neil: Man With A Storied Past," Sarasota Herald-Tribune, 20 June 1971, 26.

26 Dateline Sarasota, interview by Kerry Kirschner on Youtube, 1998.

27 "Black Tigers Play Negro Business Men," Sarasota Herald-Tribune, 26 August 1930, 8.

28 "At The Edwards This Week," Sarasota Herald-Tribune, 27 April 1930, 6.

29 "Black Tigers to Play Black Giants Monday," Sarasota Herald-Tribune, 5 April 1931, 8.

30 Ibid.

31 "Black Tigers Defeat Sebring Team, 9 to 1," Sarasota Herald-Tribune, 5 June 1932, 4

32 Wulf, Steve & Conrads, David. (1996). I Was Right on Time, Buck O'Neil, 40.

33 Wulf, Steve & Conrads, David. (1996). I Was Right on Time, Buck O'Neil, 42.

34 https://www.notablebiographies.com/supp/Supplement-Mi-So/O-Neil-Buck.html#ixzz71utcwvDy

35 "Jacksonville Nine Beats Miami Giants," Miami Herald, 2 April 1934, 8.

36 "Jacksonville Nine Beats Miami Giants," Miami Herald, 28 May 1934, 6.

37 "Colored Teams Divide Honors," Key West Citizen, 8 June 1934, 3.

38 "Favors New Ball Field," Key West Citizen, 9 June 1934, 3.

39 Wulf, Steve & Conrads, David. (1996). I Was Right on Time, Buck O'Neil, 44.

40 "Colored Baseball and Sports Monthly," October 1934, 16.

41 Ibid.

42 "Richmond Negroes Meet Miami Giants," Richmond Virginia Times Dispatch, 14 August 1934, 12.

43 "Miami Giants Too Tough For Capital City Stars," Richmond Times Dispatch, 15 August 1934, 11.

44 "Negro Baseball Teams Vie at Island Tonight," Richmond Times Dispatch, 17 August 1934, 17.

45 "Black Sox meet Bacharach Today," Chester Times, 25 August 1934, 13.

46 "Baseball Tonight," Syracuse Herald, 5 September 1934, 18.

47 "Hillsdales Meet Fla. Team in Balto., Baltimore Afro-American, 8 September 1934, Sports.

48 "Miami Giants Meet Edisons In Park Test," Schenectady Daily Gazette, 18 September 1934, 14.

49 "Miami Giants to play Richmond Stars Today," Richmond Times Dispatch, 28 September 1934, 18.

50 "Yellowjackets to Meet Miami Giants in Double Header," Burlington Daily Times-News, 3 October 1934, 2.

51 Wulf, Steve & Conrads, David. (1996). I Was Right on Time, Buck O'Neil, 47.

52 Wulf, Steve & Conrads, David. (1996). I Was Right on Time, Buck O'Neil, 51.

53 Ibid.

54 Wulf, Steve & Conrads, David. (1996). I Was Right on Time, Buck O'Neil, 52.

55 https://livinghistoryfarm.org/farminginthe30s/water_07.html

56 Ibid.

57 http://law2.umkc.edu/faculty/projects/ftrials/scottsboro/SB_acct.html

58 Wulf, Steve & Conrads, David. (1996). I Was Right on Time, Buck O'Neil, 54.

59 Wulf, Steve & Conrads, David. (1996). I Was Right on Time, Buck O'Neil, 55.

60 "Satchel Paige to Be Magnet for Fans on Night's Feature," Wichita Eagle, 15 August 1935, sports.

61 "Arizona Club in Tourney Victory," Wichita Eagle, 16 August 1935, sports.

62 "Denver Negroes Eliminated in Wichita Meet," Denver Post, 26 August 1935, 20.

63 Ibid.

64 Wulf, Steve & Conrads, David. (1996). I Was Right on Time, Buck O'Neil, 57.

65 Wulf, Steve & Conrads, David. (1996). I Was Right on Time, Buck O'Neil, 59.

66 Ibid.

From Dunseith To Memphis, And Back Again

67 "Sports Gossip," Brandon Daily Sun, 16 May 1936, 3.

68 "Islanders Beat Colored Stars - - Farmall to Meet Andover," Rock Island Argus, 16 May 1936, 14.

69 "Acme Giants Conquer Moose Sunday, 5 to 2," Rockford Register-Republic, 18 May 1936, 16.

70 Bohn, Terry, (2019). Hired Batteries, 242.

71 https://commerce.nd.gov/uploads/8/CensusNewsletterOct2014.pdf

72 "Four Best Ball Clubs Here in Tournament," Brandon Daily Sun, 17 June 1936, 4.

73 Bohn, Terry, (2019). Hired Batteries, 243.

74 O'Neil, Wulf, and Conrads, 65.

75 "Valley City Signs Five Negro Stars; Leagues Organized," Bismarck Daily Tribune, 30 April 1936, 14.

76 "Bismarck Wins Brandon Tourney," Winnipeg Free Press, 19 June 1936, 32.

77 "Hi-Liners Conquer Local Nine in Page Tournament," Bismarck Tribune, 20 June 1936, 25.

78 "Sports scribes join Schmeling At Party Celebrating Victory," Greensboro Daily News, 21 June 1936, 35.

79 "Bismarck Scores 9-3 Triumph Over Acme Giants to Win Virden Tourney," Bismarck Tribune, 24 June 1936, 7.

80 "Bismarck Wins Portage Tourney," Winnipeg Free Press, 25 June 1936, 20.

81 "Ball Tourney," Russell Banner, 2 July 1936, 8.

82 "Negroes Win at Arlington," Omaha World-Herald, 3 September 1936, 13.

83 "Omaha Team in Title Play," Omaha World-Herald, 4 September 1936, 30.

84 "Bell Breaks Even in Double-Header," San Antonia Express, 21 September 1936, 8.

85 "All-Stars Lose Two To Spiders," San Antonia Express, 5 October 1936, 7.

86 O'Neil, Wulf, and Conrads, 66.

87 "Negroes Pay Before Entering Mexico," Detroit Tribune, 1 August 1936, 5.

88 Shreveport Times, April 12, 1937, sports.

89 Ibid.

90 Ibid.

91 "The Newest thing on the Baseball Diamond: Zulu Cannibals Set Fashions," Chicago Grafieldian, 30 July 1936, 2.

92 "Buck O'Neil: A star from a Royal Era. Kansas City Star Magazine, 15 March 1981, 14-15.

93 Ibid.

94 "North Iowa Clubs to see Action on Sunday Ticket," Mason City Iowa Globe-Gazette, 4 June 1937, 24.

95 "Zulu Baseballers here on Friday," Winnipeg Free Press, 17 June 1937, 17.

96 Wulf, Steve & Conrads, David. (1996). I Was Right on Time, Buck O'Neil, 73.

97 Ibid.

Kansas City, My Kind Of Town

98 McShann, Jay. Telephone Communication, Interview by Author, Kansas City, Missouri 1980s.

99 "Society News," Kansas City, Kansas Plaindealer, 18 February 1938, 5.

100 Kansas City, Kansas Plaindeler, 2 September 1938, 3.

101 "Monrovians Present Fashion Revue," Kansas City, Kansas Plaindealer, 15 April 1938, 8.

102 Telephone Interview with Chester Owens of Kansas City, Kansas, 5 January, 2008.

103 "Wilberforce Jubilee Concert," Kansas City, Kansas Plaindealer, 11 February 1938, 5.

104 O'Neil, John "Buck". Interview by Author. Tape recording. Kansas City, Missouri, 14 January, 1985.

105 "Jimmie Lunceford to Battle White Girls Band Here Tuesday," Kansas City, Kansas Plaindealer, 4 March 1938, 5.

106 http://cinematreasures.org/theaters/4866

107 https://www.imdb.com/name/nm0130572/

108 https://www.arts.gov/honors/jazz/andy-kirk

109 "Well-known Fight Promoter Attends Lewis-Kranz Fight," Kansas City Call, 28 May 1937, 8.

110 https://www.imdb.com/name/nm0275297/bio

111 https://www.imdb.com/name/nm0913405/bio?ref_=nm_ov_bio_sm

112 Peiss, Kathy. Zoot Suit: The Enigmatic Career of an Extreme Style, 2014.

113 http://www.encyclopediaofarkansas.net/encyclopedia/entry-detail.aspx?entryID=6277

114 Brown, Ernest L., Kansas City Call, 29 July 1938, 12.

115 "Joe Rogan, Idol of Negro Fans, Here Tomorrow Night," Topeka Daily Capital, 11 August 1938, sports.

116 "Chicago American Giants Battle Kansas City Monarchs Here Sunday," Dallas Times Herald, 24 April 1938, section 2, 5.

117 "A Poor Sport at the Negro Ball Game," The Delta Democrat-Times, 16 August 1939, 2.

118 Hiller, Holly. "A Baseball Memoir George Giles, Manhattan, Kansas Mercury, 27 May 1984, D1.

119 "Athletes Run Into Hotel Jim Crow At Chicago Big Ten Meet," Kansas City, Kansas Plaindealer, 8 July 1938, 2.

120 Finnigan, Bob. "Baseball Runs In Their Bloodline," Manhattan, Kansas Mercury, 28 June 1990, D1-D6.

121 O'Neil, John "Buck." Tape recording of Cablevision Interview in Author's collection. Overland Park, Kansas, 21 January, 1984.

The Negro American League

122 Webber, H.B and Brown, Oliver. "Play Ball!," The Crisis, May 1938.

123 "The Way We Were, with Phil S. Dixon," Kansas City Kansas Community College, 1986.

124 "Antique Dealer's Hobby Keeps Him on The Road," Springfield News-Leader, 3 May 1936, B4.

125 "Local Boy To Start Contest Here Saturday," Wichita Beacon, 14 June 1928, 11.

126 Bell, Julian. Personal Communication, 1987.

127 Cowans, Russ J., "Thru the Sport Mirror," Detroit Tribune, 12 December 1938, 7.

128 Julia Mae Jones. Personal Communication, 1984.

129 Ibid.

130 Holway, John. Voices from The Great Black Baseball Leagues, 287.

131 "Monarchs To Oppose Georgians," Kansas City Call, 3 June 1938, 6.

132 James "Gabby" Kemp. Personal Communication, 1987.

133 "Fans Meet The Memphis Red Sox Owners and Players," Chicago Defender, 23 July 1938, 9.

134 Ted "Double Duty" Radcliffe. Personal Communication, 31 May 1987.

135 https://en.wikipedia.org/wiki/Damon_Runyon

136 Ted "Double Duty" Radcliffe. Personal Communication, 31 May 1987.

137 Fullerton D. Christopher, Every Other Sunday, Boozer Press, 1999, 110.

138 Kansas City Call, 24 March 1933, sports.

139 Marlin Carter. Personal Communication, 1980s.

140 Ibid.

141 "The Mound Blues Who Will Represent Indianapolis in the American League," Indianapolis Recorder, 21 May 1938, 12.

142 Swanton, Barry, and Mah, Jay-Dell, Black Baseball Players In Canada, McFarland, 22.

143 "Jacksonville Florida Red Caps invade Chicago for the First time," Chicago Defender, 4 June 1938, 8.

144 "The Standings," Chicago Defender, 23 July 1938, 9.

Help At The Initial Sack

145 Caddo-Shreveport Health unit birth Certificate, certified copy of public records, 19 January 1942.

146 Enlisted Record and Report of Separation Honorable Discharge papers, 5 October 1945.

147 Jones, Julia Mae. Interview by Author, Personal Communication, 1984.

148 "Monarchs In West Winning Ball Games, "Kansas City Call, 19 July 1935, 6.

149 "Locals Drop 5-1 Decision To Kansas City Monarchs Team," Borger Daily Herald, 13 May 1936, Sports.

150 O'Neil, John Buck. "The Way We Were, with Phil S. Dixon," Video recording with the Author. Kansas City Kansas Community College, 1986.

151 Powers, Jimmy. "Big Leagues Ignore Colored Aces," New York Daily News, 11 September 1938, 89.

Spring Training With The Champions

152 "Monarchs In A Long Tie," Kansas City Times, 13 September 1937, 13.

153 Cowans, Russ J. "Thru the Sport Mirror," The Detroit Tribune, 14 August 1937, 7.

154 O'Neil, John "Buck." Interview by Author, Tape recording. Kansas City, Missouri, 14 January 1985.

155 Barnes, Sarah. Telephone Interview with Phil S. Dixon, 19 January 1985.

156 Marshall, William "Jack". Telephone interview with Phil S. Dixon, 17 December 1985.

157 Posey, Cumberland. Posey's All-American Ball Club!" Pittsburgh Courier, 10 October 1931, 5-section 2.

158 "Dizzy Dean to 8,000," Kansas City Times, 3 October 1933, 10.

159 "Negro Hurler Fans 14 Men, Blanks Stars," The Oklahoman, 12 October 1933, 12.

160 "Monarchs Win in Ninth," Kansas City Times, 16 October 1933, 10.

161 "Dean All-Stars Beaten 9-0 by Monarch Team," Des Moines Register, 14 October 1934, section 7, 1.

162 "Kansas City Wins 7-1 Tilt From Phillies," Chicago Defender, 16 April 1938, 8.

163 "Snappy Baseball, Colored Teams Give Fine Display In First Battle," Winnipeg Free Press, 16 July 1938, 35.

164 "C. Torrienti, Famous Ball Players, Dies," Chicago Defender, 23 April 1938, 20.

165 Foster, Willie. Interview by Chalk, Oceania, tape recording. Year unknown.

166 Gottlieb, Ferdinand. "Notes Of The Sports World," Plantation, Kansas Observer Enterprise, 31 May 1917, sports.

167 Byas, Richard "Subby." Interview by Author, Chicago, Illinois, 1980s.

168 "Monarchs, Stars to Close Out Series Here Tonight," Houston Chronicle, 12 April 1938, 26.

169 "Grays, Monarchs Divide as 3,000 Watch Twin Bill," New Orleans Times-Picayune, 18 April 1938, 18.

170 "Game Cancelled," Monroe Morning Star, 20 April 1938, 18.

Back To Texas, Headed North

171 "Negro Giants Defeat Kansas City Monarchs," 21 April 1938, Sports

172 "Negro Pro Clash on Trojan Field Thursday," Tyler Morning Telegraph, 20 April 1938, 6.

173 "Major Loop Negro Team To Play Here In Thursday Game," Tyler Courier-Times-Telegraph, 17 April 1938, 11.

174 "Negro Majors Play Friday, Matthewson Park," Marshall News Messenger, 21 April 1938, 5.

175 "Negro Teams to Play April 22," Marshall News Messenger, 14 April 1938, 5.

176 "Over 600 Fans See Kansas City Drub Chicagoans, 9-1," Marshall News Messenger, 24 April 1938, 7.

177 "Famous Negro Nine To Play At Steer Park," Dallas Express, 23 April 1938, 3.

178 "Ruth and Gehrig of big Time Negro Ball Opponents Here," Dallas Morning News, 22 April 1938, section 2, 3.

179 "Chicago Giants Beat Monarchs in Negro Clash," Dallas Times Herald, section 2, 2.

180 "Giants Drug Monarchs in Baseball; Stearnes Leads Long Range Attack," Dallas Express, 30 April 1938, 3.

181 Ibid.

182 "Negro Nines will Contest Tonight," Waco News-Tribune, 26 April 1938, 7.

183 Ibid.

184 "Kansas City Nine Downs Chicagoans," Waco News-Tribune, 27 April 1938, 7.

185 "Morgan Line Will Play Chicago Giants Tonight," Galveston Daily News, 28 April 1938, 8.

186 "Oilers To Play Bartlesville," Enid Daily Eagle, 27 April 1938, Sports.

187 "Monarchs To Battle Larks," The Hutchinson, Kansas News, 27 April 1938, 2.

188 "Cooper or Rogan Pitch Here Friday," Joplin Globe, 29 April 1938.

189 "Miners Outhit Monarchs, But Make Five Errors as K.C. Team Wins," Joplin Globe, 30 April 1938, 8.

190 "Monarchs Battle Cards Sunday," Springfield Daily News, 30 April 1938, 9.

191 "Monarchs Get Cardinals Club In Match Here," Springfield Leader and Press, 29 April 1938, 27.

192 "Weldon Faces Joplin Miners In Opening Scrap Wednesday," Springfield Daily News, 1 May 1938.

193 "Lick Monarchs Andy Van Slate To Hurl Friday," Springfield Leader and Press, 2 May 1938, 6.

194 "Springfield Cards Jolt Monarchs," Springfield Daily News, 2 May 1938, 6.

195 "Lick Monarchs Andy Van Slate To Hurl Friday," Springfield Leader and Press, 2 May 1938, 6.

Ring Around The Circuit

196 O'Neil, John "Buck." Interview by Author. Tape recording. Kansas City, Missouri, 1985.

197 "From Dixie," Pittsburgh Courier, 14 May 1938, 17.

198 "To Play Larks Tomorrow Night," Hutchinson, Kansas News, 27 April 1938, 2.

199 "The Kansas City Monarchs," Banner-Journal, 22 June 1938, 5.

200 "Monarchs meet Burnt Crackers," 6 June 1938, Wichita Eagle, 6.

201 "Thousand see Coons whip the House of David," Vernon County Censor, 28 September 1938, 5.

202 Etkin, Jack. Innings Ago, 11.

203 Hockaday, Laura R. "Baseball has changed a lot in 53 years," Kansas City Star, unknown.

204 "Antique Dealer's Hobby Keeps Him on the Road," Springfield News-Leader, 3 May 1936, B4.

205 Dryburgh. Dave. "Along the Sport Byways," Regina Leader-Post, 22 July 1938, 16.

206 Ferguson, Jay H. "Give 'Em a Tincup, Dark Goggles," Chicago Bee, 1 May 1938, 10.

207 Ibid.

208 Ibid.

209 Haupert, Michael. "MLB's annual salary leaders since 1874," https://sabr.org/research/mlbs-annual-salary-leaders-1874-2012

210 O'Neil, John "Buck." Interview by Author. Tape recording. Kansas City, Missouri, 1980s.

211 Young, Maurice "Doolittle." Interview by Author, 1980s.

212 O'Neil, John "Buck." Interview by Author. Tape recording. Kansas City, Missouri, 1980s.

213 Williams, Jesse. Interview by Author. Kansas City, Missouri, 1984.

214 Duncan, Frank Jr. Telephone Interview by Author. Kansas City, Missouri, 1984.

215 "Antique Dealer's Hobby Keeps Him on the Road," Springfield News-Leader, 3 May 1936, B4.

216 The Way We Were, Kansas City Kansas Community College, 1986.

217 "Stars new 2nd Baseman," St. Louis Argus, 17 April 1931, 7.

218 "Kansas City Monarchs, Fielding Prejudice," Vibrations, Sunday Magazine of the Columbia Missourian, 2 August 1981, 4.

219 O'Neil, John "Buck." Interview by Author. Tape recording. Kansas City, Missouri, 24 January 1985.

220 Ibid.

221 "Roundy Says...," Madison Wisconsin State Journal, 24 May 1938, 9.

222 "Double Bill Carded," The Memphis Commercial Appeal, 9 May 1938.

223 "Red Sox Victors In Double-Header," The Press-Scimitar, 9 May 1938, 10.

224 "Sox Win Twin Bill from K.C.," Pittsburgh Courier, 14 May 1938, 17.

225 "Memphis Red Sox Defeat Monarchs," The Press-Scimitar, 11 May 1938, Sports.

226 "Negro American League Teams To Play Game Here," Arkansas Gazette, 8 May 1938, 13.

227 "Monarchs in Win Over Chicago Giants," Arkansas Gazette, 12 May 1938, 17.

228 "Cancel Exhibition Go By Negro Ball Clubs," Springfield Daily News, 13 May 1938, 23.

229 "Monarchs Play Giants Tonight," Springfield Leader and Press, 12 May 1938

Winning, It's What We Do

230 Byas, Richard "Subby." Interview by Author. Chicago, Illinois, 1980s

231 "Chanute seeks to win a pair." Chanute Tribune, 14 May 1938, 8.

232 "May call Monarch game," Chanute Tribune, 15 May 1938, 8.

233 "Monarchs Edge Oilers 3 to 1," Enid Morning News, 18 May 1938, 7.

234 "Davids Next on Oiler Schedule," Enid Morning News, 19 May 1938, 9.

235 Posey, Cum. "Posey's Points," Pittsburgh Courier, 7 May 1938, 16.

Double For Your Trouble

236 Marshall L. Riddle. http://www.uky.edu/Libraries/NKAA/subject.php?sub_id=7

237 "ABC's Lose," Kansas City Call, 27 May 1938, Sports.

238 "Two for Monarchs," Kansas City Times, 23 May 1938, 11.

239 "American Giants and Monarchs in Series," Chicago Daily News, 25 May 1938, 23.

240 "Call off game," Des Moines Tribune, 23 May 1938, 2A.

241 "All-Stars conclude set with Monarchs," Peoria Star, 25 May 1938, 14.

242 "Monarchs Top A.M. Nine, 10-4," Peoria Transcript-Journal, 25 May 1938, Sports.

243 "Monarchs Top All-Stars, 6-2, Peoria Transcript-Journal, 26 May 1938, sports.

244 "Mills, Kansas City Monarchs Play Friday," Chicago Auburn Parker, 25 May 1938, 19.

245 "Kansas City has some Fun with Chicago," Chicago Defender, 4 June 1938, 9.

246 "Kaysees Victor in Mound Duel over, Chi, 3-1," Baltimore Afro American, 4 June 1938, 23.

247 Ibid.

248 "Kansas City has some Fun with Chicago," Chicago Defender, 4 June 1938, 9.

The Streak

249 "Blatz gives 6 hits as Blues win, 3-2, from Monarchs," Wisconsin State Journal, 2 June 1938, sports.

250 Brown Jr., Ernest. "Sports Chatter," Kansas City Call 10 June 1938, 7.

251 Etkin, Jack. Innings Ago, p. 103.

252 The Way We Were, Kansas City, Kansas, Community College, 1986.

253 Brown, Willard. Telephone Interview with Author, May, 1987.

254 Etkin, Jack. Innings Ago, p. 103.

255 "Great hurler will arrive with players," Pampa News, 11 May 1936, unknown.

256 "Monarchs bring fast ball team," Wichita Eagle, 5 June 1938, 5A.

257 "Negro teams meet at Moody stadium," Galveston Daily News, 10 April 1938, 16.

258 "Johnson, C. C. Sporting News Publishing Company, 7 June 1974, A compiling of Brown's minor league statistics.

259 Moore, James "Red." telephone interview, 18 July, 2007.

260 "K.C. Monarchs in shutout victory," Wichita Eagle, 7 June 1938, 6.

261 "Kansas City Wins Off Atlanta, 3-1, The Oklahoman, 8 June 1938, 12.

262 "Detroit stars seek player deal with Monarchs," Chicago Defender, 22 January 1938, 9.

263 "Detroit, Monarchs dicker for a trade," Chicago Defender, 15 January 1938, 9.

264 Rogosin, Donn. Invisible Men, p. 13.

265 "Kansas City wins 7-1 tilt from Phillies," Chicago Defender, 16 April 1938, 8.

266 "All-Stars conclude set with Monarchs," Peoria Star, 25 May 1938, 14.

267 "K.C. Lads in 12 to 3 victory," Manhattan Morning Chronicle, 9 July 1938, 3.

More Exhibitions, Less League

268 "Beat the Barons Twice," Kansas City Times, 13 June 1938, sports.

269 "Black Barons Defeated Twice By Kansas City, 5 to 1, 2 to 1," Atlanta Daily World, 15 June 1938, 5.

270 "Monarchs Take Both End of Doubleheader from Barons," Kansas City Call, 17 June 1938, Sports.

271 Gannon, Pat. "They Say in New York," Milwaukee Journal 18 September 1938, 25.

272 "Dixie Whites Would Not Quit Big Leagues if Our Men Could Play," Chicago Defender, 18 June 1938, 21.

273 "hufschmidt Defeats East St. Louis in Wild Trolley Duel, 11 to 7," East St. Louis Journal, 13 June 1938, 8.

274 "Manager says Best Hurlers Saved to Beat Local Tossers," Belleville News-Democrat, 14 June 1938, part 2.

275 Ibid.

276 "Kansas City Monarchs Nose Out East St. Louis in 10th, 6 to 5," East St. Louis Journal, June 14, 1938, 9.

277 Brisker, William. "Monarchs Stage Exciting Rally To Beat Trolley Leaders in 10 Innings," St. Louis Argus, 13 June 1938, 11.

278 http://www.americanbreweriana.org/history/bvil2.htm.

279 https://www.britannica.com/topic/Volstead-Act

280 http://en.wikipedia.org/wiki/Twenty-first_Amendment_to_ the_United_States_Constitution.

281 http://gb-beer.com/our-story

282 http://www.lib.niu.edu/ipo/1996/ihy961218.html.

283 http://www.americanbreweriana.org/history/bvil2.htm.

284 http://pre-prowhiskeymen.blogspot.com/2014/11/henry-l-griesedieck-whiskey-man-in-beer.html

285 "Stags Seeking First Victory Over Monarchs," Belleville News Democrat, 13 June 1938, Sports.

286 "President "Bud" Meyer names Sox as Tuesday night rival of Locals," Belleville News Democrat, 15 June 1938, part 2.

287 "Kansas City Monarchs swamp Chairs 20 to 4," Sheboygan Press, 3 July 1937, 13.

288 "Chairmakers defeat Memphis Red Sox 16-1," The Sheboygan Press, 17 August 1937, 12.

289 Johnson, Lloyd. The Minor League Register, p. 136.

290 "Kansas City Monarchs trip Chairmakers by 8-2 score," Sheboygan Press, 17 June 1938, 12.

Chicago, A Great Baseball City

291 "Monarchs, Giants, to Play Four Games Here," Chicago Daily News, 15 June 1938, 27.

292 "Kansas City Monarchs Win From Mills, 7 to 2," Chicago Daily Tribune, 18 June 1938, 19.

293 "Mills Play Kansas City Monarchs Sunday," Oak Park Oak Leaves, 23 June 1938, 47.

294 "Mills Seek Revenge in Tilts Sunday," Chicago Daily News, 24 June 1938, 20.

295 "Kansas City Monarchs Beat American Giants, 5 to 0," Chicago Daily Tribune, 19 June 1938, A2.

296 "Monarchs beat Giants, 7-2, then lose to Coals, 5-4," Chicago Daily Tribune, 21 June 1938, 19.

297 Ibid.

298 "Kennedy Streak Extended to Four," Flint Journal, 23, June 1938, 26.

299 "Harlem Goes Wild Over Louis Victory," Galveston Daily News, 23 June 1938, 8.

300 "Monarchs and Mills Meet in 2 Games Today," Chicago Daily Tribune, 26 June 1938, B2.

301 "Mills vs. Monarchs, Coals vs. Collegians," Chicago Daily Times, 26 June 1938, 26.

302 "Chicago Mills in Double Holiday Bills," Chicago Garfieldian, 30 June 1938, 11.

303 "Kansas City Wins 7 to 4 from Chicago," Chicago Defender, 9 July 1938, 8.

304 "Monarchs Defeat Chicago Team, 7-4," Milwaukee Journal, 29 June 1938, 23.

305 "Monarchs win 10 to 0," Black River Falls Banner Journal, 6 July 1938, Sports.

306 "Giants Wallop Texas Spiders." Mason City Globe-Gazette, 10 September 1938, 31.

307 "Kansas City Monarchs Here on Thursday," Charles City Press, 29 June 1918, sports.

Edged Out Of A Pennant

308 Foreman, Ross. "Bubba Hyde discusses baseball career," 21 June 1991, Sports Collectors Digest, 102.

309 Carter, Marlin. Interview with Author, Memphis, Tennessee, 1980s.

310 Ibid.

311 Hyde, Cowan. Telephone Interview with Author, 1980s.

312 Radcliffe, Ted. Interview with Author, Chicago, Illinois, 1980s.

313 Carter, Marlin. Interview with Author, Memphis, Tennessee, 1980s.

314 Erardi, John. "Year of the Tigers," Cincinnati Enquirer, 13 May 2007, Sports.

315 "Monarchs Take Exhibition Game," Manhattan Morning Chronicle, 6 July 1938, 3.

316 http://en.wikipedia.org/wiki/Dust_Bowl

317 "Monarchs trip Oilers 13 to 5," Enid Morning News, 7 July 1938, 6.

318 "Monarchs Nip Barons 12 to 3," Topeka Kansas Whip, 15 July 1938, 1.

319 "Mob Lynches Negro Hunted as Murdered," Arkansas Gazette, 18 October 1938, 3.

320 "Practice No longer Confined to the South," 17 November 1900, 17.

321 Missouri's Black Heritage, p. 148.

322 O'Neil, John "Buck." Tape recording of Cablevision Interview in Author's collection. Overland Park, Kansas, 21 January, 1984.

323 "Two for the Monarchs," Kansas City Times, 31 May 1937, 8.

324 "Birmingham Drops Ban on Negro-white Competition in Baseball and Football," Kansas City Call, 2 February 1954, sports.

325 "7,000 Attend Initial Night Contest Here," Dallas Morning News, 8 May 1930, 21.

326 Burnette, Merrill. "Cowboys drop 3 to 1 verdict to Monarchs," Dallas Morning News, 12 July 1938.

327 "Cowboys Play Strong Negro Team Tonight," Sioux City Journal, 11 July 1938.

328 Burnette, Merrill. "Cowboys drop 3 to 1 verdict to Monarchs," Dallas Morning News, 12 July 1938.

329 "A new catcher," Kansas City Sun, 11 June 1921, 8.

330 Duncan, Frank Jr. Telephone Interview with Author, 15 November 1986.

331 Ibid.

332 Ibid.

333 Bell, Julian. Telephone Interview with Author, 1980s.

334 Grayson, Harry. "The Payoff," Altoona Mirror, 30 August 1938, 13.

Into Minnesota And Beyond

335 "Monarchs and Giants," Crookston Daily Times, 14 July 1938, 2.

336 "K.C. Monarchs Beat Giants," 18-3, St. Paul Pioneer Press, 13 July 1938, 15.

337 Fitzgerald, Eugene. "More than 3,000 see Chicago Colored Club Beat Monarchs," 14 July 1938, unknown

338 "Chicago In Ninth Inning Rally to Win," Chicago Defender, 23 July 1938, 9.

339 "Giants One Of Oldest Negro Teams Playing," Crookston Daily Times, 11 July 1938, 2.

340 "Colored Clubs Here Thursday For Loop Game," Crookston Daily Times, 12 July 1938, 2.

341 "Monarchs and Giants," Crookston Daily Times, 14 July 1938, 2.

342 "Giants defeat Monarchs, 4-1, Crookston Daily Times, 15 July 1938.

343 "Snappy Baseball," Winnipeg Free Press, 16 July 1938, 35.

344 "Four-Run Homer Gives Giants Opening Game," Winnipeg Tribune, 16 July 1938, 16.

345 "Monarchs Win Two," Chicago Defender, 30 July 1938, 8.

346 "Colored Teams Please Fans at Portage," Winnipeg Free Press, 20 July 1938, 12.

347 "Kansas City Monarchs and Chicago Giants to Play Tonight," Brandon Daily Sun, 20 July 1938, 2.

348 "Monarchs lose in 10-inning ball thriller," Regina Leader-Post, 22 July 1938, 16.

349 Ibid.

350 Dryburgh, Dave. "Along the Sport Byways," Regina Leader-Post, 22 July 1938, 16.

351 "Kansas City Monarchs signed to play in Bismarck," Bismarck Tribune, 24 July 1938, 8.

352 Byas, Richard "Subby." Interview by Author. Chicago, Illinois, 1980s

353 "Newt Allen Ill," The Kansas City Call, 5 August 1938, Sports.

354 "Monarchs Win From Chicago," Fargo Forum, 26 July 1938, page unknown.

355 1935 Indiana State Yearbook. 102.

356 Dixon, Phil. Negro Baseball Leagues: A Photographic History, p. 184.

357 "Giants Beat Monarchs, 11-4," Des Moines Register, 29 July 1938, page unknown.

358 "Kansas City Here For Two Tilts Sunday," Chicago Defender, 7 July 1938, 20.

359 "Today's Sportalkie," Chicago Daily News, 17 October 1938, 17.

Baseball, Bigotry And Turkey Stearnes

360 "Memphis Here For 3 Games with Chicago," Chicago Defender, 9 July 1938, 9.

361 "Jake Powell is suspended for careless air remarks," Logansport Indiana Press, 31 July 1938, 6.

362 Brown, Ernest "Hipps" Jr. "Sports Chatter," Kansas City Call, 5 August 1938, 8.

363 "Turkey Stearnes: One of the Best," Watertown New York Daily Times, 11 August 1979, 4.

364 Holway, John B., Blackball Stars, p. 248.

365 "Monarchs Play Tonight," Kansas City Times, 8 August 1938, 9.

366 Brown, Sam R. "Disastrous Trip Sees Grays Win Nine In Row," Atlanta Daily World, 5 August 1938, 5.

367 Radcliffe, Ted "Double Duty." Interview by Author, May 31, 1987.

368 McNary, Kyle P., Ted "Double Duty" Radcliffe, p. 139

369 Carter, Marlin. Interview by Author, 1980s.

370 Radcliffe, Ted "Double Duty." Interview by Author, August 2, 1987.

371 "Kansas City Monarchs, fielding prejudice," Vibrations, Sunday Magazine of the Columbia Missourian 2 August 1981, 3.

372 "Monroe Monarchs to meet Links Monday," Lincoln Nebraska Star, 29 July 1934, 5.

373 "A no-hit, no run game," Kansas City Times, 17 May 1937, 11.

374 "Base Ball Season. Opening Game Tonight," Negro Star, July 29, 1938, 3.

375 Carter, Marlin. Interview by Author, 1980s.

376 O'Neil, John "Buck." Tape recording of Cablevision Interview in Author's collection. Overland Park, Kansas, 21 January, 1984.

377 Taylor, Turk. Telephone Interview by Author, 1980s.

378 "Crack Negro Nikes Clash," Daily Oklahoman, July 31, 1938, 2B.

379 Johnson, Bryon. Telephone Interview by Author, November 12, 1987.

380 http://www.nndb.com/people/486/000160006/

381 Milan, Bob. Interview by Author, November 15, 2018.

382 "The stuff is here," Chicago Defender, 9 July 1938, 21.

383 "Red Sox Beaten, 7-0," The Commercial Appeal, 8 August 1938.

384 "Memphians Split Two," The Commercial Appeal, 9 August 1938.

Baseball, Bios And Ted Strong

385 Jenkins, Sherman L. Ted Strong Jr., The Untold Story Of An Original Harlem Globetrotter, 6.

386 "Famous colored ball club to appear for first time in the city," Sheboygan Press, 23 November 1938, 12.

387 "Indianapolis A's in Negro American League," Indianapolis Recorder, 7 May 1938, 12.

388 De Leighbur, Don. "A star gives advice to the kids coming along in baseball: Ted Strong is his name," Kansas City Call, 15 June 1945, sports.

389 "Famous colored ball club to appear for first time in the city," Sheboygan Press, 23 November 1938, 12.

390 O'Neil, John "Buck." Interview by Author. Tape recording. Kansas City, Missouri, January 24, 1985.

391 Marcus Haynes, Interview by Author, September 25, 2007.

392 O'Neil, John "Buck." Interview by Author. Tape recording. Kansas City, Missouri, January 24, 1985.

393 "Girl's attacker pleads guilty," Chester Times, 5 October 1938, 2.

394 "Kranston, Armstead likely Moundsmen," Topeka Daily Capital, 12 August 1938, sports.

395 "The Mound Blues who will Represent Indianapolis in The American League," Indianapolis Recorder, 21, May 1938, 12.

396 Ibid.

397 "Monarchs Here," St. Joseph Gazette, 15 August 1938, 5.

398 Ibid.

399 "Monarchs win game at Le Loup," Ottawa Herald, 17 August 1938, 10.

400 "Negro Outfits here Tuesday," Chanute Tribune, 15 August 1938, 8.

401 "Henry Armstrong becomes first man to hold three boxing Championships," Winnipeg Free Press, 18 August 1938, 17.

402 "Monarchs Crush South Ends, 14-1," St. Louis Globe-Democrat, 19 August 1938, 18.

403 "Negro Giants Whip Monarchs, 10-5," St. Louis Globe-Democrat, 20 August 1938, 12.

404 Jesse Askew, Interview by Author, March 21, 1989.

A Wake-Up Call

405 Holway, John. Voices from the Great Black Baseball Leagues, 331.

406 O'Neil, John "Buck". Interview by Author. Kansas City, Missouri, 26 April 1988.

407 Jones, Lucius L., "Sports Bug," Atlanta Daily World, 31 August 1938, 5.

408 "Monarchs to Play Atlanta Club in K.C., MO., Today," Kansas City Kansan, 21 August 1938, unknown.

409 "Monarchs Lose Twin Bill," Kansas City Times, 22 August 1938, unknown.

410 "Atlanta Pitchers in Form," Kansas City Call, 26 August 1938, unknown.

411 Jones Lucius L. "Sport Bug," Jackson Advocate, 13 June 1942, 8.

412 Holway, John. Voices from the Great Black Baseball Leagues, 330.

413 Holway, John. Voices from the Great Black Baseball Leagues, 332.

414 O'Neil, John "Buck". Interview by Author. Kansas City, Missouri, 26 April 1988.

415 "Select Negro Star Line-ups," Milwaukee Journal Sentinel, 19 August 1938, 22.

416 "Negro All-Stars Play 8 to 8 Tie," Milwaukee Journal Sentinel, 22 August 1988, 11.

417 Spalding's Official Base Ball Guide, 60.

418 Kountze, Mabe "Doc. "50 Sports Years Along Memory Lane. " Mystic Valley Press, Medford, Massachusetts, 1970.

419 Ibid.

420 "Cracker Rally Beats Monarchs," Junction City Union, 23 August 1938, 2.

421 Evans, Felix "Chin". Interview by Author. May 11, 1990.

422 "Colored Team Here," The Chanute Tribune, 24 August 1938, 8.

423 Maclary, Fletcher, "Chanute Takes Worst Defeat Of The Season," The Chanute Tribune, 25 August 1938, 9.

424 Ibid.

425 Lake, John. "Brickbats and Bouquets," Chicago Defender, 3 September 1938, 9.

426 "Pair Negro Teams Tangle At Landis," Lincoln State Journal, 14 September 1938, 11.

427 "Panthers Get Taste of Defeat Thursday," Macon Chronicle-Herald, 27 August 1938, 4.

428 http://www.elmer-missouri.com/elmer-s-famous-baseball-team.html

429 "Locals Load For Negroes," The Keokuk Daily Gate City, 25 August 1938, 4.

430 "Monarchs Top Indians 3-1," The Keokuk Daily Gate City, 26 August 1938, 4.

431 Ibid.

432 "St. Paul and Kansas City neck and neck in attendance race," Kansas City Star, 16 August 1938, 8.

433 "Kansas City and Chicago Divide Pair," Chicago Defender, 3 September 1938, 9.

434 "Oklahoma History," https://www.okhistory.org/publications/enc/entry.php?entry=TU013

435 "Monarchs Unbeaten Pitcher to Face Crax," Atlanta Daily World, 30 August 1938, 5.

436 "Crax Shell Red Sox At Macon For Ninth In Row; Score 12-6, Atlanta Daily World, 31 August 1938, 5.

437 Jones, Lucius L., "Sports Bug," Atlanta Daily World, 31 August 1938, 5.

438 Roberts, Ric. "Crax Nip Monarchs, 4-3; Ladies Free Tonight," Atlanta Daily World, 1 September 1938, 5.

439 Robert, Ric, "Crackers Blank Monarchs in Night Battle," Atlanta Daily World, 2 September 1938, 5.

440 Ibid.

Simple Mathematics

441 O'Neil, John "Buck." Interview by Author. Tape recording. Kansas City, Missouri, 24 January 1985.

442 "United States Census, 1910," database with images, GenealogyBank (https://genealogybank.com/#), Norman Starnes, Nashville Ward 14, Davidson, Tennessee, United States. (Original index: United States Census, 1910, FamilySearch, 2014)

443 https://www.theclio.com/web/entry?id=4022

444 Murray, Dr. R. Smith. Joe Engel, The Lookouts' "Baron of Baloney," 30 August 2011 http://www.engelfoundation.com/in-the-news/2011/08/joe-engel-the-lookouts-baron-of-baloney/

445 Worcester Democrat and the Ledger-enterprise, Pocomoke City, Maryland, 22 July 1938, 1.

446 Trouppe, Quincy. 20 years too soon, 114.

447 Ibid.

448 Brown, Willard. Telephone Interview by Author, 23 August 1986.

449 Senior Anvil yearbook, Washington High School 1929, page 374

450 "Charleston puts his okay on Henry Milton," Kansas City Call 18 April 1932, sports.

451 "9 records broken at Tuskegee," Chicago Defender, 16 May 1931, 9.

452 "Monarchs' Unbeaten Pitcher to Face Crax," Atlanta Daily World, 30 August 1938, 5.

453 "Chicago, Kansas City, and Memphis in double-header," Louisville Leader, 10 September 1938, 6.

454 "Monarchs To Meet Red Sox Sunday, June 20th," Kansas City, Kansas Plaindealer, 18 June 1948, 4.

455 Brown Jr., Ernest. Kansas City Call 16 September 1938, 8.

456 Haslam Texas. https://tshaonline.org/handbook/online/articles/hlh31

457 "United States Census, 1930," database with images, GenealogyBank (https://genealogybank.com/#), Fred Bankhead, Precinct 16, Walker, Alabama, United States. (Original index: United States Census, 1930, FamilySearch, 2014)

458 Bankhead, Wilma wife of Fred Bankhead telephone interview by author in the 1980s.

459 "Red Sox and Atlanta Open Title Set Today," Commercial Appeal, 18 September 1938, 25.

460 "Clubs Should Develop More Young Men," The Detroit Tribune, 2 October 1937, 7.

461 White, Sol. History of Colored Base Ball, P. 18.

462 "Atlanta Black Crackers clinch second half in American League," Pittsburgh Courier, 17 September 1938, 17.

463 "Georgia nine to play for championship," Chicago Defender, 10 September 1938, 20.

464 O'Neil, John "Buck." Interview by Author. Tape recording. Kansas City, Missouri, 24 January 1985.

465 "Memphis leads in playoff for championship, Chicago Defender, 24 September 1938, 20.

Barnstorming With The House Of David

466 "Old Pete's in Hall of Fame," Omaha World-Herald, 19 January 1938, 15.

467 "Alex Proud To Have Earned Niche In Hall Of Fame But Says Tavern Is Good Enough," Houston Chronicle, 19 January 1938, 15.

468 "Benton Harbor remembers cult destroyed by sex scandal" Detroit Free Press, 13 November 2016, https://www.freep.com/story/news/columnists/john-carlisle/2016/11/13/house-of-david-benton-harbor/93069448/

469 Ollie Marquardt, https://sabr.org/bioproj/person/ollie-marquardt/

470 "Big Six again possesses group of outstanding football centers," Nebraska State Journal, 29 September 1938.

471 http://www.baseballinwartime.com/in_memoriam/keller_art.htm

472 "House of David club plays here," Arkansas City Daily Traveler, 24 May 1937, 8.

473 "Monarchs and Davids Clash," Daily Oklahoman, 2 October 1938, 4b.

474 O'Neil, John "Buck." Tape recording of Cablevision Interview in Author's collection. Overland Park, Kansas, 21 January 1984.

475 Polk's Directory for Rock Island and Its neighbor to the east, Moline, page 22 for Aldridge, page 67 for Brown.

476 "Rock Island," Chicago Defender, 1 October 1938, 20.

477 "Bearded Team Faces Colored Stars Tonight," The Rock Island Argus, 20 September 1938, 12.

478 "Bearded Team Beats Colored Stars by 5 to 1, "The Rock Island Argus, 21 September 1938, 15.

479 Ibid.

480 "Hawks edge out Acme Giants by score of 4 to 3," Waterloo Daily Courier, 15 September 1936, 11.

481 "Charles City Lions end baseball card," Waterloo Daily Courier, 23 September 1938, 15.

482 "Don't Forget the Big ...Vernon County Fair, September 20 to 23," Vernon County Censor, 7 September 1938, 1.

483 "Thousands see Coons whip the House of David," Vernon County Censor, 28 September 1938, 5.

484 Scherwitz, Harold, Sportlights, San Antonia Light, 23 September 1938, 12.

485 "Attend Night Ball Game," Plattsmouth Journal, 3 October 1938, 2.

486 "Few Missions Left In Town," San Antonio Light, 27 September 1938, 8.

487 "Monarch and House of David Teams Here," The Kansan, 22 September 1938.

488 "Monarchs Won Last Evening," The Kansan, 24 September 1938.

489 "Monarchs Play Here Tomorrow," Manhattan Kansas Mercury, 29 September 1938, 8.

490 "Monarchs Win 13-3," Manhattan Morning Chronicle, 1 October 1938, 2.

491 "Monarchs won 13 to 3 In Last Night's Game," Manhattan Kansas Mercury, 1 October 1938, 6.

492 "Monarchs to Play in Tulsa, Kansas City, Kansas Plaindealer, 30 September 1938, 3.

493 "Monarchs and Davids Clash," Daily Oklahoman, 2 October 1938, 4-B.

494 "Stars Beaten By Monarchs," Daily Oklahoman, 7 October 1938, 17.

495 "Stars' Will Face Negroes," Daily Oklahoman, 9 October 1938, B5.

496 "Monarchs Capture Two More from City All-Stars," Daily Oklahoman, 10 October 1938, 16.

Index

Made in the USA
Las Vegas, NV
07 August 2022

52876107R00186